APJ

D1823316

English Travel Writing from Pilgrimages to Postcolonial Explorations

Barbara Korte

Translated by Catherine Matthias

First published in English in Great Britain 2000 by
MACMILLAN PRESS LTD
Houndmills, Basingstoke, Hampshire RG21 6XS and London
Companies and representatives throughout the world

A catalogue record for this book is available from the British Library.

ISBN 0–333–77041–2

First published in English in the United States of America 2000 by
ST. MARTIN'S PRESS, INC.,
Scholarly and Reference Division,
175 Fifth Avenue, New York, N.Y. 10010

ISBN 0–312–22663–2

Library of Congress Cataloging-in-Publication Data
Korte, Barbara, 1957–
[Englische Reisebericht. English]
English travel writing from pilgrimages to postcolonial
explorations / Barbara Korte ; translated by Catherine Matthias.
    p.   cm.
"Chapter 8 on postcolonial travel writing is an addition to the
German version and was newly written for the present volume"–
–Prelim. note.
Includes bibliographical references and index.
ISBN 0–312–22663–2 (cloth)
1. Travelers' writings, English—History and criticism.
2. British—Travel—Foreign countries—Historiography. 3. English
prose literature—History and criticism. 4. Postmodernism
(Literature)—Great Britain. 5. Pilgrims and pilgrimages in
literature. 6. Decolonization in literature. 7. Travel in
literature. I. Title.
PR756.T72K6713   1999
820.9'355—dc21   99–15877
                                                             CIP

This book is printed on paper suitable for recycling and made from fully managed and sustained
forest sources.

10   9   8   7   6   5   4   3   2   1
09 08 07 06 05 04 03 02 01 00

Printed and bound in Great Britain by Antony Rowe Ltd, Chippenham, Wiltshire

English Travel Writing from Pilgrimages to
Postcolonial Explorations

Also by Barbara Korte

ANGLISTISCHE LEHRE AKTUELL: Probleme, Perspektiven, Praxis (*co-editor with Klaus Peter Müller*)

BODY LANGUAGE IN LITERATURE

EINFÜHRUNG IN DIE ANGLISTIK (*with Josef Schmied and Klaus Peter Müller*)

KÖRPERSPRACHE IN DER LITERATUR: Theorie und Geschichte am Beispiel des englischsprachigen Romans

MANY VOICES – MANY CULTURES: Multicultural British Short Stories (*co-editor with Claudia Sternberg*)

MODES OF NARRATIVE: Approaches to American, Canadian and British Fiction (*co-editor with Reingard M. Nischik*)

TECHNIKEN DER SCHLUSSGEBUNG IM ROMAN: Eine Untersuchung englisch- und deutschsprachiger Romane

UNITY IN DIVERSITY REVISITED? British Literature and Culture in the 1990s (*co-editor with Klaus Peter Müller*)

Contents

Preliminary Note

This is a revised and augmented translation of my book *Der englische Reisebericht: Von der Pilgerfahrt bis zur Postmoderne*, published in Germany in 1996.

I should like to thank the German publisher, Wissenschaftliche Buchgesellschaft, Darmstadt, for their permission to have the original book translated, and to Catherine Matthias for doing the translation.

Chapter 8 on postcolonial travel writing is an addition to the German version and was newly written for the present volume.

Introduction: Travelling Pleasure – Reading Pleasure

The literature of travel is gigantic; it has a thousand forms and faces.
(Percy G. Adams, 1983, p. 281)

People have travelled since time immemorial and for many reasons; accounts of travel – or travelogues[1] – have thus been produced in various cultural contexts.[2] The present book is intended to provide an introduction to English travel writing, with its main forms and traditions. Even though the travelogue is a genre not easily demarcated, a basic understanding of its characteristic features has evolved over the centuries: accounts of travel depict a journey in its course of events and thus constitute narrative texts (usually composed in prose). They claim – and their readers believe – that the journey recorded actually took place, and that it is presented by the traveller him or herself. Within this basic frame of definition, accounts of travel manifest themselves in a broad formal spectrum, giving expression to a great variety of travel experience.

The English-speaking world has proved particularly fertile ground for travel writing, perhaps because the cultural contexts of Britain and its (former) colonial empire represented a special challenge to travel. According to Paul Fussell (1980):

> The geographical and linguistic insularity of the English is one cause of their unique attraction–repulsion to abroad, but another reason they make such interesting travelers is the national snobbery engendered by two centuries of wildly successful imperialism.... Significantly, there is no Travelers' Club in New York. There is one in London. Its original requirement for membership was an achievement of travel a thousand miles from London. (pp. 74, 76)

1

However, a particular disposition of the English nation to travel was noted well before the emergence of the British Empire; in the late Middle Ages, it was even accounted for astrologically, as in the *Travels of Sir John Mandeville*: 'We are in a climate under the rule of the moon, which is a planet that moves quickly – the traveller's planet' (p. 120).[3] At certain times, British wanderlust was so pronounced that it was even mocked by other nations. In Goethe's *Faust Part II*, Mephistopheles is astonished *not* to find any British travellers amid the griffins, sphinxes and other fantastical creatures of the Classical Walpurgis-Night: 'Are there any Britons around? / They have a mania for antiquity; / Walking the ground / Of old battle fields; / Staring at scenically pleasing waterfalls, / And dreary old ruins / With crumbling walls; / They'd love it here for their holidays' (Act II, Scene iv).

The ranks of British peacetime travellers who have written accounts of their journeys comprise many important representatives of English literature. Quite irrespective of their authors' literary standing, however, travel writing has always been popular with the reading public. Between the eighteenth and early twentieth centuries, accounts of travel were among the texts most commonly read and, for all the swansongs of certain contemporary critics, the travelogue today is in no way a 'dead' genre. To the contrary: despite mass tourism abroad, television documentaries about foreign countries and increased 'multi-culturalism' at home, the genre is actually booming – in the English-speaking world at least. The shelves of British book-shops are packed with the travelogues of contemporary writers like Patrick Leigh Fermor, Bruce Chatwin and V. S. Naipaul, Freya Stark, Dervla Murphy and Jan Morris, as well as numerous new editions of older travel books. Television, too, has seized on the genre, with Michael Palin, for example, emerging as a vastly successful globe-trotter for the BBC.

Even though the genre has enjoyed great popularity and its authors include many writers in 'established' fields of English literature, literary studies have taken comparatively little interest in travel writing until fairly recently[4] – unless it related to 'recognized' works of literature.[5] Only since the 1970s, under the growing influence of the cultural studies approach, have travelogues been increasingly analysed for their projection of culture-specific mentalities, their representations of 'otherness' and imaging of foreign countries, or as phenomena of inter-culturality. While these areas have, by now, been covered quite intensively, the literariness of travel writing has been an issue widely neglected. As yet, neither a poetics nor a comprehensive history of the genre has been written. The history of travel writing is naturally bound up with the history of travel itself – its various forms, circumstances and cultural contexts, so that any study of travel writing necessitates an interdisciplinary approach. However, accounts of travel are not only cultural documents. Rather, they have to be considered as texts written according to particular strategies – including specific artistic principles and designs. They thus not only represent cultural history, but have their own history as a particular form of writing.

Given the scarcity of critical studies to date, and in view of the vast spectrum of travel writing itself, the present introduction cannot avoid being sketchy and will have numerous omissions. Its prime focus is on travel writers from the British Isles (mostly England), but Chapter 8 gives a comprehensive survey – the first of its kind – of travel writing from former British colonies. US-American authors (with important representatives such as Mark Twain and Paul Theroux) could not be included. Even with such limitations, English travel writing presents itself as a vast and rather amorphous field. Understandably, most monographs to date are therefore confined to accounts of travel to particular regions (Italy, North America or the East), about a particular mode of travel (the Grand Tour or voyages of exploration), of specific periods, or by individual authors. Such studies have the advantage that they can explore their subject in detail and with a suitable degree of differentiation. They cannot, however, provide an overview of a genre which is fascinating precisely in its great variance and its several lines of historical development.

The aim of the present volume is to offer such an overview. Its time-frame spans texts of the late Middle Ages to the present; within this frame, the most important subgenres of English travel writing are identified. As far as its pace and detail are concerned, this enterprise may be compared with a tour around the world in eighty days. Quite understandably, trips of this kind have been criticized by passionate globetrotters, since they hardly leave a profound impression of the countries visited; nevertheless, a superficial impression may kindle the desire to go back and explore a region more thoroughly at a later date. In the same spirit, this introduction hopes to inspire the academic reader to return to certain aspects of travel writing and conduct a more in-depth analysis. It is also addressed to the general reader, however, who wishes to discover this textual terrain for his or her armchair travels. For this kind of reader, each of the chronological chapters is preceded by a selection of representative excerpts from the kind of travelogue to be discussed, and, wherever possible, quotations are taken from paperback editions currently in print. For the sake of readability, Middle and Early English texts are quoted in translated or modernized editions.

Chapters 2 to 8 delineate the most important types in which English travel writing has evolved over the centuries, including its 'feminine', 'postmodern' and 'postcolonial' varieties. Chapter 1 establishes a set of features which allow us to recognize the account of travel as a distinct literary genre and to appreciate its specific qualities – including a striking potential to be continually revitalized.

1
Charting the Genre

There are no books which I more delight in than in Travels.
(Joseph Addison, 1759, p. 363)

Travel literature is a neglected literature; compared to the samples of canonical genres, it can hardly offer something like 'works'.
(Charles Grivel, 1994, p. 256)

The theme and functions of travel accounts

Undoubtedly, the popularity of travel writing is due to its theme, which truly encompasses the world. As we shall see, in some periods and for some types of journey, travellers were bound by directions which prescribed the course of their journeys and, in turn, affected the content and manner of their accounts. There are also, however, numerous accounts which let their travellers roam the world freely and which illustrate the genre's particular potential to assemble a wealth of observations, experiences and reflections. It is no accident that the term *omnium-gatherum* is found repeatedly in studies of travel writing: in the medley of a travel account, everything can potentially be included which the traveller/writer sees fit.

More acutely than any other genre, then, travel writing is defined by the interaction of the human subject with the world. Naturally, this world will often be 'foreign', but the traveller's own country may equally be the object of his or her investigation. Accounts of travel let us participate in acts of (inter)cultural perception and cultural construction, in processes of understanding and misunderstanding. These processes are undergone by the traveller on the journey and later as he or she writes the account; they are also, however, experienced by the reader as he or

5

she is perusing the text. Travel writing thus provides us not only with an impression of the travelled world, but the travelling subject is always also laid bare: accounts of travel are never objective; they inevitably reveal the culture-specific and individual patterns of perception and knowledge which every traveller brings to the travelled world. As Manfred Pfister (1996) points out for 'The Italies of British Travellers':

> The Italy for which the traveller sets out is never a *tabula rasa* but always already inscribed with the traces of previous texts, i.e. prescribed by his or her culture. And the traveller's perception of it . . . is filtered through the home country as a perceptual foil of comparison and contrast, and scripted through established routes and canonized sights. The traveller's Italy is constructed through, and in, such sets of preconceptions, prejudices, stereotypes, anticipations and preferences, which articulate themselves in what we have come to call 'discourses'. (p. 4)

The relation, in an account, between references to travelling subject and travelled world can vary to a great extent. Where an account is object-orientated, that is where the imparting of geographical and anthropological knowledge is foregrounded, the subjectivity of the traveller will often be hardly discernible. At the other end of the spectrum, the travelling subject is firmly at centre stage. To Norman Douglas (1926), for example, travel writing was an attractive genre precisely because of its capacity to be subject-orientated and to render the *personal* experience of travel:

> It seems to me that the reader of a good travel-book is entitled not only to an exterior voyage, to descriptions of scenery and so forth, but to an interior, a sentimental or temperamental voyage, which takes place side by side with that outer one; and that the ideal book of this kind offers us, indeed, a triple opportunity of exploration – abroad, into the author's brain, and into our own. (p. 11)

Closely related to the theme of travel writing is the long-standing debate surrounding the genre's function and, in particular, its 'usefulness'. In fact, the texts themselves are shot through with questions of this nature. Accounts with a strong focus on the travelled world instruct their readers in a very obvious manner: they furnish useful information about a country's topography, population and culture. Some forms of travel writing, for example accounts about the medieval pilgrimage or the educational Grand Tour, also include explicit advice to future travellers. In the eighteenth and nineteenth centuries, appendices giving factual information and statistics were part and parcel of the standard travel account. Last but not least, travel writing can also be educational in as much as it allows the reader to accompany the traveller and to be influenced and perhaps even transformed by his or her experience.

However, thanks to their very content matter, accounts of travel are also capable of giving delight. They satisfy the reader's curiosity about foreign countries and 'strange' experiences; depending on the type of journey and the place involved, they may also fulfil a need for adventure. Henry Fielding's *Journal of a Voyage to Lisbon* (1755) is one of the first examples of English travel writing in which the genre itself is discussed. According to Fielding's preface, the travel writer should strive to be entertaining, for it is only then that the reader's attention is also drawn to the informative and edifying aspects of the text:

> But all his pains in collecting knowledge, all his judgment in selecting, and all his art in communicating it, will not suffice, unless he can make himself, in some degree, an agreeable as well as an instructive companion. The highest instruction we can derive from the tedious tale of a dull fellow scarce ever pays us for our attention. (p. 221)

The problem which can arise for the writer as he or she is torn between the need to be instructive and the need to be 'agreeable' is illustrated by one of the first and best-known accounts of a British explorer in Africa. In 1795, Mungo Park, a Scottish surgeon, travelled through Africa on behalf of the Association for Promoting the Discovery of the Interior Parts of Africa (or the African Association), which was founded in 1788. The aim of his expedition was to locate the Niger, unseen by European eyes up to that point, and to gather all kinds of information that might be used for the benefit of British overseas trade. In his preface to *Travels in the Interior Districts of Africa* (1799), Park stresses the 'profit' derived from his journey: 'It is a plain unvarnished tale, without pretensions of any kind, except that it claims to enlarge, in some degree, the circle of African geography' (p. xv). The information gain claimed here is not to be underestimated. The interest in reading Park's account today, however, is not so much in the observations he puts together, as in the numerous adventures which he depicts in a lively and surprisingly humorous manner:

ambushes, imprisonment by Ali, 'the Moorish king of Ludamar', life-threatening illness and near starvation. By including such episodes, Park allows his readers to experience the journey along with him. What is striking about the text, though, is the author's obvious awkwardness in combining the informative and adventurous components of his report. Park prefers to present facts in special chapters that are set apart, rather abruptly, from the account of the journey proper, so that his text is neatly split into chapters with a focus on narration and chapters with a focus on description. The abruptness of this change in presentation is even highlighted in transitions such as the following:

> Believing, therefore, that I should certainly find the means of escaping from Jarra, if I should once get thither, I now freely indulged the pleasing hope that my captivity would soon terminate; and happily not having been disappointed in this idea, I shall pause in this place to collect and bring into one point of view such observations on the Moorish character and country, as I had no fair opportunity of introducing into the preceding narrative.   (p. 113)

As far as its theme and content matter are concerned, the travel account has not emerged as a genre hermetically sealed off from other kinds of writing. Many novels, for example, specifically deal with the theme of travel; English literature alone provides us with numerous classic examples, including Thomas Nashe's *The Unfortunate Traveller*, Aphra Behn's *Oroonoko*, Daniel Defoe's *Robinson Crusoe*, Jonathan Swift's *Gulliver's Travels*, Henry Fielding's *Tom Jones*, Robert Louis Stevenson's *Treasure Island*, Virginia Woolf's *The Voyage Out* or E.M. Forster's *A Passage to India*. Works of 'non-fiction' also treat the journey in various forms. Guidebooks in the manner of Murray or Baedeker belong to the nineteenth and twentieth centuries, but manuals for travellers, to be read before or during the journey, are considerably older: medieval pilgrims had itineraries, and the sixteenth century saw a proliferation of apodemic writing, that is treatises on the art of travelling. Other instructive texts are devoted to the mere results or 'returns' of a journey, for example the observations gathered during a voyage of exploration. Clearly, then, its content matter does not suffice to establish the travel account as a genre of its own. The next section will treat the question of whether travel writing is distinguished by a specific manner of presentation or particular text modes.

Text modes of travel writing

Travel writing characteristically fuses various modes of presentation: in very different proportions, narration is intermingled with description, exposition and even prescription. Mungo Park, as we have seen, combines the report of his adventures with a thorough stocktaking of Africa, and in accounts of the Grand Tour the story of the journey is habitually accompanied by advice to future travellers. Guidebook elements, pointing the reader to relevant sights, abound in accounts of tourist travel since the mid-nineteenth century; they are anticipated in texts about the so-called scenic or picturesque tour, that is the journey devoted to the enjoyment of landscape. Crossovers with the essay, the letter, reportage, the sketch, anecdote or treatise are frequent, and occasionally an account will even contain sections of poetry. It is hardly surprising, then, that travel writing has been characterized as an essentially 'hybrid' or 'androgynous' literary form.[1] To Jonathan Raban (1987), 'travel writing is a notoriously raffish open house where very different genres are likely to end up in the same bed' (p. 253).

Nevertheless, despite this generic hybridity and flexibility, one formal feature sets the tone: a text about a journey is not normally considered an *account* unless the journey is narrated. Travel accounts or travelogues are defined by a narrative core; they always tell the story of a journey. This is also true of travel books which present the reader with a great deal of factual information, such as Charles Darwin's *Voyage of the Beagle* (1839). Despite the considerable attention paid to descriptions of the natural world, this account of Darwin's famous voyage as the *Beagle's* official naturalist is even insistent in its purpose of storytelling:

> [Darwin's] aim, of course, was not merely to recount the events of his voyage ... but to communicate his scientific information in an accurate and lively manner while sustaining his readers' interest in the whole narrative. One might call it a problem of narrative integration, and Darwin solved it by developing a recognizable story line and an appealing voice for himself as storyteller. He seems to have constructed his plot using two main strategies: first, he rearranged the chronology of his trip, and second, he severely abridged his diary to emphasize certain types of material. ... Finally, he composed his text from a consistent point of view, creating a narrative persona that is both engaging and 'respectable'.
>
> (Tallmadge, 1980, pp. 330–1)[2]

The element of storytelling in travel writing is closely related to another genre characteristic, namely its element of fictionality. At first sight, this fictional element might appear to contradict the criterion that travel accounts depict journeys which have actually taken place. Certainly the stamp of authenticity may well be what makes travel writing attractive to many readers (as it does in autobiography and historiography). To many writers, too, the distinction between authentic and 'fantasized' accounts is essential. Charles Grivel (1994), for example, denies the fictionality of travel writing categorically: 'The travel report is not a fictional genre. Its referential object is precise and stands out. . . . I describe, impressions reach me, the "prose of the world" flows from my pen' (p. 256). Ultimately, however, a reader's sense of reality only lies in his or her *assumption* that the text is based on travel fact, on an authentic journey, and this assumption can only be tested beyond the text itself. As far as the text and its narrative techniques are concerned, there appears to be no essential distinction between the travel account proper and purely fictional forms of travel literature.[3]

Notwithstanding their authentic and factual element, reports of travel necessarily re-*create* the experience of the journey on which they are based. Thus travelogues produced long after the completion of a journey often include extensive passages of dialogue which – at least in the days before tape recordings – can only be reconstructions of the traveller's actual conversations. Similarly, patterns, lines of development, cross-references, emphases and other structural elements may arise in the account which, in all probability, were not part of the original experience of the journey itself.[4] The experience of travel is translated, in the text, into a travel *plot*. As a result, reports of one and the same journey by various authors can be very different – without one being more 'true' than the other. In his own travelogue, *Journey to Kars* (1984), Philip Glazebrook compares the parallel accounts of two Victorian travelling companions and concludes: 'A single event, thus shaped by two men, may be made to serve two different purposes, and so emerge in a different form in each of their accounts: yet neither lies' (p. 167).[5]

References to the creativity of the travel writer abound in texts of the twentieth century. Thus Evelyn Waugh, at the opening of *Ninety-Two Days* (1934), stresses his role as re-creator and translator of the original travel experience:

> Just as a carpenter, I suppose, seeing a piece of rough timber feels an inclination to plane it and square it and put it into shape, so a

writer is not really content to leave any experience in the amorphous, haphazard condition in which life presents it; and putting an experience into shape means, for a writer, putting it into communicable form. . . . for myself and many better than me, there is a fascination in distant and barbarous places . . . It is there that I find the experiences vivid enough to demand translation into literary form.

So for the next month or two I shall be reliving my journey in Guiana and Brazil. (pp. 10–11)

Similarly, Jonathan Raban (1987) regards the journey itself as 'a shapeless, unsifted, endlessly shifting accumulation of experience'; only when shaped by the writer does it become a meaningful story:

The first thing it needs is an ending, for only in retrospect (and often in long retrospect) will the dust of travelling settle and the journey begin to emerge as a story, of sorts. . . .
For travelling is inherently a plotless, disordered, chaotic affair, where writing insists on connection, order, plot, signification. It may take a year or more to see that there was any point to the thing at all, and more years still to make it yield an articulate story. Memory, not the notebook, holds the key. . . .
Memory . . . is always telling stories to itself, filing experience in narrative form. It feeds irrelevancies to the shredder, enlarges on crucial details, makes links and patterns, finds symbols, constructs plots. (pp. 246–8)

The actual experience of a journey is reconstructed, and therefore fictionalized, in the moment of being told. This is even the case with accounts in the form of (more or less private) diaries and letters written during a journey, in which the interval between the experience and its telling is smaller than in retrospective travelogues, which narrate a journey after – even years after – it has been completed. Travelogues which emphasize the delay between the original experience and the reporting make the process of fictionalizing particularly clear. In *A Time of Gifts* (1977), for example, Patrick Leigh Fermor depicts his peregrinations in Europe almost four decades after they actually took place. His memory of the journey is therefore scanty ('only a few scattered fragments remain', p. 68), and he must repeatedly call on his imagination as he recreates his experiences: 'I think the inn where I found refuge was called *Zum Schwarzen Adler*. It was the prototype of so many I fetched up in after the day's march that I must try to reconstruct it' (p. 44). The fictional element of Fermor's report is evident above all in relation to the diaries which he had kept during his journey. His use of these diaries, while composing his retrospective account, is very limited, as he no longer had them in complete form. However, when he comes across an old diary which he assumed he had lost, he chooses to quote from it, thus laying bare the distinction between his present act of recreation and the more spontaneous record of his earlier, travelling self:

> It was an exciting trove; a disturbing one too. There were some discrepancies of time and place between the diary and what I had already written but they didn't matter as they could be put right. The trouble was that I had imagined – as one always does with lost property – that the contents were better than they were. ... But, with all its drawbacks, the text did have one virtue: it was dashed down at full speed. I know it is dangerous to change key, but I can't resist using a few passages of this old diary here and there. (p. 261)

This example also illustrates another distinctive feature of travel writing as we understand it today, namely its autobiographical element (which is, of course, closely related to the element of authenticity). The narrator of the account and the travelling persona in the plot are fused in the union of first-person narration; the autobiographical nature of the text arises from the further extension of this union to the author him or herself. The reader of a travelogue assumes that the Marco Polo or Bruce Chatwin in the respective texts are basically identical to Marco Polo or Bruce Chatwin as they really were.

Notwithstanding this assumption, a narratological analysis of travel writing must distinguish between the author, the narrator and the travelling persona of an account. The voice narrating the journey may appear quite distinct from the 'real' author, for example when the narrator is posing or controlling him or herself in accordance with certain aims or social expectations. The narrator may also, just as the first-person narrator of a novel, create a certain distance from himself as persona in the travel plot. The metatext of Philip Glazebrook's *Journey to Kars* explores the manner in which the Victorian travelogue tended to construct its travellers as 'heroes': 'There was a good deal of artifice in it' (p. 18). This is followed by a general comment on 'the traveller's need to construct himself as he would most like to be' (p. 20). This element of artifice and construction is also apparent where the aim is not necessarily to produce a heroic persona. In *Travels in West Africa* (1897), for example, Mary Kingsley occasionally sets herself up as a comical character who is couched in irony through the narrating voice. Her 'performance' in the following episode is thus not only one for the audience within the travel plot, but she also performs to the reader of her text:

> I scrambled along, the men yelled and shouted and hauled the canoe, and the inhabitants of the village, seeing we were becoming amusing again, came ... after us, young and old, male and female, to say nothing of the dogs. Some good souls helped the men haul, while I did my best to amuse the others by diving headlong from a large rock on to which I had elaborately climbed, into a thick clump of willow-leaved shrubs. They applauded my performance vociferously, and then assisted my efforts to extricate myself, and during the rest of my scramble they kept close to me, with keen competition for the front row, in hopes that I would do something like it again. But I refused the *encore*, because, bashful as I am, I could not but feel that my last performance was carried out with all the superb reckless *abandon* of a Sarah Bernhardt, and a display of art of this order should satisfy any African village for a year at least.
>
> (p. 58)

Apart from the first-person traveller, other characters within the travel plot are also frequently subjected to obvious manipulations. A famous eighteenth-century instance of parallel travel accounts, by the great Dr Johnson and his admirer Boswell, provides us with a very clear example. In Samuel Johnson's *A Journey to the Western Islands of Scotland* (1775), the country, its inhabitants and history are at the centre of attention; Johnson himself appears largely as observant onlooker and commentator. In James Boswell's version of the Scotland trip, *The Journal of a Tour to the Hebrides* (1786), our attention is directed as much towards Boswell's travelling companion as towards Scotland itself. As in his later, classic biography of Johnson, Boswell takes every opportunity to 'glean *Johnsoniana*' (p. 354) and assumes the role of admiring (and sometimes tongue-in-cheek) eyewitness, who sets his famous friend quite clearly at centre stage: 'Dr Johnson, mounted on a large bay mare without shoes, and followed by a foal, which had some difficulty in keeping up with him, was a singular spectacle' (p. 344).

The generic features considered here are evident, in varying degrees, throughout the history of travel writing. Quite apart from evaluating the 'literariness' of the travel account, these features shed light on its characteristic textual practices, and they allow us to investigate their handling through the genre's history and in its various subgenres.

The debate surrounding the literariness of travel writing normally goes hand in hand with a narrow view of the genre. In the *Cambridge History of English Literature* (1916), for example, F.A. Kirkpatrick confines his survey of travel writing to those texts 'in which the personality and literary power of the writer count for more than his theme'; he has to admit that 'such books are, relatively, few' (p. 240). To Gertrud Kalb (1981), the 'literary' travelogue does not emerge until the eighteenth century, when the genre was taken up by professional writers such as Smollett and Fielding. These, she claims, were the first travel writers to recreate their journeys with particular, authorial aims in mind:

> A literary travel account is 'self-sufficient', autonomous. It is neither a vehicle for scientific observation and research nor a collection of eclectic remarks of a personal kind, but rather a rounded, harmonious, independent whole ... A literary travel account is therefore more than a simple report of a journey. The 'primary information' in it is reconstructed in such a way as to fit particular authorial aims.
>
> (pp. 84, 86; my translation)[6]

Such definitions exclude a large proportion of travel writing, especially accounts of early periods. Neither do they do justice to the particular attraction of the genre which lies in its very heterogeneity in matters of form and content.

The view that travel writing is only literature if couched in 'literary' language or 'poetic prose' (Segeberg, 1983, p. 26), is equally restrictive. Some accounts are certainly marked by a special poetic quality, as is a monumental example from the nineteenth century, *Travels in Arabia Deserta* (1888) by the English poet and scholar Charles M. Doughty. In the company of Bedouins, Doughty travelled through the Arabian peninsula between 1876 and 1878. His account, which runs into more than a thousand pages, is highly informative: it describes people, places, farming practices, the climate and cave drawings, and, in this respect, is not unlike most other contemporary accounts of exploration. However, to convey the archaic quality of nomadic life, Doughty chose to compose his text in an old-fashioned English reminiscent of Chaucer and the Elizabethan poets:

A bare dish of dates was set before us; and the good-man made us thin coffee: bye and bye his neighbours entered. All these were B. Temîm, peasant-like bodies in whom is no natural urbanity; but they are lumpish drudgers, living honestly of their own – and that is with a sparing hand. When I said to one of them, 'I see you all big of bone and stature, unlike the (slender) inhabitants of Hâyil!' – He answered, dispraising them, 'The Shammar are *Beduw*!' Whilst we sat, there came in three swarthy strangers, who riding by to Hâyil alighted here also to drink coffee.

(vol. 2, pp. 261–2)

Even though the language of a travelogue clearly deserves our attention, the analysis of travel writing must not be confined to texts whose style strikes one as particularly 'literary'. Again, focusing on only a select group of texts makes the scholar blind to important historical developments and general generic features. Moreover, the heterogeneous content matter characteristic of much travel writing often goes hand in hand with a hybridity in terms of text modes and style. Charles Darwin, for example, expressly described his account of the *Beagle* voyage as 'my first literary child'.[7] Large portions of the text are, however, dedicated to observations of a scientific nature, and passages such as the description of the Galapagos finches could hardly be considered 'poetic' prose:

The general character of the plumage of these birds is extremely plain, and like the Flora possesses little beauty. Although the species are thus peculiar to the archipelago, yet nearly all in their general structure, habits, colour of feathers, and even tone of voice, are strictly American. The following brief list will give an idea of their kinds. First: A buzzard, having many of the characters of Polyborus or Caracara; and in its habits not to be distinguished from that peculiar South American genus; ... ninth: A group of finches, of which Mr Gould considers there are thirteen species; and these he has distributed into four new sub-genera. These birds are the most singular of any in the archipelago. They all agree in many points; namely, in a peculiar structure of their bill, short tails, general form, and in their plumage. The females are gray or brown, but the old cocks jet-black. All the species, excepting two, feed in flocks on the ground, and have very similar habits. It is very remarkable that a nearly perfect gradation of structure in this one group can be traced in the form of the beak, from one exceeding in dimensions that of the largest gros-beak, to another differing but little from that of a warbler.   (pp. 275–6)

The point of view here is clearly scientific, and the description is correspondingly sober and sequential. In contrast, other passages of *Voyage of the Beagle* reveal Darwin's subjective sensibility, and the tone loses its sober quality, both in terms of syntax and in terms of diction. In the following extract, the emphasis in Darwin's description of Tierra del Fuego is on the particular mood of the landscape described:

> I continued slowly to advance for an hour along the broken and rocky banks; and was amply repaid by the grandeur of the scene. The gloomy depth of the ravine well accorded with the universal signs of violence. On every side were lying irregular masses of rock and up-torn trees; other trees, though still erect, were decayed to the heart and ready to fall. The entangled mass of the thriving and the fallen reminded me of the forests within the tropics; – yet there was a difference; for in these still solitudes, Death, instead of Life, seemed the predominant spirit. I followed the water-course till I came to a spot where a great slip had cleared a straight space down the mountain side. By this road I ascended to a considerable elevation, and obtained a good view of the surrounding woods.   (p. 175)

This description is clearly affected by the Romantic aesthetics of landscape, and it appears more 'poetic' and 'rhetorical' in style than the description of the Galapagos finches. Both passages, nevertheless, are parts of *one* account. Obviously, the question of the 'literariness' in travel writing must be treated with the same flexibility as the genre in general.

The selection of texts

The richness and variety of travel writing is part of what attracts us to the genre. For the purposes of this book, however, this wide spectrum results in a problem of selection. Which texts provide us with a genuine overview of the genre, representing its main forms and lines of development? The long-standing marginalization of travel writing by literary scholars has meant that there is no canon of texts at our disposal, even if the travelogues of established men and women of letters have received somewhat greater attention and acclaim than those of the many occasional writers who have contributed to the genre. Nevertheless, a handful of the latter's texts, such as Alexander Kinglake's *Eothen* (1844), were so consistently popular that they went into many editions and thus escaped oblivion.

The absence of a canon is not, in itself, problematic. Quite the contrary: travel writing offers the reader literary ground which is previously untrodden and unmapped, and in which there is a lot to discover for oneself. At the same time, the wealth of travel writing published throughout the centuries[8] may easily become an embarrassment of riches. However, this wealth is not easily accessible; although a veritable flood of travelogues is currently being published, many older texts are only available in libraries, and sometimes only in special collections. This problem of availability has lead me to concentrate, for the benefit of the general reader, primarily on texts which are not only representative of the areas I wish to discuss, but which are also in print or easily accessible in libraries. As one might expect, the selection thus includes texts which have attained a certain status through their treatment in other critical studies or through intertextual references within the genre of travel writing itself. To counteract canon formation, however, these 'classics' will be complemented with a series of lesser known examples.

The historical overview

Chapters 2 to 7 give a historical survey of the main varieties of travel writing in the British Isles. I have resisted starkly dividing the genre into periods, since there are many parallel lines of development; furthermore, some of these lines are more clearly manifested in accounts about certain kinds of travel than in others. Travel writing of whatever age is typically multiple in form, resulting in part from the kinds of travel possible in any age.

Chapters 2 and 3 trace the gradual emergence, from the Middle Ages to the eighteenth century, of two features of travel writing as we understand it today. The first concerns the object orientation of the travel account, in particular its claim to represent the travelled world authentically and empirically; reports of travel in foreign countries, especially by explorers and scientists, will serve to illustrate the development of this generic feature. The second feature concerns the degree to which travel writing is subject-orientated and reveals the personality and individual experience of the traveller; the emergence of this feature manifests itself most clearly in accounts about the Grand Tour, that is educational travel on the Continent. In Chapter 4, an analysis of texts about domestic travel illuminates these two lines of development in a different context.

By the late eighteenth century, travel writers had the full range of possibilities for writing about travel at their disposal, and the genre can be considered more or less consolidated. The nineteenth century was a heyday of British travel throughout the world; Chapter 5 considers two varieties of the travelogue most characteristic of this period: accounts of exploration (in the service of the Empire) and of the newly emerging tourist trip. The nineteenth century is also particularly significant as far as women's travel and travel writing are concerned. It seems appropriate, therefore, to dedicate Chapter 6 to the special concerns and the tradition of 'feminine' travelogues. Chapter 7 is devoted to British travel writing of the twentieth century, ranging from the critique of civilization in travel books around the First World War to recent texts of a postmodern kind; in particular, the twentieth century brings with it a conscious inter- and metatextual reflection on the conventions of travel writing. Despite the problems of definition which the genre has known throughout the centuries, what emerges in this chapter thus is, at the very least, a *self*-consciousness within the genre itself. The final chapter goes beyond the British Isles to explore how English travel writing has evolved in the so-called postcolonial world of the twentieth century, committed to generic traditions, but also innovative.

2
Paths to the Real World

[1] *There are many different kinds of people in these isles. In one, there is a race of great stature, like giants, foul and horrible to look at; they have one eye only, in the middle of their foreheads. They eat raw flesh and raw fish. In another part, there are ugly folk without heads, who have eyes in each shoulder; their mouths are round, like a horse-shoe, in the middle of their chest. In yet another part there are headless men whose eyes and mouths are on their backs. And there are in another place folk with flat faces, without noses or eyes; but they have two small holes instead of eyes, and a flat lipless mouth. In another isle there are ugly fellows whose upper lip is so big that when they sleep in the sun they cover all their faces with it. ... In another, people have feet like horses, and run so swiftly on them that they overtake wild beasts and kill them for their food. In another isle there are people who walk on their hands and their feet like four-footed beasts; they are hairy and climb up trees as readily as apes. ... There is still another isle where the people have only one foot, which is so broad that it will cover all the body and shade it from the sun. They will run so fast on this one foot that it is a marvel to see them. There is also another isle where the people live just on the smell of a kind of apple; and if they lost that smell, they would die forthwith. Many other kinds of folk there are in other isles about there, which are too numerous to relate.*

(*The Travels of Sir John Mandeville,* mid-fourteenth century, p. 137)

[2] *It rests I speak a word or two of the natural inhabitants, their natures and manners ...*

They are a people clothed with loose mantles made of deer skins, and aprons of the same round about their middles, all else naked; of

19

such a difference of statures only as we in England; having no edge tools or weapons of iron or steel to offend us with, neither know they how to make any. Those weapons that they have are only bows made of witch-hazel and arrows of reeds; flat-edged truncheons also of wood about a yard long. Neither have they anything to defend themselves but shields made of barks, and some armours made of sticks wickered together with thread.

   Their towns are but small, and near the sea coast but few, some containing but ten or twelve houses; some twenty. The greatest that we have seen has been but of thirty houses. . . .

   Their houses are made of small poles, made fast at the tops in round form after the manner as is used in many arbours in our gardens of England; in most towns covered with barks, and in some with mats made of long rushes, from the tops of the houses down to the ground. The length of them is commonly double the breadth, in some places they are but twelve and sixteen yards long, and in others we have seen twenty-four.

   ('Hariot's Brief and True Report', 1588, pp. 126–7)

The prehistory of European travel writing

The emergence of empirically 'true' accounts manifests itself most conspicuously in texts about travel to 'foreign' worlds. Travel writing naturally represents a wide range of encounters with the foreign; in fact the literature of travel has been pre-eminent in the European construction of the 'other' or 'exotic' worlds.[1] Thus it exemplifies how complex any notion of foreignness or 'other'ness actually is – not only in our present, globalized world in which cultural interference and interaction have become a commodity of everyday existence. Recent research in anthropology, cultural studies, psychoanalysis and other disciplines has established that all concepts of the 'other' are projections of the 'self' and thus essentially slippery, relational and relative.[2] The foreignness of a travelled country is always the result of an act of construction on the part of the perceiver, who defines the country's otherness against his or her own sense of identity, his or her own familiar contexts.

   The other cultures do, of course, exist in their own right; only in their otherness are they constructions of external observers. For them, they function as projection screens for their own anxieties and desires. The Other . . . helps both the individual and a culture to establish and maintain identity by serving as a screen onto which the self projects its unfulfilled longings, its repressed desires and its darker sides which it wishes and sees itself constrained to exorcise. ... In a word: the Other is fascinating. One feels drawn towards and into it and at the same time shies away from it; it is alluring and repellent at the same time.   (Pfister, 1996, pp. 4–5)

The degree of unfamiliarity with a travelled country varies, then, not only from traveller to traveller, but also between the countries visited by one particular traveller. Even though any impression of 'foreignness' is thus necessarily relative and subjective, we may still assume that countries which are not the traveller's own present a special challenge to his or her usual modes of perception – in particular when the foreign world, to European eyes, is an entirely 'new' one. The Americas, of course, were not the first region outside Europe which Europeans had travelled and whose otherness had been depicted in accounts of their travels.

The period dealt with at the beginning of this chapter, the late Middle Ages, can only in fact be termed a *pre*history of the travelogue in Europe. In Europe, more specifically in England, our contemporary understanding of the travelogue as the account of authentic, autobiographical travelling experience does not emerge until the Early Modern period, and many earlier texts are not compatible with the modern conception of the genre. Nevertheless, some travel writing of the Middle Ages has proved so influential that it should not be omitted from a historical survey. The inclusion of these texts reveals, above all, how veracity becomes an increasingly important feature of the genre over the centuries. Medieval travel writing, however, also has its own precursors.

Documents about peacetime travel have been in existence for thousands of years. Inscriptions on Egyptian tombs, for example, bear witness to journeys of exploration and mercantile travel. The European tradition was predominantly influenced by the travel writing of the classical period.[3] The Greeks and Romans, colonizers of Europe and the Middle East, were avid travellers; they accordingly produced many geographical writings as well as travel texts. The periegesis, a genre particularly popular in the Hellenistic period, was specifically dedicated to travel, depicting countries, towns and sights in the form of an imaginary guided tour. Pausanias' *Guide to Greece* (*Perihēgēsis tēs Hellados*, 160–80 AD) is a 'Baedeker of the Ancient World' (Casson, 1974, p. 292), a detailed ten-volume description of

Greece, its geography and cultural monuments, as well as the related myths, legends and biographies. Apart from this specialized genre, accounts of travel were also incorporated into the great encyclopedic works of the classical period. Substantial information about ancient travel, foreign countries and customs can thus be found in the *History* of Herodotus (fifth century BC), or the elder Pliny's monumental *Historia naturalis* (77 AD).

The travel writing of Greek and Roman antiquity paved the way for the genre's medieval and Early Modern developments in two respects. In the first place, the encyclopedic character of this writing anticipates the *omnium-gatherum* of later travelogues and collections of travel records. Secondly, classical travel writing presents a world which is, at the same time, empirically observable *and* fantastical. Some Greek and Roman travel writers were certainly well travelled; Herodotus, for example, knew Italy, the Black Sea, the Danube, the Don, Persia and Egypt from personal experience. However, since their descriptions of foreign countries often formed part of encyclopedias, they were not only based on authentic experience, but were also, and more commonly, the result of intensive reading. Classical travel writing drew on (pseudo-)scientific literature as well as on myths, anecdotes and life histories which were considered authoritative if only because they had been handed down the generations – even if their descriptions were not empirically attestable. What had been written in a text was understood to be true; empirical verification was of less significance in the claim to truth than it was to become in later periods. As Mary Campbell (1988, p. 139) points out in her study of early European travel writing: 'A fact and the words in which it was encapsulated were much more clearly identical than they are now: for all practical purposes a change in wording was a change in fact, a mistranslation could alter the world.' Thanks to the authority attached to texts of writers such as Pliny the Elder or Gaius Julius Solinus (third century AD),[4] fabulous creatures whom the Greeks and Romans believed to inhabit foreign worlds lived on into the travelogue of the Middle Ages (see excerpt 1) and even the Early Modern period. In these later texts, they often appear in a manner that seems very strange to the modern reader – in perfect parallel with a foreign world that was indeed observable and observed. The great importance attached to textual authority – as opposed to autobiographical experience – accounts for the deficit in verisimilitude that characterizes much early travel writing. It also explains the lack of subjectivity that marks the early travelogue: handing down traditions was as important as, and often more important than, *personal* experience of travel.

Travel writing in the late Middle Ages

Medieval travellers came from various social groups. Vagrants roamed aimlessly and thus formed a little respected group of travellers. Those who travelled with a purpose enjoyed greater respect, but they, too, had to endure danger and hardships: kings and their courtiers travelled for reasons of government business, sometimes accompanied by their entire household; students and scholars peregrinated from university to university, apprentices from one master craftsman to another; merchants were a very active and fairly large group among travellers with a secular aim. In cultures deeply rooted in Christianity, travels with a religious motive – missionary travel, crusades and pilgrimage – were particularly esteemed. The pilgrimage is one of the most important forms of medieval travel, around which, in the late Middle Ages, there even evolved an early form of tourist industry; pilgrims' travel became a highly organized affair and mobilized a fairly large proportion of the populace: 'In 1434, Henry VI. granted licences to 2433 pilgrims to the shrine of St James of Compostella [*sic*] alone. The numbers were so large that the control of their transportation became a coveted business enterprise' (Howard, 1914, p. 3). Apart from Santiago de Compostela in Spain, further destinations favoured by English pilgrims were Rome and, above all, Jerusalem. Sacred places abroad were popular not least because of the considerable indulgences to be obtained in reaching them; more modest pilgrimages took English travellers to holy sites on home territory, including Canterbury's shrine of Thomas à Becket.

The travels of merchants, missionaries and pilgrims were the kinds of journey most frequently written about in the Middle Ages,[5] and they will also be the focus of our attention. Most examples, however, will be taken from a text which would not qualify as a travelogue according to the modern conception of the genre. The *Travels of Sir John Mandeville* (hereafter *Mandeville's Travels*) is a fictional rather than a factual text; 'John Mandeville', the first-person narrator and traveller, is only a creation of the text's real author whose identity – despite much speculation – has never been ascertained. For centuries, however, *Mandeville's Travels* was thought to be the account of an actual journey, remaining a recognized authority up to the sixteenth century. It was widely read by the explorers of the Early Modern period; the copy owned by Columbus, with his handwritten notes in the margin, still exists. In its various versions (the original manuscript was in French), *Mandeville's Travels* was certainly the most famous travel text, and generally one of the most popular works of prose of late medieval Europe.[6] Furthermore, *Mandeville's Travels* also compiled the existing authentic travel accounts of the time[7] and, as such, provides an adequate illustration for the purposes of this chapter. Mandeville's departure on his travels is dated, in the text, as Michaelmas Day 1332. The countries visited are listed in the prologue: Turkey, Armenia, Tartary, Persia, Syria, Arabia, Egypt, Libya, Chaldea, Ethiopia, Amazonia, India and its surrounding islands, as well as China, where the traveller is received at the court of the Great Khan. The journey starts out as a pilgrimage to the Holy Land, but it then leads the traveller beyond Palestine, to the Far East, which, in the thirteenth and fourteenth centuries, was visited by European missionaries and merchants.

The pilgrimage

In accordance with its relative frequency, the pilgrimage gave rise to a wealth of specialist literature which, in turn, helped to standardize this form of travel. The purely factual writing on the pilgrimage included handbooks with practical tips for the journey (for example on routes, costs, rates of exchange or provisions) and lists of indulgences. The so-called itineraries often only gave routes and distances between stations, but some narrated the course of actual pilgrimages, as, for example, the *Itineraries* of William Wey. Apart from the account of his journeys, Wey's text also contains large sections of useful information for future pilgrims:

> William Wey was a fellow of Eton College, and there is a record dated 1457 of his permission to go on the 1458 pilgrimage. His work survives in a unique manuscript preserved at the Bodleian Library. It contains a table of money changes, a warning about practical details, some mnemonic verses naming places, a list of motives for going to the Holy Land, two narratives of a Jerusalem pilgrimage (one in English and one in Latin) dated 1458 and 1462, word lists of Greek and Hebrew, answers to questions about relics, lists of places, indulgences and shrines, an itinerary to Compostella, a pilgrims' song with music – in short, it is an *omnium-gatherum* of pilgrimage information.
>
> (Howard, 1980, pp. 20–1)

In keeping with its 'real' models, the pilgrimage part of *Mandeville's Travels* supplements the account of the journey with information and advice. The reader learns about distances between places and foreign alphabets (which are, incidentally, fabricated), and prospective pilgrims are warned of deceivers such as Cypriot monks who falsely claim to own half of the holy cross 'in order to get offerings' (p. 46). Advice is also given on how to recognize authentic balm, a popular but expensive souvenir from the Holy Land: 'You must know that balm which is natural and good is a clear yellow and has a strong sweet smell. If it is thick, red, or black it is adulterated' (p. 66).

In most pilgrim accounts, the holy places are given more significance than the act of travelling itself. Consequently, the narration of the pilgrim's journey is subordinated to the description of places and a relation of the holy stories associated with them. The pilgrim's personal experience of travel appears equally marginal; with its standardized routes, the pilgrimage served, after all, a purpose prescribed not only to the individual traveller, but to all pilgrims – and in fact all Christians: attaining the grace of God. An impression of the pilgrimage as a kind of travel virtually pre-*scribed* emerges clearly – among other examples – from a famous autobiography, *The Book of Margery Kempe*, which includes descriptions of various pilgrimages. Kempe, a most avid pilgrim, dictated her text to a priest, who gives 1436 as the date of the recording. Throughout the text, Kempe is referred to in the third person. When depicting her journey to Jerusalem, Kempe reports how monks would shepherd the pilgrims, taking them to the holy places, where the relevant Scriptural stories were told to them. The travelling experience remains, at least in the way it is reported, strictly bound by the purposes of the pilgrimage, and any personal reaction rendered in the text is also purely religious in nature:

> Then they went to the Church of the Holy Sepulchre in Jerusalem, and they were let in on the one day at evensong time, and remained until evensong time on the next day. Then the friars lifted up a cross and led the pilgrims about from one place to another where our Lord had suffered his pains and his Passion, every man and woman carrying a wax candle in one hand. And the friars always, as they went about, told them what our Lord suffered in every place. And this creature [Kempe] wept and sobbed as plenteously as though she had seen our Lord with her bodily eyes suffering his Passion at that time.   (p. 104)

Margery Kempe's experience (as presented in the text) appears to be determined more by the Holy Scriptures than by what she perceives

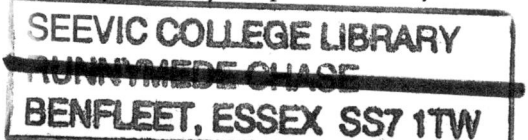

with her own corporeal eye. Since the pilgrims' experience of travel was thus heavily influenced by texts handed down to them, it is not surprising that pilgrim accounts frequently take their descriptions of holy places from other texts – the predestined nature of the pilgrim's experience makes a fresh description unnecessary, and perhaps even impossible. Thus pilgrims' accounts are particularly uniform and, curiously for the modern reader, many of them hardly record the experience of a foreign, an 'other' world, at all.

Palestine was the most distant country which a significant number of Western Europeans tended to visit. Occasionally, pilgrims' texts suggest that curiosity about these foreign parts was not insignificant in a decision to take part in a pilgrimage to Jerusalem.

> Pilgrims might endure hardship and physical dangers, but their journey could be as often a vacation as a penance, and, like any travelling vacationers, they saw new lands and peoples, heard strange tales, experienced different ways of thinking and living. Too frequently the pilgrim garb of the late Middle Ages was but a mask for the *curiosus*.
>
> (Zacher, 1976, p. 53)[8]

Officially, however, *curiositas* – that is an enthusiasm for this world rather than the one hereafter – was held by Christian doctrine to be a suspect motive for travelling, particularly unfitting to the pilgrimage. Thus many texts about the journey to Jerusalem impart little or nothing of the traveller's estrangement through the travelled world; the otherness of a world unfamiliar in its materiality – its topography, flora, fauna and inhabitants – is rarely emphasized. Instead, the focus of attention is on those aspects which other texts had already made familiar – not only the wealth of pilgrim literature, but above all the Bible that is a text which formed the keystone of the pilgrim's *own* culture. Locations in Palestine are of primary interest not for their topography, but rather for their association with events in the Bible. Pilgrim accounts do not focus so much on Palestine as a *foreign* country as on the country as the *Holy* Land: 'Palestine has little significant present tense, and the significance of its past tense is overwhelming – we might say blinding' (Campbell, 1991, p. 6).

Mandeville's Travels is a text which, seen as a whole, conveys the pleasure of travel and curiosity for foreign lands. Thus the following passage on Greece lays particular emphasis on the thrill of its otherness for the pilgrim from Western Europe:

And although these things do not bear on teaching you the way to the Holy Land, nevertheless they do touch on what I promised to show you, that is to say the customs, manners and *diversities* of countries. And since the land of Greece is the nearest country that *varies* and is *discordant* in faith and writing from us and our faith, I have therefore put it in here so that you may know the *differences* between our belief and theirs. For many men desire to hear of *unfamiliar* things and take pleasure in them.   (p. 52; my italics)

Although this passage is taken from the pilgrimage section of *Mandeville's Travels*, it is clear that the description of Greece goes against the grain of the pilgrim account proper. The text itself draws attention to this deviation from convention: 'although these things do not bear on teaching you the way to the Holy Land'. In the description of the Holy Land itself, however, Mandeville is more orthodox and hardly reports about any worldly sights, as Stephen Greenblatt (1991) also notes:

The Holy Land for Mandeville is the place of sacred metonymy: one Biblical story or holy legend is propped tightly against another, and it seems as if the major events of Jesus' life, along with careers of the patriarchs and prophets, transpired in a confused rush within a space of some ten square meters.   (p. 41)

The impression of a rush from site to site is particularly intense in Mandeville's description of the route from Bethlehem to Jerusalem, which contained the highlights of the pilgrimage. The shortest leg of the journey appears to be virtually congested with holy places which the pilgrim feels obliged to visit:

From Bethlehem to Jerusalem is only two miles. On the road to Jerusalem, half a mile from Bethlehem, is a church, where the angels told the shepherds of the birth of Christ. And on that road is the tomb of Rachel, mother of Joseph the Patriarch; and she died as soon as she had borne Benjamin. There was she buried; and Jacob her husband set twelve great stones over her, betokening the twelve Patriarchs. Half a mile from Jerusalem the star appeared again to the Three Kings. And on this road to Jerusalem are many churches, by which pilgrims go to Jerusalem.   (p. 76)

Mandeville's Travels thus follows authentic pilgrimage texts in its description of a Palestine travelled with Biblical blinkers. The only section of the pilgrim part of the *Travels* to display a more in-depth interest in the 'other' is Mandeville's long conversation with the Sultan of Jerusalem. Here, however, the prime interest is religion; Christianity and Islam are compared in detail, with explicit reference even to Christian sins.

Curiosity is given full rein only when Mandeville goes beyond the Holy Land and progresses from the Middle into the Far East. Here, in its second part, the book follows a more worldly – and 'entertaining' – type of travel writing: reports of missionary and mercantile travel to the Far East. This kind of travel writing, of which Marco Polo's account is the most famous example, was based – at least in large part – on the travellers' own experiences. It became common in the late Middle Ages, when the East opened up under the Khans of the Mongol Empire.

Travel to the Far East

Travellers to the Far East, such as Marco Polo or the missionary William of Rubruck, set off on their journeys unguided by itineraries and handbooks. In contrast to the pilgrims, they did not travel on routes that were prescribed and, in their own accounts, they provided much less information for future travellers. Nevertheless, the Far East, too, was no unwritten territory. From the classical authorities, late medieval travellers had inherited the image of a marvellous East populated by fabulous creatures – an image also disseminated by the Alexander romance and the (forged) 'Letter' of Prester John, the legendary priest-cum-king. The 'monstrous races' (Friedman, 1981) authorized by this tradition are mentioned even in the texts of the actual travellers to the East.[9] In fact, in accordance with the great value placed on textual tradition, the incredible marvels included in Marco Polo's account appeared more believable to his contemporary audience than did the empirical – yet previously unrecorded – observations he had actually made.

The wonders of the East are also encountered in the second half of *Mandeville's Travels*; excerpt 1 presents a cumulative list of the 'monsters' described by Pliny and others. However, precise descriptions of these unseen creatures are significantly absent, and in other respects, too, the presentation in this part of *Mandeville's Travels* is often imprecise. Most marvellous places, for example, are only vaguely localized: 'From this country men go through the Great Sea Ocean by way of many isles and different countries, which would be tedious to relate' (p. 127).[10]

Apart from wonders unseen, however, the texts of actual travellers to the Far East which Mandeville followed included many descriptions rooted in empirical observation. William of Rubruck and Marco Polo, for example, meticulously record the merchandise and natural resources of the areas travelled, and the Khan and his subjects are depicted in their actual living circumstances. The travellers seek out contact with the countries' inhabitants, and they engage in conversation with them to gather more information about their customs.

Mandeville is indebted to Marco Polo, for example, for his account of the use of paper money in the realm of the Great Khan. Here, the description is far more detailed than in his report of the unobservable monsters:

> This Emperor can spend as much as he wishes to, for he coins no money except from leather, or paper, or the bark of trees. When this money gets old, and the printing on it is defaced by heavy use, it is brought to the King's treasury and his treasurer gives new for old. This money is printed on both sides, like money is in other countries, and it is current throughout the Great Khan's lands. They make no money there of gold and silver, when it is brought thither by different nationalities from other lands, but the Emperor has his palace adorned with it and makes useful things of it as he pleases. (p. 153)

In keeping with the tradition of missionary and mercantile travel, such passages present a Far East whose inhabitants it was possible and necessary to *deal* with, to establish contact with – if only for practical reasons. The travelogue resulting from this kind of travel experience is thus not only object-orientated, but it also claims to represent this object truthfully and accurately.

In the English-speaking world, this line of travel writing was consolidated in the accounts of exploration and discovery in the sixteenth century. The assumption that foreign parts were marvellous and populated by fabulous races was certainly long-standing,[11] but the empirically orientated travelogue took an increasingly stronger hold. *Mandeville's Travels* went from being an authority to a text reputed to be a monstrous hoax – just as there developed a general suspicion of (old-style) travel writing as a genre prone to lie. This unfavourable image finds expression, for example, in Shakespeare's *The Tempest* (1610). When Prospero conjures up a banquet for the visitors stranded on his island (Act III, Scene iii), a clear association is made between the travelogue and the fantastical. Faced with Prospero's incredible spectacle, the shipwrecked visitors will now even believe the accounts of travellers: 'And I'll be sworn 'tis true: travellers ne'er did lie, / Though fools at home condemn 'em' (lines 26–7).

At the same time, however, Shakespeare's sources for *The Tempest* include contemporary reports of an actual shipwreck in the Bermudas, that is the 'new' world. Indeed, it was the reporting home about America which gave European travel writing a significant new impetus. Early Modern voyagers to America were motivated by fresh political, economic and sometimes even scientific aims; above all, the New World called for new paradigms of perception. Stephen Greenblatt (1991, p. 24) describes this development as a shift 'from medieval wonder as a sign of dispossession to Renaissance wonder as an agent of appropriation'. Mary Campbell (1988) also underlines the material moment of the emerging new paradigms:

> [America] was becoming the locus par excellence of commercial activity, political expansionism, new scientific knowledge. It was a bunch of real, palpable atoms, in furious spin. It could not be Paradise (does one *mine* Paradise or organize commerce with the *locus amoenus*?), and it had to be something. Writers had to convey this Something without the help of classical authority or popular legend.   (p. 224)[12]

The caesura in the given world-view thus goes hand in hand with an essential change in the textual strategies of the travel account. The material interest in the 'discovery', exploration and colonization of America causes the travellers to scrutinize this foreign world, to perceive it in all its empirical qualities – and to write home about it in meticulous detail.

Early Modern accounts of discovery and exploration

Not until the second half of the sixteenth century did the English catch up with the Spanish and Portuguese in the race for the New World. Their voyages to America were motivated primarily by economic factors: the acquisition of wealthy possessions overseas and the discovery of new routes for their traditional trade in Asia (whose development was to be furthered by the foundation, in 1600, of the East India Company).[13] In 1576, Martin Frobisher embarked on the first search for the Northwest Passage to Asia. In 1577, Francis Drake set out on the voyage which would make him the first Englishman to circumnavigate the globe. The first attempt to set up an English colony in North America was made by Sir Richard Grenville in 1585.

The travels of explorers, merchants and colonizers of the Early Modern period gave rise to a panoply of travel writing throughout Europe, which was collected in extensive compilations.[14] Among the most significant of these collections was Richard Hakluyt's *Principal Navigations, Voyages and Discoveries of the English Nation* (1589). The compiler was a geographer with considerable political influence at the court of Queen Elizabeth I. As Urs Bitterli (1991, p. 240) points out, Hakluyt's monumental collection sprang from both scientific interest and a desire to promote overseas expansion and the colonization of North America. The former made him acknowledge the geographical and naturalist discoveries of other seafaring nations. At the same time, Hakluyt was convinced that England was destined to take on the leading role in the exploration of the world, and he thus collated the knowledge gathered by his countrymen with particular care, demonstrating the extent to which England had already adopted this new role. Hakluyt's compilation was avidly read, as were all European travel compendia; the 1600 edition of *Principal Navigations* already ran into three volumes. Hakluyt's enterprise was even expanded by Samuel Purchas, in his equally successful collections, *Purchas his Pilgrimage* (1613) and *Hakluytus Posthumus or Purchas his Pilgrimes* (1625).

In addition to the compilations of travel writing, new knowledge about the world was recorded in ever more precise atlases and cosmographies. Artefacts and natural objects from distant lands appeared in the so-called cabinets of curiosities (precursors of the modern museum) as tangible proof of the reality of these lands which were 'marvellous' in an entirely new way.[15] Travellers even kidnapped, shipped home and displayed the inhabitants of the foreign world.[16] Accounts of travel to this world were thus becoming increasingly verifiable – not only by other travellers, but also by readers back home. Mary Campbell (1988) summarizes the consequences this had on the travel writer, who was not so much obliged to follow old 'authorities' as to present a credible eyewitness account:

He need not be comprehensive beyond his own experience . . . He need not organize his data according to conceptual categories. Others would do that for him. His most essential contribution had become the first-person narrative of experience, a work whose claim to the reader's attention had to do with the more properly literary features of story and personae. And the situation that made the encyclopedias and collections possible – the new accessibility of other worlds and the frequency of travel to them – also put a new pressure of veracity on the traveler. His reports could be, would be, verified or exposed.   (p. 218)

The following section will examine some strategies of presentation which helped to enhance the effect of authenticity in a number of texts from Hakluyt's collection dedicated to voyages to North America and the first English attempts to colonize it.[17] The most famous text relating to this enterprise is Thomas Hariot's 'Brief and True Report of the New Found Land of Virginia', one of the most important early sources on the climate, nature, resources and inhabitants of the North American continent, and the opportunities it offered to the English.

All these texts are written in the first person and are indeed autobiographical, composed by members – though not always the leaders – of the respective expeditions. Invariably, these first-person reporters are distinguished by a strong sense of the realities of the New World and a keen awareness of its difference from Europe. Thomas Hariot, for example, makes explicit reference to 'the difference we found in our travels' (p. 134). The empirical otherness of the New World requires a representation rooted in actual observation. Not surprisingly, the voyages of exploration yielded many precise visual records of America and its inhabitants, such as the famous drawings, tinted with watercolour, by John White. The written equivalent of these illustrations is a high amount of detailed description in travel texts. However, in order to depict phenomena which had been previously undescribed and for which their own language often had no vocabulary, it was necessary for the writers to find or develop the appropriate expressions. Comparison with the old world was one way in which the writers tried to conceptualize the new; they also borrowed words from the indigenous languages of America, or they created new words.

> The Renaissance explorer had only the elemental words of sense experience. Even some phenomena we now consider 'elemental' had to find new names. American nature was mountainous, riverine, tempestuous. *Waterfall, cataract, lagoon, whirlpool, swamp, keys, hurricane, tornado, thunderstorm*: as vernacular English words, all joined the language during the first century of the period of English exploration.
>
> (Campbell, 1988, p. 226)

Not only were individual new words necessary to represent the foreignness of America – a whole new discourse was developed by the Elizabethan explorers: a discourse characterized by an insistence on precision, vividness and verifiability. Places, for example, are often located according to latitude, as in Edward Hayes's report of 'Sir Humphrey Gilbert's Newfoundland Voyage', which also explicitly emphasizes the intent of an *'exact* discovery':

> Many voyages have been intended, yet hitherto never any thoroughly accomplished by our nation of exact discovery into the bowels of those main, ample and vast countries, extended infinitely into the north from 30 degrees, or rather from 25 degrees of septentrional latitude. (p. 21)

As the Elizabethan voyagers depict the differentness of America from Europe in great detail, the foreign world is not generalized and reduced to '*the* other' as it was in ancient and medieval accounts of the fabulous East. Nowhere is the interest in *concrete* differentness clearer than in Hariot's 'Brief and True Report'. Hariot is also quite open about the reason for his meticulous stocktaking of America, namely the New World's potential for trade and colonization:

> The Treatise wherof I will divide into three special parts. In the first I will make declaration of such commodities there already found or to be raised ... These commodities, for distinction sake, I call Merchantable.
>
> In the second I will set down all the commodities which we know the country by our experience yields of itself for victual and sustenance of man's life ...
>
> In the last part I will mention such other commodities as I think behoveful for those that shall inhabit and plant there to know of; which specially concern building, as also some other necessary uses. With a brief description of the nature and manners of the people of the country. (pp. 109–10)

Throughout Hakluyt's collection of explorers' accounts, North America is depicted as a country of anticipated and, above all, actual wealth. Common to all the following extracts is an emphasis on the abundance of natural resources:

> The soil along the coast is not deep of earth, bringing forth abundantly peas, small yet good feeding for cattle. (Hayes, p. 37)

Here we arrived about the midst of June at the east end, and rode in eighteen fathom water in fair white sand and very good anchorage, and for trial heaved a line overboard and found wonderful great cod fish.   (Wyet, p. 59)

This island had many goodly woods full of deer, conies, hares, and fowl, even in the midst of summer in incredible abundance. The woods are not such as you find on Bohemia, Moscovy, or Siberia, barren and fruitless, but the highest and reddest cedars of the world, far bettering the cedars of the Azores, of the Indies, of Lebanon; pine, cypress, sassafras, the lentisk, or the tree that bears the mastic; the tree that bears the rind of black cinammon, of which master Winter brought from the straits of Magellan, and many other of excellent smell and quality.
                                          (Amadas and Barlow, p. 67)

So abounding with sweet trees that bring such sundry rich and pleasant gums, grapes of such greatness, yet wild, as France, Spain nor Italy have no greater; so many sorts of apothecary drugs, such several kinds of flax, one kind like silk, the same gathered of a grass as common there as grass is here.   (Lane, p. 84)

Similarly, descriptions of the inhabitants of the New World reveal a precise anthropological interest, as in excerpt 2 from Hariot's report. Of course, this interest was partly determined by the travellers' need for contact with these populations. The North American Indians, for example, are not portrayed as fabulous creatures, but as human beings strongly resembling the European visitors: 'of such a difference of statures only as we in England', Hariot describes them in the passage in question.[18] He displays a clear interest in the indigenous way of life – its social organization, religion and myths. In conversations with the Indians, he interviews them systematically, and when rendering these conversations in his text, he makes use of many indigenous terms:

They think that all the gods are of human shape, and therefore they represent them by images in the forms of men, which they call *kewasowok*, one alone is called *kewas*. Them they place in houses appropriate or temples, which they call *machicomuck*, where they worship, pray, sing, and make many times offering unto them. In some *machicomuck* we have seen but one *kewas*, in some two, and in others three. The common sort think them to be also gods.

They believe also the immortality of the soul ...

For the confirmation of this opinion they told me two stories of two men that had been lately dead and revived again. (pp. 128–9)

In this passage, the beliefs of the indigenous people are presented from a Christian perspective, but the author nevertheless attempts to grasp the otherness of this religion in precise terms. Hariot is further-more respectful of the Indians' practical abilities, not measuring them against European standards, but relative to 'their own manner':

In respect of us they are a people poor, and for want of skill and judgement in the knowledge and use of our things, do esteem our trifles before things of greater value. Notwithstanding in their own manner (considering the want of such means as we have), they seem very ingenious. For although they have no such tools, nor any such crafts, sciences and arts as we, yet in those things they do, they show excellence of wit. (pp. 127–8)

To summarize, the accounts of Elizabethan exploration consoli-dated the genre – as we understand it today – in the following respects: they are based on empirical observation and are autobiographical reports of actual journeys. As far as the relationship between the subject and object of travel is concerned, however, there remains, despite the texts' autobiographical character, a heavy emphasis on the object, that is the country travelled. The peripheral status in the account of the traveller's *personal* experience may be explained, at least in part, by the travellers' mentality as explorers and colonizers: the travellers/writers, as far as they present themselves in their texts, largely identify with the official purpose of their voyages. Nevertheless, with its accounts of discovery and exploration, the Elizabethan era introduced a type of travelogue which is already very close to our modern understanding of the genre, and which was continued in the centuries to follow with various points of emphasis.

The writing of scientific travel

R. W. Frantz (1934, pp. 7–8) sets the end of the 'heroic period' of English exploration at around 1600, claiming that subsequent over-seas travel – and its kind of travelogue – was predominantly scientific in nature: 'In the seventeenth century, . . . the English voyager was seized by a great soberness. The Elizabethan adventurer and explorer was replaced by the Restoration buccaneer and scientist.' However, even the Elizabethan account of exploration, with its focus on empirical experience, belonged to a new scientific discourse. Thomas Hariot, for example, was a mathematician and astronomer, whom Sir Walter Raleigh made a scientific adviser for the expedition to Roanoake Island (1583–6). As early as 1605, in *The Advancement of Learning*, Francis Bacon included the voyages of exploration in his concept of a new, empirically based science: 'And this proficience in navigation and discoveries may plant also an expectation of the further proficience and augmentation of all sciences; because it may seem they are ordained by God to be coevals, that is, to meet in one age' (p. 78).[19]

It was not until the second half of the seventeenth century, however, in the age of the New Science, that travel for scientific purposes gained an influential basis. In 1665/6, the Royal Society [for the Improvement of Natural Knowledge] published a 'Catalogue of Directions' for travellers in its *Philosophical Transactions*. This catalogue closed with notes on 'General Heads for the Natural History of a Country, Great or Small', drawn by the chemist Robert Boyle, a founder member of the society. Later, other scientific societies as well as the British admiralty sponsored scientific expeditions, with strict instructions for the instruments to be used and observations to be made.[20]

Travel for scientific purposes was encouraged to such an extent that, in the late seventeenth century, it even became bound up with the adventures of buccaneers. Thus Lionel Wafer, a surgeon who accompanied a number of privateering expeditions, wrote his *New Voyage and Description of the Isthmus of America* (1699) not to entertain, but chiefly to inform his readers about this region of America. A rather cursory narration of the course of the voyage is therefore interspersed with chapters on purely scientific matters: 'Mr. Wafer's Description of the Isthmus of America', 'Of the Trees, Fruits, &c. in the Isthmus of America', 'Of the Animals: And first of Beasts and Reptiles', 'The Birds, and Flying Insects', 'Of the Indian Inhabitants: Their Manners, Customs, &c.'

The career of William Dampier also displays a mixture of privateering adventures and the pursuit of science. Dampier was one of the most famous buccaneers of his time, and the accounts of his expeditions, such as *A New Voyage round the World* (1697), were greatly popular with the contemporary reader. However, Dampier also put his voyages to scientific and nautical use, and his accounts are often marked by a focus on description, to which the subtitle of the *New Voyage* actually draws attention: 'Describing particularly, The *Isthmus* of *America*, several Coasts and Islands in the *West Indies* . . . the *Cape* of *Good Hope*, and *Santa Hellena*. Their Soil, Rivers, Harbours, Plants, Fruits, Animals, and Inhabitants. Their Customs, Religion, Government, Trade, *etc.*' Compared with the extensive descriptive passages of the text, adventurous episodes of the voyage often appear to be played down by being narrated somewhat soberly and in haste, as in the following passage on an encounter with the Spaniards in California:

> While we lay here, Captain *Swan* went into this lake again, and landed 150 Men on the N.E. side, and marched into the Country: About a mile from the Landing-place, as they were entring a dry *Salina*, or Salt-pond, they fired at two *Indians* that crost the way before them: one of them being wounded in the thigh fell down, and being examined, he told our Men, that there was an *Indian* Town 4 or 5 leagues off, and that the way which they were going would bring them thither. While they were in discourse with the *Indian*, they were attacked by 100 *Spanish* Horsemen, who came with a design to scare them back, but wanted both Arms and Hearts to do it. Our Men past on from hence, and in their way marched through a Savannah of long dry Grass. This the *Spaniards* set on fire, thinking to burn them; but this did not hinder our Men from marching forward, though it did trouble them a little. They rambled for want of Guides all this day, and part of the next, before they came to the Town the *Indian* spake of. There they found a company of *Spaniards* and *Indians* who made head against them; but were driven out of the Town of a short dispute.   (p. 265)

The famous European explorer-scientists of the late eighteenth century include Louis Antoine de Bougainville, Georg Forster, Alexander von Humboldt and James Cook. The records of their expeditions do not altogether lack a sense of adventure, but their emphasis is chiefly on the scientific merit of the enterprise. They embarked on their voyages with precise instructions for observations in the realms of geography, astronomy, meteorology, botany, anthropology and so on. They were equipped with various instruments, specialized naturalists and scientists, assistants responsible for collecting and preserving samples of flora and fauna, as well as artists who produced maps and visual records. The work of these artists would later form an important component of the voyagers' accounts.

The aim of the factual travel account was to spread graphically before the reader and viewer a great range of exact information about the world. This alliance between science and art suggested that accurate text wedded to precise image would offer a progressivist paradigm for understanding the physical processes at work in the universe.

(Stafford, 1984, p. 59).[21]

In order to be as precise as possible, the scientific observer, as Stafford notes, 'looke[d] at, not over, that which he explore[d]' (p. 40). The following extract from Cook's *Journal* about his third and last voyage around the world is an exemplary illustration of the great value placed on *close* observation – and the exact recording of it. The foreign world is scrutinized even in minute details – such as the Arctic ice which Cook 'examined' in 1778, and which he describes in his text with exact numerical data:

> Having but little wind, I went with the boats to examine the state of the ice, and found it consi[s]ts of loose pieces of various extent, and so close together that I could hardly enter the outer edge with a boat ... I took Notice that it was all pure transparent ice, except the upper surface which was a little porous. It appeared to be intirely [sic] composed of frozen Snow and had been all formed at sea ... The pieces of ice that formed the outer edge of this feild [sic] were from 40 to 50 yards in extent to 4 or 5 and I judged that the larger pi[e]ces reach'd 30 feet or more under the surface of the Water. It appeared to me, very improbable that this ice could be the produce of the preceding Winter alone, but rather that of a great many, or that the little that remained of the summer would distroy [sic] the tenth part of what now remained, sence [sic] the Sun had already exerted the full influence [of] his rays.   (pp. 424–5)

Due to their purpose, accounts by explorer-scientists are marked by a strong focus on the object of travel, as was also noted in Chapter 1 of Darwin's *Voyage of the Beagle*. It will be shown (pp. 61–2) that, in the course of the eighteenth century, the account of scientific travel reveals increasing attention to the traveller's subjective experience. Even then, however, the distinctive tone in this type of travelogue is set by its representation of the travelled world.

It is clear that scientific exploration demands a programme of travel and a systematic analysis and presentation of its results. Nevertheless, travelling and writing with a method is by no means confined to this type of journey, and it also appears before the age of the New Science. In the sixteenth century, a comprehensive literature on the methodology of travel concentrated not so much on overseas travel as on journeys within the 'old' world – in particular those journeys whose prime intent was to foster the traveller's education and personal development. From the sixteenth to the eighteenth centuries, an institutionalized form of travel for education, the Grand Tour, was of particular cultural significance. This tour of certain European countries did not take the English traveller to territories entirely foreign, but rather – at least in its original form – to countries abroad and yet familiar. In the writing based on this kind of journey, a travelogue emerges in the course of the eighteenth century which displays a marked concern with the traveller's personal, subjective experience.

3
Paths to the Self

[1] *I was imbarked at Dover, about tenne of the clocke in the morning,
the fourteenth of may, being Saturday and Whitsuneve, Anno 1608,
and arrived in Calais (which Caesar calleth Ictius portus, a maritime
towne of that part of Picardy, which is commonly called le pais
reconquis; that is, the recovered Province, inhabited in former times
by the ancient Morini.) about five of the clocke in the afternoone,
after I had varnished the exterior parts of the ship with the excre-
mentall ebullitions of my tumultuous stomach, as desiring to satiate
the gormandizing paunches of the hungry Haddocks ... with that
wherewith I had superfluously stuffed my selfe at land, having made
my rumbling belly their capacious aumbrie.*

(Thomas Coryat, *Coryats Crudities*, 1611, p. 152)

[2] *My time [in Bologna] then has been past thus – every morning from
about ten to two I have been employed in seeing pictures, churches,
and palaces – then I'd up to go to the Marshal's. He generally
contrives to have some one of learning or merit at dinner. I stay there
till between 6 and 7. Then a Marquis Morini ... comes by the order
of the Countess to attend me to some conversation or assembly.
There I meet her, and play at loo or primiera very low a couple of
hours, then I go home write my journal or notes critical in the
margins of my books of painting etc[.] and go to bed. I have besides
this an hour in the morning for the same employment.*

(Letter of Rev. Norton Nicholls, 1771, cited in Black, 1991, p. 39)

[3] *Thus the whole circle of travellers may be reduced to the following*
Heads.

40

Idle Travellers,
Inquisitive Travellers,
Lying Travellers,
Proud Travellers,
Vain Travellers,
Splenetic Travellers.
Then follow the Travellers of Necessity,
The delinquent and felonious Traveller,
The unfortunate and innocent Traveller,
The simple Traveller,
And last of all (if you please) The
Sentimental Traveller (meaning thereby myself).

(Laurence Sterne, *A Sentimental Journey through France and Italy*,
1768, p. 15)

The Grand Tour

The Early Modern period was not only the age of the explorer; it also saw the Humanist leaning towards Old and New Learning and the resulting educational reform. In this context, travel as a part of education emerges – a purpose hitherto uncommon except for the scholar's peregrination to European universities. A type of journey associated with a particular value for the traveller's formal education and his personal development was the Grand Tour: a social institution which took English travellers to certain countries of the Continent, particularly France and Italy, but also Germany, the Low Countries and Switzerland.[1] Italy – as the origin of European culture and civilization – was generally considered the highlight of the journey, not only during the Humanist period. In the slightly mocking words of Dr Johnson, who deeply regretted never having been to Italy himself, '[a] man who has not been in Italy, is always conscious of an inferiority, from his not having seen what it is expected a man should see.'[2] In the eighteenth century, particularly during the Enlightenment, the educational journey was widely practised and avidly discussed, as for instance in the chapter on travel of Rousseau's influential didactic novel, *Émile* (1762). The universalist, pan-European spirit of the Enlightenment fostered travel as a means of edification, and the Grand Tour saw its heyday after the Peace of Utrecht (1713–14) which concluded the War of the Spanish Succession.

Many important political and intellectual figures in Britain from the sixteenth to the nineteenth centuries had, as young men, taken the trip round Europe, its cabinets or museums, libraries, academies and various other institutions of public life. Among other things, the tour helped to polish the traveller's cosmopolitan manners and to shape his aesthetic taste in, for example, architecture (the Palladian style comes to mind) and interior design, collecting art or appreciating opera; 'standards were high in general and tourism served to enrich the British elite culturally' (Black, 1985, p. 229). Men of letters alone travelled in great numbers: Sir Philip Sidney, John Milton, Samuel Johnson, James Boswell, Henry Fielding, Arthur Young, James Thomson, Horace Walpole and Thomas Gray, William Beckford, Robert Southey, William Wordsworth, William Hazlitt and Lord Byron, to name just some of the most famous.

The intention of the Grand Tour was to add – after the traveller's student years – the finishing touches to his education and the process of his socialization. Originally, it had also been a part of the courtier's professional training, preparing him for a career in a political, or more commonly, diplomatic office: 'in the sixteenth century there were no schools of political economy, of modern history or modern languages at the universities. A sound knowledge of these things had to be obtained by first-hand observation' (Howard, 1914, p. 23). Henry VIII thus financed the tour of many promising young courtiers and later English monarchs continued this practice. The stay on the Continent, which could last a number of years, enabled the traveller to familiarize himself with foreign customs, laws, forms of government and modern languages, as well as to establish contacts.[3]

Because of their journey's eventual benefit to the nation, tourists of the Continent were also known as *patriotic* travellers. In his *Instructions for Forreine Travell* (1642), James Howell explicitly numbers the tourist's patriotic obligations:

The most materiall use therefore of *Forreine Travell* is to find out something that may bee applyable to the publique utility of one's own Countrey, as a *Noble Personage* of late yeares did, who observing the uniforme and regular way of stone structure up and down *Italy*, hath introduced that *forme* of building to *London* and *Westminster*, and else where . . .

Another seeing their *Dikes*, and draynings in the *Netherlands*, hath been a cause that much hath beene added, to lengthen the skirts of this *Island*.

Another in imitation of their *aqueducts* and *fluces*, and conveyance of waters abroad, brought *Ware-water* through *London streets* . . .

(p. 73)

The tour served the encyclopedic collection of all kinds of knowledge that could be potentially useful for England or Britain and its relationship with other nations; along with the areas named above, this included observations on climate, trade, agriculture or fortifications. Curiosities and details of everyday life were also recorded with great care. Thomas Coryat's *Crudities* (1611), for example, registers the unusual height of beds in Savoy ('so high that a man could hardly get into his bedde without some kinde of climing', p. 225), or the habit of Italians to 'alwaies at their meales use a little forke when they cut their meat' (p. 236). While Coryat considers the latter highly recommendable ('seing all mens fingers are not alike cleane', ibid.), he did not relish the Italians' custom to eat their meats 'sprinkled with cheese' (ibid.).

The Grand Tour was for a long time a male preserve, and initially confined to the aristocracy. Following the Napoleonic Wars and the blockade of the Continental System (1806–15), which prevented the English from conducting the tour, travelling in Europe became less expensive, easier and safer, thanks, in part, to a well-developed European stagecoach network. This led to a marked increase in continental travel, which was now open to the bourgeois class as well. Since the late eighteenth century, even women went on the trip through Europe, though they were mostly accompanied by their husbands and families. By now, edification was no longer the main motive for travelling the Continent, and the Grand Tour in its archetypal form merged into tourism as we understand it today.

As early as the sixteenth century, the Grand Tour and its purpose were the subject of a lively debate surrounding its advantages and risks. These risks included, for example, the temptations presented by inns and brothels beyond the scope of parental control. John Evelyn, who stayed in Naples in 1644, makes a note in his diary of the abundance of local prostitutes to which he was exposed: 'the town is so pestered with these cattle, that there needs no small mortification to preserve from their enchantment' (p. 103). Roman Catholicism, too, was considered a dangerous allurement to Protestant English travellers; in the sixteenth and early seventeenth centuries, their travel licences often explicitly barred their entry to Catholic regions.[4] Apart from the distractions offered by wine, women and papists, the tourist could also be tempted by pure wanderlust and by the same curiosity which had already threatened to lead the medieval pilgrim astray. The pleasures of travel and seeing foreign lands are mentioned both in accounts of the Grand Tour themselves and in treatises on the tour. Thomas Coryat, for example, admits in his *Crudities* how much he enjoyed travel for travel's sake: 'Yea such is the exuberancie and superfluity of these exoticke pleasures, that for my owne part I will most truly affirme, I reaped more entire and sweet comfort in five moneth travels of those seven countries mentioned in the front of my booke, then I did all the dayes of my life before in England, which contayned two and thirty yeares' (p. 9). James Howell, too, names curiosity as a motivation for travel, and, in the second edition of his *Instructions for Forreine Travell* (1642), includes an appendix dedicated to travels in Turkey and the Levant – that is, areas clearly beyond the traditional domain of a Grand Tour. This appendix was aimed chiefly at travellers whose curiosity was not satisfied by the standard trip: 'If my *Travellers* curiosity hath a further extent, and that Europe cannot bound the largnes[s] of his desires' (p. 82). Fynes Moryson was one such traveller for whom the bounds of Europe were too narrow. As recorded in his *Itinerary* (1617), he set off on a ten-year journey at the age of twenty-three, after completing his academic studies, and travelled as far as Turkey and Jerusalem. His travels were expressly intended not only to prepare him for a career in the legal profession, but also to satisfy his inborn passion for travel – 'as well for the ornament of this profession, as out of my innated [*sic*] desire to gaine experience by trauelling into forraigne parts' (Part I, p. 1).

Curiosity as a *sole* motivation for going on a Grand Tour was generally disapproved of. A healthy curiosity, however, was defended, as in Laurence Sterne's sermon on 'The Prodigal Son'. To Sterne, it is precisely a sense of curiosity which makes a person educable in the first place. Nevertheless, this curiosity was to be channelled in order to make travel a rewarding and profitable experience:

> The love of variety, or curiosity of seeing new things, which is the same, or at least a sister passion to it, – seems woven into the frame of every son and daughter of Adam; we usually speak of it as one of Nature's levities, though planted within us for the solid purposes of carrying forward the mind to fresh inquiry and knowledge. Strip us of it, the mind (I fear) would doze for ever over the present page, and we should all of us rest at ease with such objects as presented themselves in the parish or province where we first drew breath.
>
> It is to this spur, which is ever in our sides, that we owe the impatience of this desire for travelling; the passion is no way bad, but, as others are, in its mismanagement or excess; – order it rightly, the advantages are worth the pursuit; – the chief of which are, – to learn the languages, the laws and customs, and understand the

government and interest, of other nations, – to acquire an urbanity and confidence of behaviour, and fit the mind more easily for conversation and discourse; – to take us out of the company of our aunts and grandmothers, and from the track of nursery mistakes; and, by shewing us new objects, or old ones in new lights, to reform our judgements; – by tasting perpetually the varieties of Nature, to know what is *good*, – by observing the address and arts of man, to conceive what is *sincere*; – and, by seeing the difference of so many various humours and manners, – to look into ourselves, and form our own.   (p. 446)[5]

As Sterne states quite clearly, a person who travels subjects the structures of his personality, his mind and his emotions to a new process of experience, which may, in extreme cases, destabilize the traveller's previous world-view. This extreme was, however, not in the spirit of the Grand Tour, which, as an institutional form of educational travel, was intended to lead the traveller safely back to the bosom of his mother country, whose values and customs he was expected to readopt. In no way was the Grand Tour intended to estrange him from his homeland. Fynes Moryson, in the third part of his *Itinerary*, expressly refers to the necessity for the returning tourist to fully reintegrate into English society:

As Souldiers in a good Common-wealth, when the warre is ended, returne to the works of their calling . . . , so that he returning home, lay aside the spoone and forke of *Italy*, the affected gestures of *France*, and all strange apparrell, yea, euen those manners which with good iudgement he allowes, if they be disagreeable to his Countrey-men: For we are not all borne reformers of the World.

(p. 35)

Similarly, Francis Bacon explicitly warns the traveller at the end of his essay 'Of Travels' (1625): 'let it appear that he doth not change his country manners for those of foreign parts; but only prick in some flowers of that he hath learned abroad into the customs of his own country' (pp. 81–2). Travellers who ignored such admonitions and cultivated continental mannerisms on their return were the exception to the rule and generally ridiculed.

In adopting foreign fashions of dress and affected pronunciations of English words, Englishmen, . . . often went to the most extravagant lengths and made themselves the laughing-stock of all sensible people. Young exquisites who had traveled in Italy, and who, as Walpole says, wore 'long curls and spying-glasses,' founded the Macaroni Club, to which no one could be admitted who had not traveled abroad. ... they speedily attracted attention by their absurd style of dress and exaggerated foreign manners.

(Mead, 1972, p. 397)

The Macaronis were apparently incapable of balancing their experience of the foreign with the demands of life at home. They could not cope with a situation which Dennis Porter (1991) has described as the basic paradox of the Grand Tour: 'The tour was both a form of higher education and an instrument of social reproduction that required an extended absence from paternal surveillance and an exposure to temptation that risked subverting the institutional goals' (p. 51).

In light of this paradox, however, the traditional Grand Tour was also designed to safeguard the traveller from being led entirely astray. In its original and canonized form, it did not embrace lands which were completely foreign. The tour was a journey through European cultures and civilizations which were far more familiar to the culture back home than the worlds encountered by the contemporary explorer. To Thomas Coryat, Venice was 'the most resplendent Mirrour of Europe' (*Crudities*, p. 2), and in classical Italy, travellers recognized their own cultural heritage. The tour thus took its travellers to a world whose otherness was clearly circumscribed and whose effect on a young gentleman's development was therefore calculable. Moreover, like the medieval pilgrimage, it normally led its travellers on paths well-trodden and well-depicted in numerous accounts and other texts. If they did not wish to, Grand Tourists were not obliged to involve themselves fully in the foreign country but could appreciate it through the filter provided by the prescribed educational programme. The travelled world was considered particularly edifying where it was in harmony with the aesthetic and ethical values of the traveller's home culture – or where it had provided the classical model for this culture in the first place.

For a 'proper' journey, where the educational purpose was at the fore, there was, moreover, a variety of aids to hand. Francis Bacon's essay 'Of Travels' recommended the guidance of an experienced tutor and the keeping of a detailed diary:

That young men travel under some tutor, or grave servant, I allow well; so that he be such a one that hath the language, and hath been in the country before; whereby he may be able to tell them what things are worthy to be seen in the country where they go; what acquaintances they are to seek; what exercises or discipline the place yieldeth. For else young men shall go hooded, and look abroad little. It is a strange thing, that in sea voyages, where there is nothing to be seen but sky and sea, men should make diaries; but in land-travel, wherein so much is to be observed, for the most part they omit it; as if chance were fitter to be registered than observation. Let diaries therefore be brought in use. The things to be seen and observed are, the courts of princes, specially when they give audience to ambassadors; the courts of justice, while they sit and hear causes; and so of consistories ecclesiastic; the churches and monasteries, with the monuments which are therein extant; the walls and fortifications of cities and towns, and so the havens and harbours; antiquities and ruins; libraries; colleges, disputations, and lectures, where any are; shipping and navies; houses and gardens of state and pleasure, near great cities; armories; arsenals; magazines; exchanges; burses; ware houses; exercises of horsemanship, fencing, training of soldiers and the like; comedies, such whereunto the better sort of persons do resort; treasuries of jewels and robes; cabinets and rarities; and, to conclude, whatsoever is memorable in the places where they go.

(Bacon, 1908, pp. 79–80)

Where the travellers were not accompanied by tutors, they could resort to the extensive apodemic literature available since the 1670s, which outlined a 'profitable' – since methodical – way of travelling and registering the travel experience.[6] Among the most influential works of travel theory was James Howell's *Instructions for Forreine Travell*, to which reference has already been made (see p. 42, 44). Some of these manuals were so detailed, in fact, that they clearly overshot the mark. As Justin Stagl (1983b, p. 27) points out, no traveller could ever have heeded all the recommendations itemized in Leopold Graf Berchtold's *An Essay to Direct and Extend the Inquiries of Patriotic Travellers* (1789), which included a system of 2443 questions concerning all conceivable aspects of the country travelled. As well as such specialized literature, many tour accounts, too, included extensive advice to future travellers; the third part of Fynes Moryson's *Itinerary*, for example, is dedicated to general information about travelling and all kinds of information about the countries travelled.

The high proportion of apodemic instruction for the Grand Tour and the 'proper' way of recording it means that accounts of this type of journey tend to reveal only little or nothing about the traveller's subjective experience – even though edification is a process essentially directed at the subject. The persona of the traveller/writer clearly fades into the background, in favour of the 'objective' material gathered systematically and carefully noted in the traveller's diary. The focus on remarkable and memorable knowledge about the countries travelled was so prominent that accounts of the tour were often even enriched with material accumulated from other books rather than actual experience. Coryat openly refers to this practice in his *Crudities*: 'For seeing I made very short aboade in divers faire Italian Cities ... and thereby was barred of opportunity to note such things at large as were most memorable; I held it expedient to borrow some few notes from a certaine Latin booke printed in Italie' (p. 4). Fynes Moryson, too, had started out compiling additional, historical information about the areas he covered in his travels. However, as he writes in the preface of his *Itinerary*, he later chose to suppress the historical abstracts rather than 'to make my gate bigger then my Citie'. Nevertheless, Moryson's account includes so much instructive material that the author was afraid of boring a reader interested in entertainment. He thus took pains to draw his reader's attention to the more delightful aspects of the book: 'which Treatise in some obscure places is barren and vnpleasant ... but in other places I hope you will iudge it more pleasant, and in some delightfull, inducing you fauorably to dispence with the barrennes [sic] of the former, inserted only for the vse of vnexperienced Trauellers passing those waies.' The 'pleasant places' in Moryson's *Itinerary* include the depiction of spectacular and curious sights, and above all passages which narrate the incidents of his journey rather than giving descriptions. At the beginning of his text, for example, Moryson gives a lively report of his quarrel with a German coachman. Generally, however, the traditional account of the Grand Tour is distinguished by its strong focus on what is worth noting and knowing. Many texts of this sort are thus not concerned so much with the traveller's personal experience as with that which he was *supposed* to see if he travelled methodically. Joseph Addison's *Remarks on Several Parts of Italy* (1705) exemplify the withdrawal of the subject even in accounts of the early eighteenth century.

The methodical account

During his university years at Oxford, Joseph Addison distinguished himself as a classical scholar. His travels on the Continent (financed by a treasury grant) followed his studies, between 1699 and 1704, by which time Addison was, at around thirty years of age, already quite old for such an enterprise. Following his journey, Addison was offered a post in government service.

Addison's *Remarks on Several Parts of Italy* is clearly object-orientated in the spirit of apodemic recommendations, and characterized by an encyclopedic breadth in its coverage of the areas travelled. The chapters are dedicated to particular places in Italy, Switzerland and Austria; the time element of the journey, Addison's movement between and within the places themselves, plays a significantly minor role in the text compared with its many descriptions and expositions. The chapters are dominated by depictions of what Addison, as a patriotic traveller, considered 'remarkable'. This included all kinds of aesthetic experience; in Florence, Addison went to the opera (the eighth performance he saw on Italian soil) and visited the famous art collection, whose highlights are enumerated in an extensive list. In Venice, Addison was suitably impressed with the city's art and monuments, its trade, history and political organization, and not least with its military defence, which he described in particular detail:

> Having often heard *Venice* represented as one of the most defensible cities in the world, I took care to inform my self of the particulars in which its strength consists. And these I find are chiefly owing to its advantagious [*sic*] situation; for it has neither rocks nor fortifications near it, and yet is, perhaps, the most impregnable town in *Europe*. It stands at least four miles from any part of the *Terra Firma*, nor are the shallows that lye about it ever frozen hard enough to bring over an army from the land-side; the constant flux and reflux of the sea, or the natural mildness of the climate, hindering the ice from gathering to any thickness; which is an advantage the *Hollanders* want, when they have laid all their country under water. On the side that is exposed to the Adriatic, the entrance is so difficult to hit, that they have marked it out with several stakes driven into the ground, which they would not fail to cut upon the first approach of an enemy's fleet. ... Nor could an ordinary fleet, with bomb-vessels, hope to succeed against a place that has always in its arsenal a considerable number of gallies and men of war ready to put to sea on a very short warning. (p. 52)

Addison's English patriotism is particularly evident in his denunciation of Roman Catholicism and the Pope's despotic rule in contemporary Italy:

[T]here is not a more miserable people in *Europe* than the Pope's subjects. His state is thin of inhabitants, and a great part of his soil uncultivated. His subjects are wretchedly poor and idle, and have neither sufficient manufactures, nor traffick to employ them. These ill effects may arise, in a great measure, out of the arbitrariness of the government, but I think they are chiefly to be ascribed to the very genius of the *Roman* catholick religion, which here shews it self in its perfection. It is not strange to find a country half unpeopled, where so great a proportion of the inhabitants of both sexes is tyed under such vows of chastity, and where at the same time an inquisition forbids all recruits out of any other religion. Nor is it less easy to account for the great poverty and want that are to be met with in a country which invites into it such swarms of vagabonds, under the title of Pilgrims, and shuts up in cloisters such an incredible multitude of young and lusty beggars, who ... consume the charity that ought to support the sickly, old and decrepid. The many hospitals, that are every where erected, serve rather to encourage idleness in the people, than to set them at work; not to mention the great riches which lye useless in churches and religious houses, with the multitude of festivals that must never be violated by trade or business.   (p. 93)

Above all, however, Addison went on his tour as a 'classic' traveller, in keeping with the contemporary enthusiasm for Graeco-Roman antiquity. While Papist Italy was something Addison abhorred, classical Italy he revered. In general, English neoclassical travellers to Italy were particularly interested in the remains of Roman greatness, and Addison's studies in classical literature led him to prepare this stage of his continental journey with special care: 'He was well aware that what he was going to observe and write about would be connected with what he had previously read ... He went through the Latin writers for remarks on Italian topography and Roman buildings' (Stoye, 1982, pp. 147–8; my translation). In Addison's *Remarks*, classical authors are thus repeatedly cited in the Latin original, and Rome features as a highlight of the journey largely because it reminded Addison of texts he had read before: 'for a man who is in *Rome* can scarce see an object that does not call to mind a piece of a *Latin* Poet or Historian' (p. 140). In Rome, Addison studied, among other things, antique statues – not only in respect of their aesthetic value, but also for their anthropological significance:

Notwithstanding there are so great a multitude of cloathed statues at *Rome*, I could never discover the several different *Roman* garments, for 'tis very difficult to trace out the figure of a vest, through all the plaits and foldings of the drapery; besides, that the *Roman* garments did not differ from each other, so much by the shape as by the embroidery and colour, the one of which was too nice for the statuary's observation, as the other does not lye within the expression of the chissel. I observed, in abundance of *Bas Reliefs*, that the *Cinctus Gabinus* is nothing else but a long garment, not unlike a surplice, which would have trailed on the ground had it hung loose, and was therefore gathered about the middle with a girdle. (p. 151)

In spite of the preoccupation with particulars revealed in this extract, Addison was reluctant, however, to depict in detail what had already been described in many earlier accounts: 'I shall say nothing of the *Via Flaminia*, which has been spoken of by most of the voyage writers that have passed it' (p. 86). Comments like this suggest quite clearly how mechanical the Grand Tour and its account had become by the early eighteenth century; Addison was well aware that he was treading worn paths. Equally striking is the lack of attention which Addison's account pays to his personal travel experience. It is thus difficult to tell from his text whether the journey had left an impact on his mind and personality – whether it had actually been an 'edifying' experience.

Although the methodical account of the Grand Tour had already exhausted itself by the beginning of the eighteenth century, this manner of writing about travel was longstanding and, as late as 1760, provoked the criticism of Dr Johnson:

The greater part of travellers tell nothing, because their method of travelling supplies them with nothing to be told. He that enters a town at night and surveys it in the morning, and then hastens away to another place, and guesses at the manners of the inhabitants by the entertainment which his inn afforded him, may please himself for a time with a hasty change of scenes, and a confused remembrance of palaces and churches; he may gratify his eye with a variety of landscapes; and regale his palate with a succession of vintages; but let him be contented to please himself without endeavour to disturb others. Why should he record excursions by which nothing could be learned, or wish to make a show of knowledge which, without some power of intuition unknown to other mortals, he never could attain.

(Johnson, 1963, pp. 298–9)

By the time Johnson formulated this criticism, however, travel writing was already tending towards a greater emphasis on subjective experience. This was in part due to developments in the Grand Tour itself; in the course of the eighteenth century, continental travel for educational purposes was becoming less and less necessary.

It was no longer necessary to live in foreign countries to understand them. With the foundation of the chairs of modern history at Oxford and Cambridge by King George the First in 1724, one great reason for travel was lost. Information about contemporary politics on the Continent could be had through the increasing number of news-journals and gazettes. As for learning the French language, there had been no lack of competent teachers since the Revocation of the Edict of Nantes in 1685 sent French Protestant refugees swarming across the channel to find some sort of living in England. Therefore the spirit of acquisitiveness dwindled and died down, in the absence of any strong need to study abroad, and an idle, frivolous, darting, capricious spirit controlled the aristocratic tourist.

(Howard, 1914, p. 190)

The Grand Tour thus increasingly came to be regarded as suspect, to the point of being considered more a corrupting than an edifying experience. 'Led by my hand, he saunter'd Europe round / And gather'd ev'ry Vice on Christian ground', are the words of a tour tutor in Alexander Pope's verse satire, *The Dunciad* (completed in 1743).[7] Even where the travellers did not succumb to the temptation of various vices, the Grand Tour frequently degenerated into a simple tour of sights or a routine of social visits, as in excerpt 2 from the letters of quite an ordinary tourist.

In the context of this development, travellers of the mid-eighteenth century started to tour the continent in a new manner not predefined in apodemic writing or by previous travellers. This meant, for example, that new areas in Europe were 'discovered'. In the 1760s, James Boswell went not only to France and Italy, but also ventured into the interior of Corsica, and this part of his journey was indeed the only one he chose to write about in his *Account of Corsica* (1768) – with great success. Boswell opens the narration of his journey (that is the *Journal* part of his book) with the motive for choosing his unusual destination:

> Having resolved to pass some years abroad, for my instruction and entertainment, I conceived a design of visiting the island of Corsica. I wished for something more than just the common course of what is called the tour of Europe; and Corsica occurred to me as a place which no body else had seen, and where I should find what was to be seen no where else, a people actually fighting for liberty, and forming themselves from a poor inconsiderable oppressed nation, into a flourishing and independent state. (p. 15)

In 1773, Patrick Brydone published his *Tour through Sicily and Malta*. The Iberian peninsula, too, was increasingly visited and described, as for example in Robert Southey's *Journals of a Residence in Portugal* (1800–1). Mary Wollstonecraft published her letters from another unusual destination: *Letters Written during a Short Residence in Sweden, Norway, and Denmark* (1796).

The most fundamental factor in the development of the Grand Tour account in the course of the eighteenth century was the new value attached to subjective experience – a value which manifested itself in a variety of areas, but in particular in philosophy and literature. Thus in travel writing, too, the depiction of the travelled world *as such* is of declining importance; what becomes important instead is the way in which the traveller relates to this world in his own individual way. It is not a coincidence that travel writing is now frequently published in the form of the diary, the journal or the letter – autobiographical forms which are particularly suited to the immediate expression of personal experience.

The subjective account

A shift towards the travelling subject can be detected, from the middle of the century, even in accounts which depict journeys to the familiar regions of the Continent, such as Tobias Smollett's *Travels through France and Italy* (1766). Smollett did not conduct his journey for the purpose of edification; he travelled to France and Italy as an elderly man, for the sake of his health, and accompanied by his family. Nevertheless, his text follows some conventions of the traditional Grand Tour account. For example, he displays a stark patriotism, which at times degenerates into plain chauvinism; remarks like the following explain the outrage with which Smollett's *Travels* was received in France:

> Notwithstanding the gay disposition of the French, their houses are all gloomy. In spite of all the ornaments that have been lavished upon Versailles, it is a dismal habitation. The apartments are dark, ill-furnished, dirty, and unprincely. Take the castle, chapel, and garden all together, they make a most fantastic composition of magnificence and littleness, taste and foppery. After all, it is in England only, where we must look for cheerful apartments, gay furniture, neatness, and convenience. (p. 45)

Furthermore, Smollett's original title suggests a methodical and factual account: '. . . Containing Observations on Character, Customs, Religion, Government, Police, Commerce, Arts, and Antiquities. With a particular Description of the Town, Territory, and Climate of Nice.' At the end of the book, Smollett even includes a meticulous register of the weather for each day of his journey – in two different systems of measurement (Réaumur and Chateauneuf).

However, Smollett's account is no longer confined to a description of the countries travelled. The text also exposes the personality and the emotions of the travelling subject, who appears as a fully developed, dramatized persona with strongly individual traits.

> Smollett presents himself as a somewhat awkward and ill-humoured character whose temper is provoked by everything not running according to plan. To a certain extent, this self-presentation is intended to entertain Smollett's readers; it may be assumed that a good number of his observations are exaggerated in order to produce a humorous effect, especially as Smollett seems to encounter any and every conceivable misfortune along the way.
>
> (Kalb, 1981, p. 55; my translation)

The journey, then, is interesting in itself, in its specific course of events, not only for the remarkable observations it has yielded. Smollett's travelogue is distinguished by a travel plot which consists of many lively episodes such as the following:

> When I rose in the morning, and opened a window that looked into the garden, I thought myself either in a dream, or bewitched.

All the trees were cloathed with snow, and all the country covered at least a foot thick. 'This cannot be the south of France, (said I to myself) it must be the Highlands of Scotland!' At a wretched town called Muy, where we dined, I had a warm dispute with our landlord, which, however, did not terminate to my satisfaction. I sent on the mules before, to the next stage, resolving to take post-horses, and bespoke them accordingly of the aubergiste, who was, at the same time, inn-keeper and post-master. We were ushered into the common eating-room, and had a very indifferent dinner; after which, I sent a loui'dore to be changed, in order to pay the reckoning. The landlord, instead of giving the full change, deducted three livres a head for dinner, and sent in the rest of the money by my servant. Provoked more at his ill manners, than at his extortion, I ferretted [sic] him out of a bed-chamber, where he had concealed himself, and obliged him to restore the full change, from which I paid him at the rate of two livres a head. He refused to take the money, which I threw down on the table; and the horses being ready, stepped into the coach, ordering the postilions to drive on. Here I had certainly reckoned without my host. The fellows declared they would not budge, until I should pay their master; and as I threatened them with manual chastisement, they alighted, and disappeared in a twinkling.   (pp. 107–8)

The traveller makes a formal complaint to the consul of the town but is ultimately forced to give in and pay the landlord's original price: 'and I was obliged to travel in the night, in very severe weather, after all the fatigue and mortification I had undergone' (p. 109). In episodes such as this, the account is clearly focused on the traveller – his individual experiences and thoughts, moral judgements and emotions. What is depicted here was neither experienced and described by earlier travellers, nor will it be relived by future travellers.

The subjectivity of the travelling experience is also underlined in the personal letters which James Boswell wrote about his tour of Italy, Corsica and France (conducted between 1764 and 1766). In particular, Boswell draws attention to the effect which the journey had on his powers of imagination and sensibility. In a letter to Jean-Jacques Rousseau of 3 October 1765 he writes: 'It was my imagination that needed correction, and nothing but travel could have produced this effect' (p. 3). A letter to John Johnston of 11 May 1765 highlights the journey's sentimental effect: 'I have experienced during this last half year such changes of sentiment as would hardly be conceived to arise in a mind where judgement was not totally overthrown' (pp. 81–2).

Developments in English travel writing were catalysed by a text which is today regarded as a novel rather than a travel account – Laurence Sterne's *A Sentimental Journey through France and Italy* (1768). In 1765, Sterne had spent eight months travelling through France and Italy, gathering material for the book. However, the text is not directly autobiographical; its protagonist and narrator is not 'Laurence Sterne' but the parson Yorick, a fictive character who also appears in Sterne's novel *Tristram Shandy* and in some of his sermons. According to the criteria delineated in Chapter 1, *A Sentimental Journey* does thus not qualify as a travelogue in the strict sense of the term. Nevertheless, the book had a significant influence on the genre's history, especially its increase in subjectivity – not least because Sterne also expressed this subjectivity in a highly idiosyncratic manner.

Yorick does not make much progress in his journey. In France he does not get much further than Lyons; the title 'through France and Italy' is clearly misleading, and we cannot be sure even today whether Sterne's original plans were ever for a longer work. The published text is in any case fragmentary: it ends in mid-sentence, just as it opens *medias in res*, right in the middle of a dialogue. In typical Sternean manner, the 'Preface' does not appear until the seventh chapter.

According to his own classification of travellers in this preface (see excerpt 3), Yorick is a sentimental traveller who is quite conscious of how this quality distinguishes him from other kinds of traveller:

> I am well aware . . . , as both my travels and observations will be altogether of a different cast from any of my fore-runners; that I might have insisted upon a whole nitch [*sic*] entirely to myself – but I should break in upon the confines of the *Vain* Traveller, in wishing to draw attention towards me, till I have some better grounds for it, than the mere *Novelty of my vehicle.*   (pp. 15–16)[8]

The special quality of *A Sentimental Journey* as a piece of travel literature is essentially derived from Yorick's sensibility. As traveller and narrator of his journey, Yorick is deeply affected by everything he experiences; in particular, he emerges as a sensitive, empathetic and benevolent observer of human behaviour. His emotional reactions and human interest are at the core of Yorick's travelling experience – and thus at the core of Sterne's text.[9] Yorick's journey does not edify in a classical sense; its purpose is to enhance one faculty only – the traveller's sensibility. Accordingly, readers of the *Sentimental Journey* learn almost nothing about France; the amount of factual information in the text is negligible. Instead, everything revolves around the moods and feelings triggered by Yorick's chance encounters, which are presented in a loose sequence of scenes and observations. The *Sentimental Journey* thus consolidates tendencies which were also emerging in the travelogue proper and which became an increasingly important generic feature towards the end of the eighteenth century.

In 1792, for example, Arthur Young's *Travels in France and Italy* (1792) opened with a discussion of the subject-orientated mode of travel writing – even though this account by a well-known agronomist was primarily intended to report the state of French agriculture. In his introduction, Young distinguishes between 'two methods of writing travel; to register the journey itself, or the result of it. In the former case, it is a diary, under which head are to be classed all those books of travels written in the form of letters. The latter usually falls into the shape of essays on distinct subjects' (p. 5). Young's own book consti-tutes a compromise between these two forms, neatly separating, however, the account of his travels *per se* and the presentation of the journey's factual 'return'.[10] The account itself also includes factual information, but the emphasis is clearly on the traveller's personal experience which, as stated in Young's preface, is precisely what makes the text attractive to the general reader:

> When I traced my plan, and begun to work upon it, I rejected, without mercy, a variety of little circumstances relating to myself only, and of conversations with various persons which I had thrown upon paper for the amusement of my family and intimate friends. For this I was remonstrated with by a person of whose judg-ment I think highly, as having absolutely spoiled my diary by expunging the very passages that would best please the mass of common readers; in a word, that I must give up the journal plan entirely or let it go as it was written. . . .
>
> The high opinion I have of the judgment of my friend induced me to follow his advice; in consequence of which I venture to offer my itinerary to the public just as it was written on the spot: requesting my reader, if much should be found of a trifling nature, to pardon it, from a reflection that the chief object of my travels is to be found in another part of the work, to which he may at once have recourse if he wish to attend only to subjects of a more important character. (pp. 6–7)

This justification of a subjective account still has an apologetic ring about it,[11] but Young leaves no doubt that the common reader's taste already tends towards this mode of reporting, and the text is also significantly less reserved in passages of a personal nature than the introduction would suggest.

Travels in France and Italy reflects, for example, the traveller's disappointment as his expectations cannot stand up to actual experience. Thus Young's impression of Venice corresponds neither with the descriptions of previous travellers nor with Canaletto's famous paintings. In light of such discrepancies it is not surprising that Young becomes increasingly frustrated with the traditional itinerary of the Italian tour. It offers him little personal gain, and he only completes it reluctantly through a sense of obligation: 'Another tour among palaces, and churches, and pictures; one sees too many at once to have clear ideas' (p. 260).

Dissatisfaction with the canonized Grand Tour is particularly apparent in the account of William Beckford, whose chief contribution to English literature was his Gothic novel, *Vathek* (1786). Just as this novel emphasizes the unreal and irrational, so dreams are an important element in Beckford's original account of his journey, entitled *Dreams, Waking Thoughts and Incidents*, which was completed and published in 1783 but then suppressed by his family. This text, then, may be regarded as essentially Romantic, as a 'testimony to Romantic self-expression and a subjective-emotional experience of the world, thematizing the discrepancy between the self's limited existence and its boundless hope and yearning' (Kalb, 1981, p. 135; my translation).

Beckford set out on his tour in 1782; he began his travels in the Netherlands, moving on to Germany and Austria, and then towards his final destination, Venice. It is clear from the outset that Beckford is not satisfied with his conventional, pre-set itinerary but that he is driven by a yearning for distant lands. His actual experience of countries in Western Europe only makes him long for regions more remote and exotic. In Antwerp, for example, the traveller dreams of an imagined Orient and appears disappointed when he awakes from his vision:

> My windows look full on the Place de Mer, and the sun, beaming through their white curtains, awoke me from a dream of Arabian happiness. Imagination had procured herself a tent on the mountains of Sanaa, covered with coffee-trees in bloom. She was presenting me the essence of their flowers, and was just telling me

that you possessed a pavilion on a neighbouring hill, when the sunshine dispelled the vision; and, opening my eyes, I found myself pent in by Flemish spires and buildings: no hills, no verdure, no aromatic breezes, no hopes of being in your vicinity: all were vanished with the shadows of fancy, and I was left alone to deplore your absence. But I think it rather selfish to wish you here; for what pleasure could pacing from one dull church to another afford a person of your turn? (p. 11)

If here, at the opening of his account, the Orient is established as the desired object of Beckford's travels, this desire becomes even more pronounced in Venice – that station of the traditional Grand Tour which was closest to the East:

Asiatics find Venice very much to their liking, and all those I conversed with allowed its customs and style of living had a good deal of conformity to their own. The eternal lounging in coffee-houses and sipping of sorbets agree perfectly well with the inhabitants of the Ottoman empire, who stalk about here in their proper dresses, and smoke their own exotic pipes, without being stared and wondered at as in most other European capitals.

(p. 100)

In this city, which is 'different' from all other destinations in Europe, Beckford manages to escape, through his imagination, from the prescribed itinerary of his journey, and his account allows the reader to share in these escapades. A guided tour of the Doges' Palace, for example, soon becomes tiresome for the traveller and is reported only in a very condensed manner. The conventional 'sights' of the palace, such as its picture galleries, no longer receive detailed attention. What fascinates the traveller instead are the palace's mysteries, and the text describes at length how Beckford pictures these secrets in his imagination, thus breaking away from the official sight-seeing programme:

... and was led from hall to hall, and from picture to picture, with exemplary resignation. To be sure, I was heartily tired, but behaved with decency, having never once expressed how much I wished the chef d'oeuvre I had been contemplating, less smoky and numerous. At last, I reached once more the colonnades at the entrance, and caught the sea breeze in the open porticoes which front San Giorgio

Maggiore. The walls are covered in most places with grim visages sculptured in marble, whose mouths gape for accusations, and swallow every lie that malice and revenge can dictate. I wished for a few ears of the same kind, dispersed about the Doge's residence, to which one might apply one's own, and catch some account of the mysteries within; some little dialogue between the three Inquisitors, or debate in the Council of Ten. This is the tribunal which holds the wealthy nobility in continual awe; before which they appear with trembling and terror; and whose summons they dare not disobey. Sometimes, by way of clemency, it condemns its victims to perpetual imprisonment, in close, stifling cells, between the leads and beams of the palace; or, unwilling to spill the blood of a fellow-citizen, generously sinks them into dungeons, deep under the canals which wash its foundations; so that, above and below, its majesty is contaminated by the abodes of punishment ... Impressed by these terrible ideas, I could not regard the palace without horror, and wished for the strength of a thousand ante-diluvians, to level it with the sea, lay open the secret recesses of punishment, and admit free gales and sunshine into every den. When I had thus vented my indignation, I repaired to the statue of Neptune, and invoked it to second my enterprise.   (pp. 96–7)

In this instance, Beckford's escape from the programmed route is restricted to his imagination, but he also strays from it in a literal sense. He is frequently caught roaming the streets of Venice, according to his own spontaneous interest and without any special aim:

I like this odd town of Venice, and find every day some new amusement in rambling about its innumerable canals and alleys. Sometimes I pry about the great church of St. Mark, and examine the variety of marbles and mazes of delicate sculpture with which it is covered ... I run up the Campanile in the piazza, and seating myself amongst the pillars of the gallery, breathe the fresh gales which blow from the Adriatic; survey at my leisure all Venice beneath me, with its azure sea, white sails, and long tracks of islands shining in the sun. Having thus laid in a provision of wholesome breezes, I brave the vapours of the canals, and venture into the most curious and musky quarters of the city, in search of Turks and Infidels, that I may ask as many questions as I please about Damascus, and Suristan, those happy countries, which nature has covered with roses.   (pp. 99–100)

Rambling about leisurely, as and when it pleases, is certainly not an entirely new way of travelling. Since the mid-eighteenth century, however, this 'free' mode of travel is recorded with a growing frequency and in accounts which increasingly deviate from canonized modes of travel writing, opening the genre up to new perspectives.

Subjectivity and scientific travel

The breakthrough of subjectivity in travel writing has been considered above in respect of a form of travel that was specifically intended to have an effect upon the traveller's self. The same development can also be observed in accounts of quite a different type of journey – that of the explorer-scientist. Because of the chief aims of scientific travel, its account places a strong emphasis on the realities of the travelled world. Since the late eighteenth century, however, texts about scientific travel also reveal that the explorer and scientist necessarily encounters the world as a subject. The German explorer Georg Forster wrote explicitly about the inevitable subjectiveness of his experience and the representation of this experience. Forster had accompanied James Cook on his second circumnavigation of the globe and described it in an account originally written in English, *A Voyage Round the World* (1777). In his preface to the German version, *Reise um die Welt* (1778–80), Forster emphasizes that two travellers 'rarely view any one object in the same way' (p. 13; my translation), so that all writing about travel necessarily has a subjective point of view determined by the traveller's 'sensitivity and style of thought' (ibid.). The reader thus has a right to know 'the colour of the glass through which I was looking [during my travels]' (ibid.). Only when this 'colour' is made explicit in the text, can the reader adequately judge what the writer has to say about the travelled world.[12]

Charles Darwin believed that exploration not only served scientific discovery, but also affected the traveller himself. The conclusion to his account of the *Beagle* voyage includes the following statement about the potential for travel to develop the traveller's self: 'In a moral point of view, the effect ought to be, to teach him good-humoured patience, freedom from selfishness, the habit of acting for himself, and of making the best of every thing, or in other words contentment' (p. 377). Accordingly, despite the sober depiction of natural phenomena in many passages of *Voyage of the Beagle* (1839), Darwin does not hesitate to convey reactions of a personal nature, for example when he writes about the empty landscape of Patagonia:

In calling up images of the past, I find the plains of Patagonia frequently cross before my eyes: yet these plains are pronounced by all most wretched and useless. They are characterized only by negative possessions; without habitations, without water, without trees, without mountains, they support merely a few dwarf plants. Why then, and the case is not peculiar to myself, have these arid wastes taken so firm possession of the memory? ... I can scarcely analyze these feelings: but it must be partly owing to the free scope given to the imagination. The plains of Patagonia are boundless, for they are scarcely practicable, and hence unknown: they bear the stamp of having thus lasted for ages, and there appears no limit to their duration through future time. If, as the ancients supposed, the flat earth was surrounded by an impassable breadth of water, or by deserts heated to an intolerable excess, who would not look at these last boundaries to man's knowledge with deep but ill-defined sensations?   (pp. 374–5)

It is no accident that Darwin's personal vision is here rendered in the context of a landscape experience.[13] The perception of landscape presupposes a subjective way of seeing, since landscape is always 'a construct of the mind as well as a physical and measurable entity' (Tuan, 1979, p. 6). The description of landscape thus does not enter into the travel account until an emphasis on the subject becomes increasingly established along with other traits of Romanticism.

Landscape in travel writing

In 1712, Joseph Addison wrote a series of essays for the *Spectator* which he entitled 'On the Pleasures of the Imagination'. These essays played an important role in the emergence of a new, Romantic aesthetics of landscape, in particular the perception of its beauty and sublimity. Nevertheless, in Addison's own *Remarks on Several Parts of Italy* – published seven years previously – scenic beauties had not yet featured prominently unless they were mentioned by a classical poet and therefore deserved Addison's special attention. The cursory description of the route between Pisaro and Rome, for example, suggests that landscapes without this special significance are passed through rather than lingered in:

The fatigue of our crossing the *Appenines*, and of our whole journey from *Loretto* to *Rome*, was very agreeably relieved by the variety of scenes we passed through. For not to mention the rude prospect of rocks rising one above another, of the gutters deep worn in the sides of them by torrents of rain and snow-water, or the long channels of sand winding about their bottoms, that are sometimes filled with so many rivers: we saw, in six days travelling, the several seasons of the year in their beauty and perfection. We were sometimes shivering on the top of a bleak mountain, and a little while after basking in a warm valley, covered with violets and almond-trees in blossom, the Bees already swarming over them, though but in the month of *February*.   (p. 86)

The natural environment is certainly not overlooked in Addison's account, but it remains inferior in significance if taken in relation to his *Remarks* as a whole; classical statues and monuments, for example, receive far more attention throughout the book. By contrast, when Thomas Gray and Horace Walpole went on their Grand Tour in 1739, they crossed the Alps prepared for a spectacular mountainscape, a sublime experience: 'set out from Echelles on horseback to see the Grande Chartreuse', Gray wrote in his *Journal in France 1739*, 'one of the most poetical scenes imaginable' (p. 244). The expectation of these travellers already bears the mark of a Romantic paradigm. To William Beckford, at the end of the century, the enjoyment of landscape was a natural part of the travel experience – and he knew how to enhance this aesthetic pleasure with culinary delights, as he records in *Dreams, Waking Thoughts and Incidents*:

You ask how I pass my time. Generally upon the hills, in wild spots where the arbutus flourishes; from whence I may catch a glimpse of the distant sea; my horse tied to a cypress, and myself cast upon the grass, like Palmarin of Oliva, with a tablet and pencil in my hand, a basket of grapes by my side, and a crooked stick to shake down the chestnuts.   (p. 149)

When Romantic aesthetics was at its height, the description of landscape became a set piece even in those accounts of continental travel which, by and large, adhered to the traditional mould. In the last years of the eighteenth century, Ann Radcliffe and her husband travelled the Netherlands and western parts of Germany. Radcliffe's account of the trip, *A Journey Made in the Summer of 1794 through Holland and the Western Frontier of Germany* (1795), contains many conventional elements of the Grand Tour account. The Dutch port of Helvoetsluys, for example, appears most remarkable for its fortifications:

The fortifications, we were assured upon good military authority, were in such repair, that not a sod was out of its place, and are strong enough to be defended by five thousand men against an hundred thousand, for five weeks. The sea water rises to a considerable height in a wide ditch, which surrounds them. We omitted to copy an inscription, placed on one of the walls, which told the date of their completion; but this was probably about the year 1696, when the harbour was perfected.   (p. 4)

However, the Radcliffes also travelled with the special intent of enjoying landscapes. They travelled the Rhine Valley in each direction, first by coach and back by ship, and the original title page of Radcliffe's account explicitly drew the readers' attention to this scenic stage of the journey: 'with a Return Down the Rhine.' The Valley is described in every nuance, which suggests that the travellers took just as much time to relish its beautiful, sublime and picturesque aspects as they did for other remarkable objects of the countries travelled:

About half-way to Andernach, the western rocks suddenly recede from the river, and, rising to greater height, form a grand sweep round a plain cultivated with orchards, garden-fields, corn and vineyards. The valley here spreads to a breadth of nearly a mile and a half, and exhibits grandeur, beauty and barren sublimity, united in a singular manner. The abrupt steeps, that rise over this plane, are entirely covered with wood, except that here and there the ravage of a winter torrent appeared, which could sometimes be traced from the very summit of the acclivity to the base. Near the centre, this noble amphitheatre opens to a glen, that shews only wooded mountains, point above point, in long perspective ... Along the base of this tremendous wall, and on the points above, villages, with each its tall, grey steeple, were thickly strewn, thus mingling in striking contrast the cheerfulness of populous inhabitation with the horrors of untamed nature. A few monasteries, resembling castles in their extent, and known from such only by their spires, were distinguishable; and, in the widening perspective of the Rhine, an old castle itself, now and then, appeared on the summit of a mountain somewhat remote from the shore; an object rendered sweetly picturesque, as the sun's rays lighted up its towers and fortified terraces, while the shrubby steeps below were in shade.   (pp. 154–5)

On their return from the Continent, the Radcliffes' journey was continued in England, as is also announced on the original title page:

'To Which Are Added, Observations During a Tour to The Lakes of Lancashire, Westmoreland, and Cumberland'. On home ground, too, the enjoyment of landscape had become a prime motive for travel. In travel writing, the depiction of landscape had evolved into a feature that was particularly popular with the contemporary reader and which could thus be used to advertise Ann Radcliffe's book. The 'home' part of Radcliffe's *Journey* is rich in descriptions of a scenic area which, by the end of the eighteenth century, had become a favourite destination for so-called 'picturesque' travellers. By the time this variety of domestic travel became fashionable, however, the home tour was already a well-established line of travel.

4
The Home Tour

[1] *[M]y Landlady brought me one of the West Country tarts, this was the first I met with, though I had asked for them in many places in Sommerset and Devonshire, its [sic] an apple pye with a custard all on the top . . .; they scald their creame and milk in most parts of those countrys and so its a sort of clouted creame as we call it, with a little sugar, and soe put on the top of the apple pye; I was much pleased with my supper tho' not with the custome of the country, which is a universall smoaking, . . . which was not delightfull to me when I went down to talke with my Landlady for information of any matter and customs amongst them . . .*

Halfe a mile from hence they blow their tin which I went to see: they take the oar [ore] and pound it in a stamping mill which resembles the paper mills, and when its fine as the finest sand, some of which I saw and took, this they fling into a furnace and with it coale to make the fire, so it burns together and makes a violent heate and fierce flame, the mettle [metal] by the fire being seperated [sic] from the coale and its own drosse, being heavy falls down to a trench made to receive it, at the furnace hole below; this liquid mettle I saw them shovel up with an iron shovel and soe pour it into molds in which it cooles and soe they take it thence in sort of wedges or piggs I think they call them; its a fine mettle thus in its first melting looks like silver, I had a piece poured out and made cold for to take with me. . .

(Celia Fiennes, 'My Great Journey to Newcastle and to Cornwall, 1698', pp. 204–5)

[2] *From Longleat we pursued our road through Froom to Wells. The first part of our journey presented nothing very interesting. As we approached Mendip-hills, the road divides; one branch leading over*

*those high grounds, the other under them. We chose the latter, which
afforded us, on the right, those hills for a back-ground; and on the
left, an extensive distance, in which Glastonburytor, as it is called,
is the most conspicuous feature.*

*Our approach to Wells, from the natural and incidental beauties
of the scene, was uncommonly picturesque. It was a hazy evening;
and the sun, declining low, was hid behind a purple cloud, which
covered half the hemisphere, but did not reach the western horizon.
Its lower skirts were gilt with dazzling splendor, which spread down-
wards, not in diverging rays, but in one uniform ruddy glow; and
uniting at the bottom with the mistiness of the air, formed a rich, yet
modest tint, with which Durcote-hill, projecting boldly on the left,
the towers of Wells beyond it, and all the objects of the distance,
were tinged; while the foreground, seen against so bright a piece of
scenery, was overspread with the darkest shades of evening. The
whole together invited the pencil, without soliciting the imagination.
But it was a transitory scene. As we stood gazing at it, the sun sunk
below the cloud, and being stripped of all its splendor by the haziness
of the atmosphere, fell, like a ball of fire, into the horizon; and the
whole radiant vision faded away.*

(William Gilpin, *Observations on the Western Parts of England*, 1798,
pp. 129–30)

The informative account: a speculum Britanniae

Although the previous chapters were concerned with travel abroad,
there was naturally also a tradition in the British Isles of travel within
one's own country, such as the local pilgrimage to destinations like
Canterbury. However, home tours did not come into fashion until
relatively late; as John Edmund Vaughan (1974, p. 54) suggests, the
Napoleonic Wars encouraged this kind of journey in Britain because
they made it difficult for Britons to travel on the Continent.[1] Thus
accounts of domestic travel are initially significantly fewer in number
compared with those relating to the Grand Tour. 'Before the 1750s',
writes Charles Batten (1978, p. 93), 'surprisingly few Englishmen of
wealth and social position had traveled extensively throughout their
own country, and fewer still had described their homeland in
accounts of their travels.' Notwithstanding, the British Isles were travelled with a specific historical and geographical interest as early as the
sixteenth century: 'The habit of touring their native land began in the
sixteenth century; it is a Tudor phenomenon. Better roads and

improved cartography were making travel easier and safer, but the motive force was pride in the greatness of Tudor England, and a curiosity both in the historic roots of that greatness and its contemporary manifestations' (Moir, 1964, p. xiv). In a period of an emerging national consciousness and pride, the English developed an interest for their own country as well as for lands abroad, and the former, too, became the object of meticulous study. In texts arising from sixteenth- and seventeenth-century home tours, we encounter the same purpose as in texts of the contemporary explorer and continental traveller: the travelled country is observed in great detail and recounted in an encyclopedic manner.

Between 1535 and 1543, John Leland went on a journey through England to gather material for an extensive work on the 'History and Antiquities of this Nation'. He never came to write this *magnum opus*, but the notes he made on his journey about places seen and knowledge gathered were circulated in manuscript form and published, between 1710 and 1712, as *Leland's Itinerary*. The peregrinations of the scholar William Camden actually yielded one of the most important early surveys of Britain, his *Britannia* (1586), which first appeared in Latin. In this impressive work, Camden collated – county by county – historical, topographical and much other information about 'the Flourishing Kingdoms of England, Scotland, and Ireland, and the Islands Adjacent'. The *Britannia*, however, depicts not so much Camden's journey as the information which the author gained from it.

Contemporary records of the home tour itself also had a clear instructive tone. Fynes Moryson, for example, not only travelled the Continent but was also a keen tourist of his native England and of Scotland. His *Itinerary* (1617) is just as extensively informative when dealing with these parts as for the foreign countries he visited. Occasionally, however, in the sixteenth and seventeenth centuries there also appeared short, entertaining pieces of travel writing which were directed at a wide audience and published in the inexpensive pamphlet form.

Among the popular pamphleteers of the seventeenth century was John Taylor, whose pseudonym, 'the Water Poet', arose from his main occupation as a London waterman. In verse and prose, Taylor published various accounts of his travels, which took him to the Continent (for example to Hamburg and Prague), but first and foremost through England, Scotland and Wales. The introductory passage in Taylor's *Pennyles Pilgrimage*, his text about a journey from London to Edinburgh in 1618, explicitly suggests that travel within the British

Isles is at times every bit as 'strange' (albeit verifiable) as journeys to foreign lands:

> List Lordings, list (if you haue lust to list)
> I write not here a tale of had I wist:
> But you shall heare of trauels, and relations,
> Descriptions of strange (yet English) fashions.
> And he that not beleeues what here is writ,
> Let him (as I haue done) make proofe of it.   (p. 122)[2]

Taylor's texts are often informative; the British Isles are 'discovered' for the reader. Moreover, some of Taylor's accounts served a particular patriotic purpose which is outlined in long expository passages. Thus his journey by river in a wherry from London to Salisbury, *A Discovery by Sea, From London to Salisbury*, was intended to show that, for the national interest, measures had to be taken to make the English rivers navigable. Taylor's account of his journey to Scotland informed his audience about a region which was still largely unfamiliar to the English, even if they had had a monarchy in common since 1603. Thus Taylor's aim is to travel through Scotland as an 'eye-witnes' (p. 121) and to describe it in all its remarkable aspects. Scottish castles are depicted in as much detail as is the Scottish economy. Taylor was impressed, for example, by a sea-coal mine with 'two wayes into it, the one by sea and the other by land' (p. 132), so that 'in the space of eight and twenty, or nine and twenty yeeres, they haue digged more then an English mile vnder the Sea, that when men are at worke belowe, an hundred of the greatest shippes in *Britaine* may saile ouer their heads' (p. 133).

Taylor's texts are also entertaining, however. Arguably, this quality of his accounts was facilitated by the fact that the home tourist – unlike the traveller to the Continent – normally travelled and wrote unguided by apodemic advice.[3] Taylor thus intersperses his descriptions with many humorous passages about certain episodes of his tours. It is highly probable that this entertainment value was also motivated by the commercial interest which Taylor associated with at least some of his travels. He planned and marketed them in accordance with a pattern tried and tested by an earlier traveller: in 1599, the actor William Kemp had famously morris-danced from London to Norwich and had published a pamphlet account of this enterprise: *Kemps Nine Daies Wonder* (1600), '[w]herein euery dayes iourney is pleasantly set downe' (p. 5).[4] Taylor, too, wove spectacular difficulties into some of his journeys, which he advertised in prospectuses in order to attract sponsors for his enterprise. Taylor proposed that he would be able to overcome his self-set obstacles, and in the event of the difficulties being mastered, the sponsors agreed to fund Taylor for the trouble of the journey by buying his account of it. The special complication for Taylor's journey from London to Edinburgh was that it was intended as a *Pennyles Pilgrimage* as specified in the subtitle of his account: *How He Travailed on Foot, from London to Edenborough in Scotland, not carrying any Money to or fro, neither Begging, Borrowing, or Asking Meate, Drinke or Lodging*. However, Taylor managed to attract his audience not only as a result of such spectacular wagers, but also because he catered to the contemporary interest in the 'discovery' of Britain, which was even to increase up to the eighteenth century.

If Taylor's accounts have a clear entertainment value and if Taylor constructs an interesting travel *plot*, these aspects become less significant in texts about later home tours, which are predominantly object-orientated. Following the end of the Civil War, the Restoration and the Revolution of 1688, England saw the dawn of a glorious age. The new national feeling was even intensified as the union with Scotland in 1707 brought about significant expansion in the territory of the state. In the late seventeenth and eighteenth centuries, British patriotism was thus expressed not only in the criticism of foreign countries – as in many accounts of the Grand Tour – but also in the stocktaking of what Britain itself had to offer. Travel writing became an important site for 'constructions of Britishness', for fashioning the nation 'as an imagined homogeneous community' (Feldmann, 1997, p. 31). The emphasis of the domestic travellers of this period was not only on topography, history and antiquities (areas which had already been noted by Tudor travellers) but also, as already with Taylor, on the present state of the nation, in particular its social and economic aspects. The account of domestic travel came to be a focus of attention for intellectual, political, historical, technical, scientific and aesthetic developments in Great Britain, as Ria Omasreiter (1982, p. 13) observes. This focus marks even the records of home tours which were inspired purely by private interest, such as the *Journeys of Celia Fiennes*.

Between 1685 and 1703, Celia Fiennes went on several journeys through England, briefly touching the borderlands of Wales and Scotland on the way. The accounts of her tours were written around 1702, based on Fiennes's travel notes, but were not published during the author's lifetime. Even in these semi-private texts, however, a patriotic gesture is transparent, as in the preface, in which Fiennes considers the purposes of the home tour and the account of it:

> It would also form such an Idea of England, add much to its Glory and Esteem in our minds and cure the evil itch of overvalueing foreign parts; at least furnish them with an equivalent to entertain strangers when amongst us, or inform them when abroad of their native Country, which has been often a reproach to the English, ignorance and being strangers to themselves. ... But much more requisite is it for Gentlemen in general service of their country at home or abroad, in town or country, especially those that serve in parliament, to know and inform themselves the nature of Land, the Genius of the Inhabitants, so as to promote and improve Manufacture and Trade suitable to each and encourage all projects tending thereto. (p. 32)

In general, the 'Idea of England' which Fiennes portrays is mixed. Like many of the contemporary Grand Tourists, she had an eye for everything 'remarkable' and seems to capture this in her text as it occurred to her. Excerpt 1 exemplifies how Fiennes's interest was attracted by a wide range of aspects. Her account appears to make no attempt to bring any order to the colourful and varying impressions of the traveller other than the chronology of travel. Precisely in its heterogeneity, the text thus conveys something of the pleasure which Fiennes appears to have enjoyed in the very variety of her travelling experience – ranging from local specialities like tarts with clotted cream to the procedures of the Bath spa, which Fiennes depicts in precise and vivid detail:

> [T]he Ladyes goes [*sic*] into the bath with garments made of a fine yellow canvas, which is stiff and made large with great sleeves like a parsons [*sic*] gown, the water fills it up so that its borne off that your shape is not seen, ... the Gentlemen have drawers and wastcoates of the same sort of canvas, this is the best linning, for the bath water will change any other yellow; when you go out of the bath you go within a doore that leads to steps which you ascend by degrees, that are in the water, then the doore is shut which shuts down into the water a good way, so you are in a private place, where you still ascend severall more steps, and let your canvass drop of [*sic*] by degrees into the water, which your women guides takes [*sic*] off and the meanetyme your maides flings [*sic*] a garment of flannell made like a nightgown

with great sleeves over your head, and the guides take the taile and so
pulls it on you just as you rise the steps, and your other garment drops
off so you are wrapped up in the flannell and your nightgown on the
top, your slippers, and so you are set in Chaire which is brought into
the roome which are called slips and there are chimney's [*sic*] in
them, you may have fires.   (pp. 45–6)

Despite the variety of her interest, it is nevertheless clear that
Fiennes's perception of England – like that of her contemporaries –
was determined to a great extent by economic factors. When her
preface mentions 'Manufacture and Trade', these are two areas in
which Britain had achieved great progress by the turn of the eighteenth century and which, along with a reform of agriculture, formed
the foundation of a flourishing economy. Fiennes repeatedly writes
about economic aspects, with great attention to detail. Mines are
described not only in her account of Cornwall (excerpt 1), but indeed
wherever Fiennes comes across them. The manufacture of various
goods is recorded minutely, from cloth and paper to quality teapots.
When Fiennes surveys food markets, she estimates the price and
quality of all products, assessing the standard of agriculture in her
country. Thus, even though her texts do not appear to be tightly
structured, they can at least be said to have a leitmotif.

The sense of living in a new age whose progress had to be monitored
and recorded is particularly obvious in Daniel Defoe's introduction to
his extensive *Tour through the Whole Island of Great Britain* (1724–6):

[T]he face of things so often alters, and the situation of affairs in
this great British Empire gives such new turns, even to nature it self,
that there is matter of new observation every day presented to the
traveller's eye.   (p. 44)

The observations here made, as they principally regard the present
state of things, so, as near as can be, they are adapted to the present
taste of the times. The situation of things is given not as they have
been, but as they are; the improvements in the soil, the product of
the earth, the labour of the poor, the improvement in manufactures, in merchandises, in navigation, all respects the present time,
not the time past.   (p. 45)

For Defoe, the future of a dynamic Britain rested, in particular, on the
middle class.[5] The principal intention behind his *Tour* was thus 'to bring

this role to the consciousness of the middle class, and above all to make it clear to this class how its role was, in fact, a moral duty' (Possin, 1972, p. 32; my translation). That this idea appealed to a large audience is evident in the many editions of his *Tour* in the eighteenth century alone. The economic upturn and prosperity of the middle class is emphasized, for example, in Defoe's description of Leeds, which is centred on the wealth of the town and its opportunities for trade:

Leeds is a large, wealthy and populous town, it stands on the north bank of the River Aire, or rather on both sides the river, for there is a large suburb or part of the town on the south side of the river, and the whole is joined by a stately and prodigiously strong stone bridge, so large, and so wide, that formerly the cloth market was kept in neither part of the town, but on the very bridge it self; and therefore the refreshment given the clothiers by the inn-keepers, of which I shall speak presently is called the brigg-shot to this day.

The increase of the manufacturers and of the trade, soon made the market too great to be confined to the brigg or bridge, and it is now kept in the High-street, beginning from the bridge, and running up north almost to the market-house, where the ordinary market for provisions begins, which also is the greatest of its kind in all the north of England, except Hallifax. The street is a large, broad, fair, and well-built street, beginning, as I have said, at the bridge, and ascending gently to the north. ...

At seven a clock in the morning, the clothiers being supposed to be all come by that time, even in the winter, the market bell rings, it would surprise a stranger to see in how few minutes, without hurry or noise, and not the least disorder, the whole market is filled; all the boards upon the trestles are covered with cloth, close to one another as the pieces can lie long ways by one another, and behind every piece of cloth, the clothier standing to sell it. (pp. 500–1)

In this passage, even the description of the buildings is given from the perspective of the textile trade. The old, imposing bridge, for example, is of particular importance to Defoe since it represents a former centre of this trade.

As we have already seen with Celia Fiennes's account, home tourists encountered their own country with the same attention to empirical detail as did the contemporary explorer and continental traveller. With Defoe, this attention is even more pronounced, as one would expect of a writer who – as journalist and novelist – was devoted to realism and who championed the ideals of a simple, clear style, which Bishop Thomas Sprat had laid down for the Royal Society.[6]

A strong focus on the object of travel clearly marks Defoe's programme for the *Tour*. 'A description of the country is the business here', he writes in the preface (p. 44), and the text is indeed more descriptive than it is narrative. As reporter of his tour, Defoe is significantly less interested in the subjective experience of travel and his actual travel plot than in the phenomena he has observed on his journey. However, even if the *Tour* does not offer an interesting plot, it is by no means without structure and method. To the contrary: Defoe organizes his travelogue particularly systematically in relation to his primary concern.[7] Throughout, the text is determined by a merchant's point of view – a merchant whose aim is to portray the economic state of his country in a favourable light. This programme is reflected in the structure of Defoe's account: his *Tour* is a synthesis of various journeys which Defoe undertook over several years, 'seventeen very large circuits, or journeys have been taken through divers parts separately, and three general tours over almost the whole English part of the island' (p. 45). The text presents these journeys, however, in such a way as to give the impression of a single travelling experience. Each of Defoe's circuits through particular regions of Great Britain begins and ends in London; the capital, that is the centre of British trade, thus also appears as the centre and highlight of Defoe's *Tour*. Economic strands and textual strands converge in the capital: 'As I am now near the centre of this work, so I am to describe the great centre of England, the city of London' (p. 286). To further emphasize the role of London for the nation's wealth, the *Tour* also highlights the splendour of a London newly rebuilt following the Great Fire of 1666; the descriptions of their large new houses attest to the prosperity of the middle class.

Programmes of travel and travel writing aimed at a precise record of the travelled world continued to be followed throughout the eighteenth century and beyond. The essays collected in William Cobbett's *Rural Rides* (1830) are based, for example, on journeys which Cobbett undertook between 1822 and 1826 with the prime intention of assessing the state of English agriculture and rural conditions. Among the most popular English travelogues of the later eighteenth century is Dr Johnson's *A Journey to the Western Islands of Scotland* (1775) – not least owing to the reputation of the author. In the second half of the eighteenth century, the Celtic fringe of the British Isles was brought to the attention of a wider public through a whole series of travelogues. Scotland in particular underwent such swift developments that many people wanted to travel there, to see and record something of the ancient Scotland before it would vanish entirely. Dr Johnson, too, was above all motivated by this interest; his account is thus strongly object-orientated – as were the contemporary accounts of exploration, which Johnson read avidly.

> Johnson's tour was very much a part of the exciting geographical exploration taking place in 1773. Johnson was surveying Scotland when Cook crossed the Antarctic Circle for the first time, Constantine Phipps sailed for the North Pole, and James Bruce returned from Abyssinia. . . . The Highlanders are treated as if they were Eskimos, Siberian nomads, American Indians, and Pacific savages. (Curley, 1976, pp. 184–5)

Minutely, Johnson observes and portrays the 'life and manners' (p. 54) of the Highlanders, whom he, like many of his contemporaries, considered exotic and 'wild'.[8] Johnson even tried to interview the 'native' population, although the result did not always satisfy his thirst for knowledge:

> He that travels in the Highlands may easily saturate his soul with intelligence, if he will acquiesce in the first account. The highlander gives to every question an answer so prompt and peremptory, that skepticism itself is dared into silence, and the mind sinks before the bold reporter in unresisting cruelty; but, if a second question be ventured, it breaks the enchantment; for it is immediately discovered, that what was told so confidently was told at hazard, and that such fearlessness of assertion was either the sport of negligence, or the refuge of ignorance. (p. 68)

Johnson gathered information not only about contemporary life in the Highlands, but also about Scotland's great past. His account records many visits to historical monuments, and here, too, Johnson's descriptions are marked by great precision and attention to detail:

> The monastery of Aberbrothick is of great renown in the history of Scotland. Its ruins afford ample testimony of its ancient magnificence: its extent might, I suppose, easily be found by following the walls among the grass and weeds, and its height is known by some parts yet standing. The arch of one of the gates is entire, and of

another only so far dilapidated as to diversify the appearance. A square apartment of great loftiness is yet standing; its use I could not conjecture, as its elevation was very disproportionate to its area. Two corner towers, particularly attracted our attention. Mr Boswell, whose inquisitiveness is seconded by great activity, scrambled in at a high window, but found the stairs within broken, and could not reach the top. Of the other tower we were told that the inhabitants sometimes climbed it, but we did not immediately discern the entrance, and as the night was gathering upon us, thought proper to desist. Men skilled in architecture might do what we did not attempt: They might probably form an exact ground-plot of this venerable edifice. They may from some parts yet standing conjecture its general form, and perhaps by comparing it with other buildings of the same kind and the same age, attain an idea very near to truth. I should scarcely have regretted my journey, had it afforded nothing more than the sight of Aberbrothick. (p. 40)

Johnson appears in his text, then, above all as a traveller whose aim is to gather and impart knowledge on a whole range of subjects. Nevertheless, he also emerges as an individual persona – in his formulation of judgements and comments, but also, occasionally, in landscape descriptions such as the following. With his companion Boswell, Johnson here explores the Buller of Buchan:

When we came down to the sea, we saw some boats, and rowers, and resolved to explore the Buller at the bottom. We entered the arch, which the water had made, and found ourselves in a place, which, though we could not think ourselves in danger, we could scarcely survey without some recoil of the mind. The bason [*sic*] in which we floated was nearly circular, perhaps thirty yards in diameter. We were inclosed by a natural wall, rising steep on every side to a height which produced the idea of insurmountable confinement. The interception of all lateral light caused a dismal gloom. Round us was a perpendicular rock, above us the distant sky, and below an unknown profundity of water. If I had any malice against a walking spirit, instead of laying him in the Red Sea, I would condemn him to reside in the Buller of Buchan.

But terrour [*sic*] without danger is only one of the sports of fancy, a voluntary agitation of the mind that is permitted no longer than it pleases. We were soon at leisure to examine the place with minute inspection, and found many cavities which, as

the watermen told us, went backward to a depth which they had
never explored.   (p. 46)

What begins as an exploration turns into sublime aesthetic experience
('terrour without danger') as Johnson perceives a gloomy and solemn
natural scene. However, this experience is only short-lived ('a voluntary agitation of the mind that is permitted no longer than it pleases'),
and the travellers – with the text – then return to scientific investigation: 'to examine the place with minute inspection'. In comparison
with history, anthropology and monuments, landscape is an area of
experience to which Johnson attributes minor importance. However,
a type of home tour whose particular purpose was the enjoyment of
landscape had already emerged by the time Johnson ventured into the
Highlands. It is in the writing about scenic tourism that accounts of
domestic travel also start to turn prominently subjective.

Accounts of scenic tourism

With the intensification of Romantic influences in the course of the
eighteenth century, the experience of landscape begins to play a
major role in travel and travel writing. At the end of the last chapter
we have seen that the description of landscape, towards the close of
the century, had become an essential element in the travelogue about
the continental journey, such as Ann Radcliffe's *A Journey Made in the
Summer of 1794*. First and foremost, however, the home tour became
the mode of travel most frequently and often exclusively undertaken
for the enjoyment of landscape. Among England's famous literary
landscapes is the Lake District, 'discovered' during the latter half of
the eighteenth century. It is this scenic area which the Radcliffes
visited when they returned from the Continent and where they felt
'infinite delight in the grandeur of its landscapes' (p. 499). When Celia
Fiennes stayed in this region a century previously, the appreciation of
the countryside was clearly not a significant experience to her. In her
account, her interest in Lake Windermere is above all in the breeds of
fish which could be caught there, or in whether the lake had a natural
outlet, before she moves on to a recipe for the regional 'oat Clap
bread' (pp. 166–7).

   The chief purpose of scenic tourism[9] lay in the aesthetic perception
of landscape – and travel thus became an art in itself. In his study of
Wordsworth, Russell Noyes (1968) explicitly includes travel among
the aesthetic practices which constituted landscape art as it evolved in

the course of the eighteenth century: 'So close, indeed, at moments were the poetry of Nature, landscape painting, landscape gardening, and the art of travel that they lost their isolation, as separate arts, and combined into *the art of landscape*' (pp. 2–3). In this comprehensive art, painting nevertheless took on a leading role: landscapes were considered to be of particular aesthetic value if they were reminiscent of a painted landscape, that is of a landscape *picture*, and travellers who went on their journeys for the pleasure of landscape consciously sought out views in which the landscape appeared as in a painting.

In light of the primary role which painting played in the landscape arts, it is hardly surprising that the most influential treatise on scenic travel was formulated by a painter, William Gilpin. In the first of his *Three Essays: On Picturesque Beauty; On Picturesque Travel, and on Sketching Landscape* (1792), Gilpin defines objects of picturesque beauty as those, 'which please from some quality, capable of being *illustrated by painting*' (p. 3). Landscapes which had this kind of picturesque effect were to be taken in by a traveller in the same manner he would appreciate a work of art, as Gilpin emphasizes in the second of his essays: 'We examine what would amend the composition: how little is wanting to reduce it to the rules of our art' (p. 49). As an aid to this kind of landscape perception, some travellers – such as the poet Thomas Gray – even took with them a so-called Claude glass.[10] This device was a tinted mirror which enabled the viewer to perceive an actual landscape like a picture, in a particular, 'framed' section and in shades of colour which were characteristic of the work of famous landscape painters such as Claude Lorrain, Salvator Rosa or Nicolas Poussin.

Before publishing his *Three Essays*, William Gilpin had been on several journeys through the British Isles since 1768; excerpt 2 is taken from one of his popular accounts of these tours, *Observations on the Western Parts of England* (1798).[11] Gilpin's tour books were illustrated with many plates, and their original titles always contained the phrase 'relative chiefly to picturesque beauty'. In keeping with this emphasis on the picturesque, the texts are characterized by a high degree of description of the landscape views sought out by the traveller.

Gilpin's books not only record his own particular journeys, but they are also intended to give his readers advice for their own practice of the art of travel. Specifically, Gilpin tells his readers how to look out for the picturesque qualities in a landscape. Thus the first section of his *Observations on the Mountains and Lakes of Cumberland and Westmoreland* (1786) enumerates those elements of a landscape which most likely give rise to the effect of picturesque beauty and of which a traveller should therefore be particularly aware: alongside topographical features, Gilpin includes, for example, the intermixture of wood and cultivation, the great quantity of English oak, atmospheric conditions (such as mist and fog), as well as ruins of castles and abbeys. In addition to such elements of the scenery itself, the perception of picturesque beauty also requires a particular way of seeing. As revealed simply by the terminology used in excerpt 2, the countryside is to be *looked at* like a picture, that is from a particular viewpoint and perspective, from the correct distance and with an understanding of the 'picture's' aesthetic composition such as its division into foreground and background. The perception of landscape thus depends not only on certain prerequisites in the object, but also results from the activity of the subject.

In his *Guide to the Lakes* (1835),[12] William Wordsworth dissociated himself from the fashionable aesthetics of the picturesque. As Christoph Bode has pointed out, he distanced himself from the prevailing modes of Lake Tourism, which he believed had already defaced the landscape, and set out to depict this region as one 'whose beauty is threatened because mankind has strayed from the route prescribed by Nature herself' (Bode, 1997, p. 104). Nevertheless, Wordsworth's tour book still reveals the conviction that the aesthetic enjoyment of landscape depends on a proper attitude and way of seeing. In his *Guide*, too, readers thus find tips on how the landscape should be approached in order to capture the best view of it. In this manner, as is already implied by its title, Wordsworth's text is a guidebook rather than the account of an individual travel experience:

> I shall now speak of the LAKES of this country. The form of the lake is most perfect when, like Derwent-water, and some of the smaller lakes, it least resembles that of a river; – I mean, when being looked at from any given point where the whole may be seen at once, the width of it bears such proportion to the length, that, however the outline may be diversified by far-receding bays, it never assumes the shape of a river, and is contemplated with that placid and quiet feeling which belongs peculiarly to the lake – as a body of still water under the influence of no current; reflecting therefore the clouds, the light, and all the imagery of the sky and surrounding hills; expressing also and making visible the changes of the atmosphere, and motions of the lightest breeze, and subject to agitation only from the winds. (p. 32)

In this passage, it is clear that landscape is constituted in an act of perception – when the perceiving subject views it in a particular way. Whether or not a journey through landscape becomes an aesthetic experience is thus quite dependent on the individual traveller, and a book on scenic travel will only be successful in as much as it introduces the reader himself to the proper way of seeing landscape. If scenic travel was initially intended to be an essentially individual and subjective experience, it was soon transformed into a standardized pilgrimage to selected beauty spots – not least because of the many books published about this kind of touring. Picturesque travel was methodized and, as a consequence, schematized into a round of well-known, canonized sights – just as the Grand Tour. Even in the heyday of Romanticism, at the beginning of the nineteenth century, the fashion of picturesque travel and the books about it thus attracted criticism and mockery. Thomas Rowlandson's caricatures are among the most famous examples. They appeared in 1809, as illustrations to a satirical poem by William Combe, *The Tour of Dr Syntax in Search of the Picturesque*.[13] In this text, the schoolmaster Syntax sets off on a tour of England to bolster his income:

> I'll make a TOUR – *and then I'll* WRITE IT
> You well know what my pen can do,
> And I'll employ my pencil too: –
> I'll ride and *write*, and *sketch* and *print*,
> And thus create a real mint;
> I'll *prose* it here, I'll *verse* it there,
> And *picturesque* it ev'ry where:
> I'll do what all have done before;
> I think I shall – and somewhat more.   (pp. 4–5)

Unfortunately, however, Dr Syntax meets with so many mishaps during his tour that his aesthetic pleasure is significantly reduced – he loses his way, is attacked by street robbers and a bull, and falls prey to greedy landlords. One of Rowlandson's drawings illustrates the episode when Dr Syntax, trying to sketch a picturesque ruin from the proper distance prescribed by Gilpin, plunges backwards into a lake.

Even if picturesque travel and tour books were thus derided in their early stages, the description of picturesque landscape in travel writing proved to be long-lived; it is a standard element in travelogues until well into the nineteenth century. In other respects, too, accounts of picturesque travel were influential for the genre's development.

Gilpin's definition of picturesque travel in his essay of this title explicitly emphasizes the fundamental disinterestedness in this type of journey – apart from the interest in aesthetic contemplation:

> We mean not to bring it into competition with any of the more useful ends of travelling. But as many travel without any end at all, amusing themselves without being able to give a reason why they are amused, we offer one end, which may possibly engage some vacant minds; and may indeed afford a rational amusement to such as travel for more important purposes. (p. 41)[14]

Picturesque travel and the writing about it thus contributed to the emancipation of travelling and the travelogue from the strictures of being 'useful'. In this manner, the scenic journey, alongside the Grand Tour, became a predecessor of tourism as we understand it today and which was soon to take hold – travel for pleasure, travel as a leisure activity.

Travel writing in the nineteenth century continues, in part, to be object-orientated and informative. Basically, from the end of the eighteenth century, however, the travel account spans the full spectrum from extreme object to extreme subject orientation, and from sober instruction to entertainment and aesthetic delight. Travel writers of the Victorian age have a whole range of possibilities at their disposal for their textualization of established as well as of new forms of travel.

5
Travel Writing in the Nineteenth Century

[1] *Nothing, in sooth, could be more picturesque than this first view of the Tanganyika Lake, as it lay in the lap of the mountains, basking in the gorgeous tropical sunshine. Below and beyond a short foreground of rugged and precipitous hill-fold, down which the footpath zigzags painfully, a narrow strip of emerald green, never sere and marvelously fertile, shelves toward a ribbon of glistening yellow sand . . . Farther in front stretch the waters, an expanse of the lightest and softest blue, . . . and sprinkled by the crisp east wind with tiny crescents of snowy foam. The background in front is a high and broken wall of steel-colored mountain, here flecked and capped with pearly mist, there standing sharply penciled against the azure air; its yawning chasms, marked by a deeper plum-color, fall toward dwarf hills of mound-like proportions, which apparently dip their feet in the wave. To the south, and opposite the long low point behind which the Malagarazi River discharges the red loam suspended in its violent stream, lie the bluff headlands and capes of Uguhha, and, as the eye dilates, it falls upon a cluster of outlying islets, speckling a sea-horizon. Villages, cultivated lands, the frequent canoes of the fishermen on the waters, and on a nearer approach the murmurs of the waves breaking upon the shore, give a something of variety, of movement, of life to the landscape, which, like all the fairest prospects in these regions, wants but a little of the neatness and finish of art – mosques and kiosks, palaces and villas, gardens and orchards – contrasting with the profuse lavishness and magnificence of nature, and diversifying the unbroken* coup d'oeil *of excessive vegetation, to rival, if not to excel, the most admired scenery of the classic regions.*

(Richard F. Burton, *The Lake Regions of Central Africa*, 1860,
pp. 307–8)

[2] *In New York there are street omnibuses as we have … The omnibuses, though clean and excellent, were to me very unintelligible. They have no conductor to them. To know their different lines and usages a man should have made a scientific study of the city. … The money has to be paid through a little hole behind the driver's back, and should, as I learned at last, be paid immediately on entrance. But in getting up to do this I always stumbled about, and it would happen that when with considerable difficulty I had settled my own account, two or three ladies would enter, and would hand me, without a word, some coins with which I had no life-long familiarity in order that I might go through the same ceremony on their account. The change I would usually drop into the straw, and then there would arise trouble and unhappiness. Before I became aware of that law as to instant payment, bells used to be rung at me which made me uneasy. I knew I was not behaving as a citizen should behave, but could not compass the exact points of my delinquency. And then when I desired to escape, the door being strapped up tight, I would halloo vainly at the driver through the little hole; whereas, had I known my duty, I should have rung a bell, or pulled a strap, according to the nature of the omnibus in question. In a month or two all these things may possibly be learned; – but the visitor requires his facilities for locomotion at the first moment of his entrance into the city.*

(Anthony Trollope, *North America*, 1862, vol. 1, pp. 292–3)

[3] *At last, Patagonia! How often had I pictured in imagination, wishing with an intense longing to visit this solitary wilderness, resting far off in its primitive and desolate peace, untouched by man, remote from civilization! There it lay full in sight before me – the unmarred desert that wakes strange feelings in us; the ancient habitation of giants, whose footprints seen on the seashore amazed Magellan and his men, and won for it the name of Patagonia. …*

It was not, however, the fascination of old legends that drew me, nor the desire of the desert, for not until I had seen it, and had tasted its flavour, then, and on many subsequent occasions, did I know how much its solitude and desolation would be to me, what strange knowledge it would teach, and how enduring its effect would be on my spirit. Not these things, but the passion of the ornithologist took me.

(W.H. Hudson, *Idle Days in Patagonia*, 1893, pp. 4–5)

Travel during the reign of Queen Victoria

The nineteenth century, in particular the age of Queen Victoria, was a period of intensification of travel which could be seen to emerge at the end of the previous century in the increased popularity of travel on the Continent and the fashion of scenic tourism. Travel was becoming open to more and more sectors of society. In his *Travelling Sketches* (1866),[1] Anthony Trollope – himself a well-travelled writer – portrays typical globetrotters of his time, such as 'The Family that Goes Abroad because It's the Thing to Do', 'The Man who Travels Alone', 'The Unprotected Female Tourist', 'The United Englishmen Who Travel for Fun' and even 'Tourists who Don't Like their Travels'. The most favoured destinations, whether at home or on the Continent, were often overcrowded. As early as 1820, when Maria Edgeworth arrived in Lausanne during her trip through Switzerland and France, the town was teeming with tourists and Edgeworth had great difficulty in finding a place to stay for her party.[2] Eighteenth-century travellers to the Continent had enjoyed the Alps in relative solitude. The Victorian John Ruskin, by contrast, found the summits littered with the leftovers of numerous tourists who held picnics while viewing the breathtaking panorama. As he complained in his chapter 'Of Modern Landscape' in *Modern Painters* (1856): 'Our modern society in general goes to the mountains, not to fast, but to feast, and leaves their glaciers covered with chicken-bones and egg-shells' (p. 320). In *Pictures from Italy* (1846), Charles Dickens describes how he repeatedly came across the same group of compatriots during his visit to Rome:

> We often encountered, in these expeditions, a company of English Tourists, with whom I had an ardent, but ungratified longing, to establish a speaking acquaintance. They were one Mr. Davis, and a small circle of friends. It was impossible not to know Mrs. Davis's name, from her being always in great request among her party, and her party being everywhere. During the Holy Week, they were in every part of every scene of every ceremony. For a fortnight or three weeks before it, they were in every tomb, and every church, and every ruin, and every Picture Gallery; and I hardly ever observed Mrs. Davis to be silent for a moment. ...
>
> Mr. and Mrs. Davis, and their party, had, probably, been brought from London in about nine or ten days. Eighteen hundred years ago, the Roman legions under Claudius, protested against being led into Mr. and Mrs. Davis's country, urging that it lay beyond the limits of the world. (pp. 377–8)

The closing sentences of this passage allude to the 'transport revolution' (Bagwell, 1974) which had affected travel from the end of the eighteenth century. Owing to modern means of transport such as the steamship and the railway, even distant countries were now accessible in less time and in greater comfort. These forms of transport, as other elements of the travel infrastructure, were increasingly open to middle-class travellers,[3] thus creating the prerequisites for a tourist industry in the modern sense: pre-planned mass travel as a leisure-time activity.[4] To Thomas Cook, a tour was no longer an individual experience, but a package tour, that is a journey organized to provide large numbers of travellers with speedy transport and convenient accommodation – at an affordable price. Cook opened the world's first travel agency in 1845, in 1856 organized the first 'Great Circular Tour of the Continent', and in 1872 the first ever tourist trip around the world.[5] Given the greater opportunities for travel, there was also a natural increase in the need for travel guides. As early as 1829, the first volume of the Baedeker series appeared in Germany; from 1846, the series was also available in other languages. The British equivalents were *Murray's Hand-Books* or *Murray's Red Guides*, which were launched on the book market in 1836.

For those who could not travel themselves, foreign lands could be experienced at home. The Great Exhibition in London (1851) not only presented British products to the world, but also brought the world to people who – thanks to Thomas Cook – had travelled to the exhibition from all over Britain; foreign countries, above all the British colonies, were staged in a show which the visitor could view at leisure. Thus the London exhibition can be related to another phenomenon typical of the period: the nineteenth century, especially during its first and last decades, was the heyday of the hugely popular panoramic entertainments – circular panoramas, dioramas and moving panoramas which presented a mass audience with highly naturalistic representations of Biblical and historical events, famous cities and foreign lands. In 1850, when the first wave of panoramas had already abated, the *Illustrated London News* still spoke of a contemporary 'panoramania'. Scott B. Wilcox, in his introductory essay to a catalogue compiled by Ralph Hyde, explicitly links the panorama to the contemporary craze for travel and knowledge about worlds abroad:

It satisfied, or at least helped to satisfy, an increasing appetite for visual information. A revolution in travel had made the world seem smaller. The growth of a literate middle class and the burgeoning newspaper industry meant that many more people were aware of a greater number of happenings over a larger area of the globe. It is not surprising that people should desire visual images of a world of which they were becoming increasingly aware through the printed word.   (Hyde, 1988, p. 37)

For many people, panoramas would become a cheap and comfortable substitute for travel and were even celebrated as such:

An article in *Blackwood's Magazine* in 1824 developed this idea at length: 'panoramas are among the happiest contrivances for saving time and expense in this age of contrivances. What cost a couple of hundred pounds and a half year a century ago, now costs a shilling and a quarter of an hour ... The affair is settled in a summary manner.'   (ibid., p. 38)

A moving panorama first displayed in 1860, for example, gave Englishmen an opportunity to travel from 'London to Hong Kong in Two Hours' (ibid., p. 133).[6]

In view of the success of these panoramas it is not surprising that travelogues continued to enjoy great popularity among the reading public – not only accounts of tourist journeys, which readers might even undertake themselves, but also and in particular the accounts of explorers and missionaries whose destinations were far more adventurous. Richard Burton alone, who was famous for his expeditions into Arabia and for his 'discovery' of Lake Tanganyika, furnished a voracious readership with over forty books about his enterprises.

The books that the explorers wrote took the Victorian reading public by storm. In the first few months after its publication in 1857, Livingstone's *Missionary Travels* sold seventy thousand copies and made its author wealthy and so famous that he had to avoid situations where he might be mobbed by admirers. If Livingstone was already a national hero in the late 1850s, he was a national saint by the time of his last African journey in 1872. ... Livingstone's apotheosis was complete in 1872 when Stanley, with his great journalistic scoop, published his first bestseller, *How I Found Livingstone*.[7] Stanley's other books were also bestsellers: *In Darkest Africa*, for example, sold one hundred and fifty thousand copies in English, was frequently translated, and, according to one reviewer, 'has been read more universally and with deeper interest than any other publication' of 1890.   (Brantlinger, 1985, p. 176)

Just as the great voyages of the sixteenth and seventeenth centuries grew from mercantile and colonial ambitions, Victorian explorers and missionaries were entangled in the imperialist discourse of their time. Even Charles Darwin's *Voyage of the Beagle* (1839), that is a scientific account about regions which were mostly not an object of British colonial desire, includes passages which are clear expressions of an imperialist spirit and a civilizing mission. The following extract, for example, refers to the South Seas:

> From seeing the present state, it is impossible not to look forward with high expectation to the future progress of nearly an entire hemisphere. The march of improvement, consequent on the intro-duction of Christianity throughout the South Sea, probably stands by itself on the records of history. It is the more striking when we remember that only sixty years since, Cook, whose most excellent judgment none will dispute, could foresee no prospect of such change. Yet these changes have now been effected by the philan-thropic spirit of the British nation.
>
> In the same quarter of the globe Australia is rising, or indeed may be said to have risen, into a grand centre of civilization, which at some not very remote period, will rule as empress over the southern hemisphere. It is impossible for an Englishman to behold these distant colonies, without a high pride and satisfaction. To hoist the British flag, seems to draw with it as a certain consequence, wealth, prosperity, and civilization. (p. 376)

Once Europe had 'discovered' Australia, there were no more conti-nents to be found. Darwin nostalgically reflects on a time when sea-voyagers could still hope to come across *terra incognita*: 'The whole western shores of America are thrown open, and Australia has become the metropolis of a rising continent. How different are the circum-stances to a man shipwrecked at the present day in the Pacific, to what they were in the time of Cook! Since his voyage a hemisphere has been added to the civilized world' (p. 372).

In the absence of completely 'new' landmasses, the explorers now directed their efforts to the interior of 'old' continents which were still largely unfamiliar to Europeans – the Arctic Regions, South America, Australia and, most significantly, Africa. The African Association had been founded as early as 1788, and Mungo Park had travelled on behalf of it (see Chapter 1, pp. 7–8). His *Travels in the Interior of Africa* (1799) reveal the interrelation of exploration and trade interests long before British imperialism in Africa reached its pinnacle:

> It appears that slaves, gold, and ivory, together with the few articles enumerated in the beginning of my work, viz., bees-wax and honey, hides, gums, and dye-woods, constitute the whole catalogue of exportable commodities. ... It cannot, however, admit of a doubt, that all the rich and valuable productions, both of the East and West Indies, might easily be naturalised and brought to the utmost perfection in the tropical parts of this immense continent. Nothing is wanting to this end but example, to enlighten the minds of the natives, and instruction, to enable them to direct their industry to proper objects.　　　　　　　　　　　(pp. 238–9)

In the last quarter of the nineteenth century, the British Empire reached its height: Britain took possession of extensive parts of Africa, and in 1876, India became the 'jewel' in the British crown, giving rise to the travels of many military and state officials and their families.

Of the many varieties of travel writing which emerged during the mobile age of Victoria, two will be considered in greater detail: accounts of exploration and texts relating to the new mass phenomenon of tourist travel.

Victorian accounts of exploration: adventure and imperialism

If the accounts of Victorian explorers achieved bestseller status, this is not only a result of their contribution to the discourse of the Empire or the fact that they satisfied a curiosity for foreign lands. They also met the public's taste for adventure and exciting entertainment, as was offered in the realm of 'pure' fiction, for example, in the novels of Sir Henry Rider Haggard. During the last quarter of the century, this kind of literature attracted a wide readership, not least due to a mass education programme for the less privileged classes. 'The new millions of readers liked ... to read not about themselves and their social and financial problems but about exotic places and daring deeds' (Gatrell, 1992, p. 31).

Many Victorian explorers appear in their accounts as heroes every bit as courageous and enduring as the protagonists of the contemporary adventure novel; moreover, the travelling heroes offered their readers the thrill of adventures which had actually been experienced.

Their accounts not only have an exciting travel plot, but they also make the travelling persona an interesting character within this plot. The following extract is taken from Richard Burton's *First Footsteps in East Africa* (1856), the account of his expedition to the forbidden town of Harar in Somalia. In April 1855, Burton and his companions came under serious attack by the Somalis. The figure of Burton as heroic adventurer is clearly at the core of the text when Burton as travel writer depicts the episode:

> The enemy swarmed like hornets with shouts and screams intending to terrify, and proving that overwhelming odds were against us: it was by no means easy to avoid in the shades of night the jobbing of javelins, and the long heavy daggers thrown at our legs from under and through the opening of the tent. We three remained together: Lieut. Herne knelt by my right, on my left was Lieut. Speke guarding the entrance, I stood in the centre, having nothing but a sabre. . . .
>
> After breaking through the mob at the tent entrance, imagining that I saw the form of Lieut. Stroyan lying upon the sand, I cut my way towards it amongst a dozen Somal, whose war-clubs worked without mercy, whilst the Balyuz, who was violently pushing me out of the fray, rendered the strokes of my sabre uncertain. This individual was cool and collected: though incapacitated by a sore right-thumb from using the spear, he did not shun danger, and passed unhurt through the midst of the enemy: his efforts, however, only illustrated the venerable adage, 'defend me from my friends.' I turned to cut him down: he cried out in alarm; the well-known voice caused an instant's hesitation: at that moment a spearman stepped forward, left his javelin in my mouth, and retired before he could be punished. . . .
>
> Again losing the Balyuz in the darkness, I spent the interval before dawn wandering in search of my comrades, and lying down when overpowered with faintness and pain: as the day broke, with my remaining strength I reached the head of the creek, was carried into the vessel, and persuaded the crew to arm themselves and visit the scene of our disasters.   (vol. 2, pp. 100–2)

Despite the obvious elements of adventure in their texts, the majority of Victorian explorers were nevertheless also committed to imparting information, thus adding to the archive of knowledge that was, as Thomas Richards (1993) has shown, a seminal instrument of control over the Empire. After all, many of the respective expeditions were sponsored by the Royal Geographical Society and similar 'knowledge-producing institutions' (ibid., p. 4). Thus Victorian accounts of exploration tend to include increasingly lengthy descriptions of natural and anthropological phenomena, as well as extensive scientific appendices and precise illustrations. In this manner, the explorers of the nineteenth century continued in the tradition of earlier writing of exploration and scientific travel, even if they generally displayed a more marked concern with the travel plot.

The mixture of adventure and 'serious' observation emerges clearly, for example, throughout the accounts of Richard Burton. In 1853, Burton travelled through Arabia, disguised as an Afghan pilgrim, to explore this region which was still widely unknown to Europeans. Burton's entry into the holy places of Islam, which were strictly forbidden to Christian visitors, was a particularly dangerous stage of his enterprise, and his *Personal Narrative of a Pilgrimage to Al-Madinah & Meccah* (1855–6) expresses the traveller's undisguised pride as he penetrates into the Kaaba: 'mine was the ecstasy of gratified pride' (vol. 2, p. 161). Despite his sense of personal triumph, however, the traveller is also careful to act as an exacting researcher and is explicitly cast in this role in the text. He even risks the danger of being found out in order to measure the sanctuary: 'with a piece of tape, and the simple processes of stepping and spanning, I managed to measure all the objects concerning which I was curious' (vol. 2, p. 177).

The Victorian explorers became *national* heroes if their expeditions could be claimed for the imperial cause. These travellers – particularly missionaries such as David Livingstone – were commonly considered to bring the blessings of British civilization to the 'wilderness';[8] the passage from Darwin's *Voyage of the Beagle* quoted above (p. 87) makes explicit reference to this 'philanthropic' mission of the British nation. The explorers were considered carriers of civilization even when their destination was the unpopulated ice desert of the polar regions. Thus Sir John Franklin became a national hero as he set off, in 1845, on his fatal quest for the Northwest Passage, which had still remained undiscovered since the first attempts of the Renaissance voyagers.

Franklin himself, famous after two previous expeditions, seemed to embody those English qualities that would make him overcome all difficulties. He was persistent, pious, and courageous, and he had at his command the best of British technology and science as well as the best of British manhood. Although national pride was involved

in the Franklin Expedition, the symbolic value of the expedition
went beyond mere patriotism ... The Franklin Expedition was not
simply carrying the Union Jack into the Arctic; it was carrying
Western man's faith in his power to prevail on earth. If Franklin
could find and navigate a Northwest Passage after almost three
centuries of failures, Western man would seem somehow to
demonstrate his capacity to conquer Nature at its most mysterious
and intimidating.   (Loomis, 1978, pp. 104–6)

Franklin did not forfeit his reputation as culture hero when his last
expedition failed – he was now considered as a *tragic* hero. This
heroism could even be reconciled with a discovery which was actually essentially incompatible with the British self-image. From 1847,
when Franklin's expedition party was finally considered missing, a
series of further expeditions set out to search for it. They only found
the mortal remains of a few members of Franklin's gallant crew
(Franklin himself was not among them, having died of a stroke before
the final catastrophe). Some of the bones bore irrefutable evidence
that the men, starving to death, had practised cannibalism, that is an
essentially 'savage' behaviour.[9] When reports about these findings
were published back home, the British initially reacted with outrage
and disbelief.[10] Eventually, however, even this aspect could be inte-
grated into the Franklin legend. After all, Franklin himself had
admitted to the consumption of human flesh in the account of one
of his earlier expeditions, *Narrative of a Journey to the Shores of the Polar
Sea* (1823) – without any harm to his reputation. For in this case,
cannibalism was built into a tragic travel plot, which presents
the heroes *in extremis*, freezing and starving to death. In this context,
the practice of cannibalism merely appears as the final straw in the
explorers' suffering. At length, the *Narrative* depicts the cold and
hunger pangs which Franklin and his companions have to endure
and which lead them to consume the flesh of a dead member of the
team shortly before being rescued:

Michel too arrived at the same time, and relieved our anxiety on
his account. He reported that he had been in chase of some deer
which passed near his sleeping-place in the morning, and although
he did not come up with them, yet that he found a wolf which
had been killed by the stroke of a deer's horn, and had brought a
part of it. We implicitly believed this story then, but afterwards
became convinced from circumstances, the detail of which may be

spared, that it must have been a portion of the body of Belanger or Perrault.   (p. 451)

Even if the British members of the expedition are initially unaware of what they are eating – according to the text – and thus practise cannibalism involuntarily, they certainly transgress taboos of their own civilization. This transgression is, however, not only excusable, but, as presented in the account, it even serves to intensify the tragedy of an enterprise which demands inhuman efforts in a hostile environment.

Where Franklin appears in his text as a suffering hero who fails to master the region he travels, many accounts of the High Victorian period present the explorer as a conqueror who claims the country he investigates for the Empire. The extent to which travelogues of this period promoted imperialist ideology[11] has been examined by Mary Louise Pratt, who concentrates on writings about Africa as that part of the world which provided the focus for imperialist ambitions of the late nineteenth century.[12] To Pratt (1985, p. 121), the apparently strictly object-orientated description of 'manners-and-customs', that is the anthropological component of these accounts, is a strategy which allows the writers to avoid the portrayal of culture *contact*: the text constructs an 'other' with whom the European traveller does not establish a genuine interpersonal relationship.[13] Another writing strategy of the imperialist travelogue is the strict separation of descriptions of a country's population from geographical and topographical descriptions, so that the country, which is, after all, the real object of the imperial gaze, comes across as 'unpopulated'. Such suppression of the native population is apparent, for instance, in excerpt 1 from Richard Burton's *The Lake Regions of Central Africa* (1860). The people and villages of Lake Tanganyika are here reduced to mere components of the landscape: 'Villages, cultivated lands, the frequent canoes of the fishermen on the waters, and on a nearer approach the murmurs of the waves breaking upon the shore, give a something of variety, of movement, of life to the landscape.' As Pratt (1982, pp. 146–7) also demonstrates in regard to this passage, the account of Victorian explorers frequently draws on traditional patterns of picturesque landscape depiction. Burton's presentation of Lake Tanganyika highlights its resemblance to a painted landscape simply through expressions such as 'picturesque', 'foreground', 'background', 'sharply penciled' and 'marked by a deeper plum-color'. If the picturesque perception of landscape was originally of a purely aesthetic nature, as was shown in Chapter 4, it is underpinned in explorer accounts by a very definite element of interest – landscape aesthetics is used to veil the ambition to conquer the land.

Drawing on the tradition of the picturesque, the account of Victorian explorers shares an element with another variety of contemporary travel writing: the account of the tourist trip. As suggested in the last chapter, travel for the enjoyment of the landscape may be regarded as a precursor of modern tourism, since the latter, just like Gilpin's picturesque travel, is fundamentally dedicated to pleasure, and in particular to the pleasure of looking. For Christopher Mulvey (1983), the Claude glass of the picturesque traveller may even be considered an antecedent to the photographic tourist snapshot:

> The image of the eighteenth-century gentleman on tour, Claude-glass in hand, prefigured that of the modern, democratic tourist, camera in hand, not making pictures but taking them at prearranged locations; prospect and view gave way to snapshot and postcard. . . . The tourist's job is to take pictures, and the guides tell him where to do it. (p. 254)

The pleasure of looking: accounts of tourist travel

The Victorian tourist, like the visitor of the contemporary panoramas, was principally concerned with seeing sights. It soon became habitual for tourists to document what they had seen through sending picture postcards back home, and later in the century, in snapshots they took themselves. In *North America* (1862), his account of a journey through Canada and the United States, Anthony Trollope emphasizes the importance of sights for the tourist in a passage relating to one of America's prime tourist spots – the Niagara Falls:

> Of all the sights on this earth of ours which tourists travel to see, – at least of all those which I have seen, – I am inclined to give the palm to the Falls of Niagara. In the catalogue of such sights I intend to include all buildings, pictures, statues, and wonders of art made by men's hands, and also all beauties of nature prepared by the Creator for the delight of his creatures. (vol. 1, p. 136)

Charles Dickens's *American Notes* (1842) even suggests an irresistible urge to look and stare as the traveller arrives in Boston, his first destination in the United States:

> The indescribable interest with which I strained my eyes, as the first patches of American soil peeped like molehills from the green sea ... can hardly be exaggerated. ... How I remained on deck, staring about me, until we came alongside the dock, and how, though I had had as many eyes as Argus, I should have had them all wide open, and all employed on new objects – are topics which I will not prolong this chapter to discuss.   (p. 23)

While the imperialist view is founded on an ideology which strives to possess what it has seen, the tourist seems to be driven by the pure pleasure of seeing. However, by contrast with the explorer's gaze, the tourist's way of seeing is frequently criticized for being a mere glance, superficial and imprecise (Erker-Sonnabend, 1987, p. 84), or is characterized as 'panoramic perception' in the special sense defined by Dolf Sternberger:

> Dolf Sternberger perceives the experience of travel in the nineteenth century as a virtual panoramization of the world. He thus extends the term panorama beyond its meaning in art history to cover an approach to reality which he considers characteristic of this period. When he writes of panoramic perception, he understands this as a manner of viewing which is essentially connected with the accelerated mode of perception offered by railway travel: the world passes by the traveller in colourful pictures; the panoramic view of the traveller is directed at pictures which are characterized by a sense of fleetingness, change and a foreground distorted by speed.
>
> (Schiffer, 1986, p. 134; my translation)[14]

A panoramic view in this sense, that is perception from a vehicle or vessel in motion, emerges very clearly from certain passages in Charles Dickens's *Pictures from Italy*. Through its title alone, this account emphasizes the importance of the visual, of seeing pictures, as an essential experience of tourist travel. In the following extract, the traveller is on a steamboat on the Rhône, and the landscape, with all its attractions, appears to be drawn past him like a moving panorama:

> For the last two days, we had seen great sullen hills, the first indications of the Alps, lowering in the distance. Now, we were rushing on beside them: sometimes close beside them: sometimes with an intervening slope, covered with vineyards. Villages and small

towns hanging in mid-air, with great woods of olives seen through the light open towers of their churches, and clouds moving slowly on, upon the steep acclivity behind them; ruined castles perched on every eminence; and scattered houses in the clefts and gullies of the hills; made it very beautiful. The great height of these, too, making the buildings look so tiny, that they had all the charm of elegant models; their excessive whiteness, as contrasted with the brown rocks, or the sombre, deep, dull, heavy green of the olive-tree; and the puny size, and little slow walk of the Liliputian men and women on the bank; made a charming picture.   (p. 272)

In this particular example, the scene seems to glide past the trav-eller, and the houses and people glanced at from a distance appear as miniatures; the traveller's impression indeed comes across as rather superficial. Nevertheless, the tourist account is not generally charac-terized by fleeting glances. Quite the contrary – much writing by tourist travellers is marked by great precision in its description of sights. Indeed, description is – as in the tour books about picturesque travel – the dominant mode of representation in this kind of travel writing. In Trollope's *North America*, for example, the Niagara Falls are presented in all their aspects and details, including the whole range of facilities which an already budding tourist industry provides for the traveller's views and sights:

When this state has been reached and has passed away you may get off your rail and mount the tower. I do not quite approve of that tower, seeing that it has about it a gingerbread air, and reminds one of those well-arranged scenes of romance in which one is told that on the left you turn to the lady's bower, price sixpence; and on the right ascend to the knight's bed, price sixpence more, with a view of the hermit's tomb thrown in. But nevertheless the tower is worth mounting, and money is charged for the use of it. It is not very high, and there is a balcony at the top on which some half dozen persons may stand at ease. Here the mystery is lost, but the whole fall is seen.   (vol. 1, p. 144)

You will be covered with spray as you walk up to the ledge of rocks, but I do not think that the spray will hurt you. ... If, however, you are yourself of a different opinion, you may hire a suit of oil-cloth clothes, for, I believe, a quarter of a dollar. They are nasty of course, and have this further disadvantage, that you

become much more wet having them on than you would be
without them.   (vol. 1, p. 147)

Passages like these reveal how Trollope's account is structured to
resemble typical tourist behaviour: the text moves, with the traveller,
from one view to the next, from sight to sight. Although Trollope
reports his journey retrospectively, his text thus also fulfils a guiding
function for its audience; the readers are even addressed directly and
pointed to views which they might seek out during future travels of
their own. Clearly, then, the account of the Victorian tourist journey,
just like the account of the Grand Tour or the home tour, borders on
the guidebook genre. In this manner, it contributes to what Jonathan
Culler (1988) terms a fundamental semiotic strategy of tourism, that
is the production of 'markers' for sights: 'the touristic experience
involves the production of or participation in a sign relation between
marker and sight' (p. 160). Or, as Hans Magnus Enzensberger (1990, p.
77) has put it in his theory of tourism, that which is worth seeing is
methodized for the tourist and becomes a norm or a 'must' – through
organized travel, guidebooks and travelogues.

If tourist travel is conducted superficially, this is largely to be
attributed to such forms of standardization. In extreme cases, the
tourist simply 'does' sights prescribed in a fixed programme (as in old
forms of methodized travel). The result is that, even during the first
heyday of modern tourist travel, a phenomenon can be discerned
which is closely bound up with tourism and which will become more
prominent still in the twentieth century: a strict distinction made
between 'real', individualistic travellers and 'mere' tourists, in which
the former place great importance on not being mistaken for the
latter. In this manner, even the title of Amelia Edwards's *Untrodden
Peaks and Unfrequented Valleys* (1873) – the account of a journey
through the Dolomites – expresses the traveller's concern to steer
clear of well-trodden tourist paths. The preface is even more explicit
about this concern: 'Here one escapes from hackneyed sights, from
overcrowded hotels, from the dreary routine of table d'hôtes, from
the flood of Cook's tourists' (p. xxxi). Travellers who, unlike Edwards,
prefer to keep to the canonized paths and expect to see 'asterisked'
sights, risk their expectations of these sights being disappointed – an
experience already recorded, as we have seen, by many Grand
Tourists of an earlier age.

Charles Dickens registers such disappointment in his *Pictures from
Italy*. In Rome, he not only arrives in the 'wrong' part of town, but

the view of ancient Rome which he had come to see is also blocked by the Carnival:

> The masquerade dresses on the fringe of the Carnival, did great violence to this promise. There were no great ruins, no solemn tokens of antiquity, to be seen; – they all lie on the other side of the city. There seemed to be long streets of commonplace shops and houses, such as are to be found in any European town; there were busy people, equipages, ordinary walkers to and fro; a multitude of chattering strangers. It was no more *my* Rome: the Rome of anybody's fancy, man or boy; degraded and fallen and lying asleep in the sun among the heap of ruins: than the Place de la Concorde in Paris is. (p. 365)

Not until the following day is the traveller's expectation met, when he visits the Colosseum and thus discovers the 'proper' Rome: 'Here was Rome indeed at last; and such a Rome as no one can imagine in its full and awful grandeur!' (p. 367).

Moreover, the programming of the tourist journey and particular expectations attached to it give rise to problems in textualization – another parallel with the Grand Tour. How can the tourist account present its readers with 'sights' which they have not already read about? How can this kind of travelogue go beyond a simple list of markers for sights, or at least render it in an original way? In *Pictures from Italy*, Dickens finds a fairly original solution to the problem of presenting Venice – that Italian city almost described to death by legions of travellers before him: Dickens depicts his stay in Venice as 'An Italian Dream'. Only at the end of the chapter does the text reveal that the 'dream' was, in fact, an actual visit to the town, whose name is withheld until the very last sentence: 'I have, many and many a time, thought since, of this strange Dream upon the water: half-wondering if it lie there yet, and if its name be VENICE' (p. 336).

A more common solution to the tourist writer's dilemma of repetitiveness is to focus not so much on the standard sights as on the singular aspects of the particular trip – certain episodes in the travel plot, or the tourist as an individual persona with his or her idiosyncratic reactions. To John Barrell (1991), tourist writers (as opposed to explorers and scientific writers) are specifically those 'whose accounts of the country seem often to have been judged in terms of the degree of personality displayed in what are always represented as "personal impressions" of the country' (p. 100). Anthony Trollope, for example, in *North America*, casts himself repeatedly as a clumsy foreigner, as in the New York episode quoted in excerpt 2. A personal, humorous attitude also colours his description of the countries visited and their inhabitants. In the introduction to his account, Trollope anticipates possible objections to this idiosyncratic mode of portrayal, implying that a travelogue cannot be objective in the first place and that a travel writer should therefore feel encouraged to introduce a personal note:

> But it is very hard to write about any country a book that does not represent the country described in a more or less ridiculous point of view. ... it can hardly be done by a man who professes to use a light pen, and to manufacture his article for the use of general readers. Such a writer may tell all that he sees of the beautiful; but he must also tell, if not all that he sees of the ludicrous, at any rate the most piquant part of it.   (p. 3)

With an eye for the general reader, Trollope produces an account that is certainly highly entertaining. Nevertheless, Trollope's travel writing is also still intended to provide useful information about the countries travelled – information, in fact, which goes far beyond established tourist sights. In his introduction to *North America*, this intention is pronounced explicitly: 'My wish is to describe as well as I can the present social and political state of the country' (p. 1). A good portion of the text accordingly describes – often supported by statistical data – the customs, political organization and institutions of the United States as a country in which the British were particularly interested as a social and political experiment. 'The British went to America as to a laboratory in which democracy was under investigation' (Mulvey, 1983, p. 24). Like Trollope's *North America*, many nineteenth-century accounts of tourist travel aim to entertain *and* instruct their readers, and it is quite common for them to include appendices of a purely informative nature – just like the contemporary accounts of exploration and scientific travel. Even if Victorian tourism represents a quite different form of travel from the voyage of the explorer, the respective forms of account display a number of parallels relating to their blend of description, factual information, entertainment value and the rendering of personal experience. Another aspect common to both varieties of Victorian travel writing is that they largely uphold the values and norms of the traveller's home society. Although the tourist account is less openly committed to imperialism than the texts of many explorers, the tourist writer also emerges, in the majority of cases, as a faithful British subject. As in all periods, however, travel in the age of Victoria also offered opportunities to escape from the traveller's own society.

Breaking with convention

If early Victorians saw travel as a means of breaking free from home, this is rarely made as explicit as in Alexander Kinglake's *Eothen* (1844), the account of a journey to the Orient. According to *Eothen*, every young man between 19 and 22 years of age – that is, prior to entering life in earnest – is gripped by a passion for travel, and this passion should be lived out, at least for a short while:

> If a man, and an Englishman, be not born of his mother with a Chiffney-bit in his mouth, there comes to him a time for loathing the wearisome ways of society ... – a time, in short, for questioning, scoffing, and railing – for speaking lightly of the very opera, and all our most cherished institutions. ... A little while you are free, and unlabelled, like the ground that you compass; but Civilization is watching to throw her lasso; you will be surely enclosed, and sooner or later brought down to a state of mere usefulness – your grey hills will be curiously sliced into acres, and roods, and perches, and you, for all you sit so wilful in your saddle, you will be caught – you will be taken up from travel, as a colt from grass, to be trained, and tried, and matched, and run. This in time; but first come continental tours, and the moody longing for eastern travel: the downs and the moors of England can hold you no longer; with larger stride you burst away from these slips and patches of free land – you thread your path through the crowds of Europe, and at last, on the banks of Jordan, you joyfully know that you are upon the very frontier of all accustomed respectabilities.   (pp. 119–20)

Kinglake actually travels to those eastern regions of which William Beckford, during his Grand Tour, could only dream. Since, for Kinglake, the value of travel lies in a temporary escape from the tread-mill of 'Civilization', he is glad to be misled by his guide so that he can meet nomadic Bedouins, as he had hoped for: 'My delight was so great at the near prospect of bread and salt in the tent of an Arab warrior, that I wilfully allowed my guide to go on, and mislead me' (p. 121).

It is clear from the very opening of *Eothen* that the fundamental reason for Kinglake's journey is not the seeking out of remarkable sights. Thus the account is not primarily concerned with describing the object world, but rather is intended to give expression to the traveller's subjective experience:[15]

> Now a traveller is a creature not always looking at sights – he remembers (how often!) the happy land of his birth – he has, too, his moments of humble enthusiasm about fire, and food – about shade, and drink; and if he gives to these feelings anything like the prominence which really belonged to them at the time of his travelling, he will not seem a very good teacher; once having determined to write the sheer truth concerning the things which chiefly have interested him, he must, and he will, sing a sadly long strain about Self; he will talk for whole pages together about his bivouac fire, and ruin the Ruins of Baalbec with eight or ten cold lines.   (p. 4)

In this programme for travel writing, the marking of sights and the inclusion of 'objective' information are no longer the dominant textual strategies. Instead, Kinglake's 'sadly long strain about Self' is realized, for example, in sections in which a large portion of the report is devoted to the presentation of the act of travelling itself – even in those cases in which only a monotonous passing of time can be narrated, as in the following depiction of a ride through the desert:

> The earth is so samely, that your eyes turn towards heaven – towards heaven, I mean, in sense of sky. You look to the Sun, for he is your taskmaster, and by him you know the measure of the work that you have done, and the measure of the work that remains for you to do. He comes when you strike your tent in the early morning, and then, for the first hour of the day, as you move forward on your camel, he stands at your near side, and makes you know that the whole day's toil is before you; then for a while, and a long while, you see him no more, for you are veiled and shrouded, and dare not look upon the greatness of his glory, but you know where he strides over head, by the touch of his flaming sword. No words are spoken, but your Arabs moan, your camels sigh, your skin glows, your shoulders ache, and for sights you see the pattern and the web of the silk that veils your eyes, and the glare of the outer light. Time labours on – your skin glows, your shoulders ache, your Arabs moan, your camels sigh, and you see the same pattern in the silk, and the same glare of light beyond; but conquering Time marches on, and by and by the descending sun

has compassed the heaven, and now softly touches your right arm, and throws your lank shadow over the sand right along on the way for Persia. (pp. 172–3)

Here, a travel writer takes (narrative) time to present time in his journey that was spent without any particular 'use', without looking at sights and without any particular events, but which, for the traveller, nevertheless represented a personal experience. The attraction in reading such passages is the opportunity to share this experience with the traveller, even in its temporality.

Not until the nineteenth century draws to its close do travelogues appear in large numbers which, like Kinglake's *Eothen*, present the attraction of travel *per se* and which emphasize the opportunities of escape which travel affords. Increasingly, this tendency is accompanied by open criticism of civilization, as well as anti-tourist and anti-imperialist attitudes.

In proportion with an ever greater mass of tourists, the last quarter of the nineteenth century saw a marked rise in attempts to travel unconventionally. Amelia Edwards was certainly not alone in her preference for untrodden paths. In 1876, Robert Louis Stevenson set off on a journey by canoe along the rivers and canals of Belgium and northern France (*An Inland Voyage*, 1878), before travelling the Cevennes with a stubborn donkey (*Travels with a Donkey*, 1879).[16] *An Inland Voyage* presents Stevenson's trip as quite distinct from the tourist journey. Even as his canoe, the *Arethusa*, is loaded off the ferry, it is clear that this modest vessel will not swim with the tourist tide:

Under these safeguards, portly clergymen, school-mistresses, gentlemen in grey tweed suits, and all the ruck and rabble of British touristry pour unhindered, *Murray* in hand, over the railways of the Continent, and yet the slim person of the *Arethusa* is taken in the meshes, while these great fish go on their way rejoycing. (p. 12)

For Stevenson – as for Kinglake a few decades earlier – the fundamental aim of a journey consists in the experience of travel as such, not in reaching a particular destination, and as in Kinglake this experience essentially includes the monotony of travelling, the absence of remarkable events or attractions. In fact, it is through its uneventfulness that Stevenson's 'inland voyage' allows him the leisure to find the pathway to his own self. This inner journey accordingly forms a major theme of the account:

What philosophers call *me* and *not me*, *ego* and *non ego*, preoccupied me whether I would or no. There was less *me* and more *not me* than I was accustomed to expect. I looked on upon somebody else, who managed the paddling ... Nor this alone: something inside my mind, a part of my brain, a province of my proper being, had thrown off allegiance and set up for itself, or perhaps for the somebody else who did the paddling. I had dwindled into quite a little thing in a corner of myself. I was isolated in my own skull. Thoughts presented themselves unbidden ...

This frame of mind was the great exploit of our voyage, take it all in all. It was the farthest piece of travel accomplished.   (p. 78)

Travels with a Donkey includes a similar vindication of travel without a programme or particular destination; the text moreover emphasizes the importance of travel as an escape from the familiar 'feather-bed of civilisation':

For my part, I travel not to go anywhere, but to go. I travel for travel's sake. The great affair is to move; to feel the needs and hitches of our life more nearly; to come down off this feather-bed of civilisation, and find the globe granite underfoot and strewn with cutting flints.   (pp. 130–1)

The traveller in Stevenson's accounts, who wishes to break free from his own culture, reveals a particular awareness of the fact that, in the travelled country, *he* is the foreigner, that this country is not there for him and should not be regarded chauvinistically or as an object of possession. 'There is no foreign land', writes Stevenson in *The Silverado Squatters* (1883), 'it is the traveller only that is foreign, and now and again, by a flash of recollection, lights up the contrasts of the earth' (p. 231). Expressions such as these reveal an attitude of cultural relativism towards the travelled region, which, by the end of the nineteenth century, was certainly not new. In this period, however, cultural relativism was part and parcel of a critique of European civilization and imperialism that was taking an increasingly strong hold.

It was above all in the 1890s that a counter-discourse began to make itself heard against the values and norms of Victorianism. Excerpt 3 is taken from a travelogue of this decade, W. H. Hudson's *Idle Days in Patagonia* (1893). As an ornithologist, Hudson had a strong scientific interest in Patagonia, but he was particularly fascinated by this region because of its pronounced lack of any trace of civilization: 'How often had I pictured in imagination, wishing with an intense longing to visit this solitary wilderness ... untouched by man, remote from civilization!' Some sixty years earlier, Charles Darwin had noted 'only' the particular atmosphere of the barren Patagonian landscape; to Darwin, the absence of signs of civilization seems to have held no particular attraction (see p. 62 above).

An effort to break free from conventional modes of perception and dominant modes of travel writing is particularly obvious in the account of a journey through Morocco which Robert Bontine Cunninghame Graham undertook in 1897. *Mogreb-el-Acksa*[17] (1898) appealed not only to the general readership, but also found the acclaim of many fellow writers; Joseph Conrad, for example, spoke of 'the book of travel of the century'.[18] At the end of the nineteenth century, entrance to inland Morocco was forbidden to Europeans since Morocco was afraid of falling prey to European imperialism in Northern Africa. On his trip, Cunninghame Graham therefore donned the disguise of a Turkish doctor. Nevertheless he did not reach his destination, the town of Taroudant; his true identity was revealed and, after two weeks' imprisonment, he was banished from the country.

Cunninghame Graham levelled sharp criticism at imperialism, which might at least in part have been motivated by his Scottish origin. Thus his preface to *Mogreb-el-Acksa* – despite the superficial resemblance of his enterprise to the Arabian adventures of Richard Burton – reads like an anti-programme to the conventional account of Victorian exploration. Cunninghame Graham does not report in the spirit of the Empire, but rather 'sans flag-wagging', and in his mode of writing, he also attempts to break new ground:

> I have tried to write after the fashion that men speak over the fire at night, their pipes alight, hands on their rifles, boots turned towards the blaze, ears strained to catch the rustle of a leaf, and with the tin tea mug stopped on its journey to the mouth when horses snort; I mean I strove to write down that which I saw without periphrasis, sans flag-wagging, and with no megrim in my head of having been possessed by some great moral purpose, without which few travellers nowadays presume to leave their homes.
>
> I fear I have no theory of empires, destiny of the Anglo-Saxon race, spread of the Christian faith, of trade extension, or of hinterlands ...   (p. xx)

To Cunninghame Graham, there is no prescribed method for writing about one's travels. Rather, the travelogue is a loosely structured, almost haphazard affair, 'a sack of cobwebs, a pack of gossamers, a bale of thistle-down, dragon-flies' wings' (p. xxi). What holds these 'cobwebs' together is, above all, the travelling and reporting subject. The associations and reflections of this subject, his memories of other journeys or reminiscences on his former life as a farmer in South America repeatedly cause the text to digress from the account of the Morocco trip.

The difference between Cunninghame Graham and 'imperialist' travel writers of the nineteenth century also manifests itself in his open expression of sympathy for the inhabitants and culture of the travelled country. Cunninghame Graham gives detailed portraits of his Arab travel companions, who are presented as individuals throughout. He also expresses his understanding for the Moroccans' distrust of Europeans who, he suggests, have only had a negative influence on the country up to that point:

> Guns, gin, powder, and shoddy cloths, dishonest dealing only too frequently, and flimsy manufactures which displace the fabrics woven by the women, new wants, new ways, and discontent with what they know, and no attempt to teach a proper comprehension of what they introduce; these are the blessings Europeans take to Eastern lands.   (p. 25)

Again and again, Cunninghame Graham thus casts himself as a mouthpiece for the perspective of the 'other', that is the non-European, and as a last gesture of respect for the people and culture of Morocco, the text closes with the ring of an indigenous voice – the song of a Berber shepherd:

> He stopped occasionally and burst into a strange, wild song, quavering and fitful, the rhythm interrupted curiously, so as to be almost incomprehensible to ears accustomed to street organs, pianos, bands, sackbut, harp, psaltery, and all kinds of music which we have fashioned and take delight in according to our kind, but which I take it would be as void of meaning to a Berber as is our life. I checked my horse, and sitting sideways for an instant, tried to catch the rhythm, but failed, perhaps because my ears were echoing still with the roar of cabs, whir of machinery, and the sweet stroke of hammers falling upon iron or brass, or

'Surely one suffices?' said the guide, eyeing me with disapproval;
for taking me for the wife of the man in spectacles he regarded my
desire to have a number all to myself as only one more instance of
the lengths to which the modern woman in her struggle for emancipation will go.
    The stick and sunshade were accordingly tied together.
(Elizabeth von Arnim, The Adventures of Elizabeth in Rügen, 1904,
pp. 161–2)

[3] The last arrangements were causing the usual delay, when the
    sergeant in charge of the escort turned up with his three men ...
    Behind him the three policemen stood with a little less soldier-like
    smartness, each holding his horse by the bridle. ... They were
    reviewed by the Ajuzan with some solemnity. He described in a few
    well-turned sentences the extreme consideration with which I was to
    be treated. To be treated with consideration is, in the case of female
    travellers, too often synonymous with being prevented from doing
    what one wants.
        'Must I have four men?' I asked the Ajuzan. 'I would much rather
    have only one.'
        'Three soldiers and a sergeant,' he replied, 'is the very least we can
    consider adequate to do you honour.'
        ... The Ajuzan accompanied us to the outskirts of the town. There
    he mounted his own handsome charger and watched us depart, a
    pained amusement visible on his countenance.
            (Freya Stark, The Valleys of the Assassins, 1936, pp. 177–8)

[4] 'Used to get wives travelling with us quite a bit. Not any more.' [The
    captain] gave a curt summary of women who had invaded his
    masculine world. A single man himself, he didn't exactly approve.
        'I've been travelling in West Africa,' I offered. 'I've been following
    the route of Mary Kingsley. She came here in the 1890s. I wanted to
    return as she did, on a cargo vessel.'
        'Mary Kingsley. Ah.' There had been a ship named the Mary
    Kingsley, he told me. On a voyage to West Africa in a severe
    equinoctial gale, a locomotive she was carrying had broken adrift
    from her deck and sunk to the bottom of the ocean. Now it all made
    sense. First Mary Kingsley the person. Then Mary Kingsley the ship.
    Now me.
                            (Dea Birkett, Jella, 1992, p. 22)

The 'femininity' of travel writing

F.A. Kirkpatrick, in his survey of travel writing in the *Cambridge History of English Literature* (1916), took it for granted that travelogues are aimed primarily at a male audience: 'They have provided the substance of a thousand books for boys ... And every reader, whether boy or man, finds in his favourite books of travel some image of himself and some hint towards moulding himself' (p. 256). Kirkpatrick similarly assumed that travelogues are normally also written by men. Although he makes reference to Mary Kingsley, his reader is left with the overall impression that the genre is a male domain. This kind of suppression of travel writing by women is a thing of the past. On the contrary, a large proportion of recent and current research is devoted to aspects of the genre related to women, and, as the result of a feminist 'archaeology' of texts, many travelogues by women have come to light again or have been discovered in archives.[1] Today, it may even be claimed that travel writing, as a marginalized genre, has always been particularly attractive to women writers:

> Its very hybridity ... has prevented it from being taken seriously as literature and has, at the same time, protected it from normative generic rules and thus preserved for it a greater freedom of experimentation. No wonder it has become one of those genres in which the traces of female writing have inscribed themselves particularly early and particularly insistently.   (Pfister, 1996, p. 13)

As the excerpts at the beginning of this chapter suggest, the circumstances, motivation and significance of travel were and to some extent still are different for women than for the 'stronger' sex. For a long time, prejudices stood in the way of women travelling and writing about their travel experiences. If only for this reason, some particular ways of seeing and manners of articulation have emerged in the travel writing of women. Today, a feminine identity and gender-specific aspects of travelling are often made explicit in travelogues by women writers. In *Jella* (1992), for example, Dea Birkett reports her journey on a cargo ship from Africa back to England, during which she experiences a profound sense of confusion regarding her role behaviour. As the sole woman on board, she is particularly disorientated as far as her gender role is concerned. In excerpt 4 above, it is clear that the attitude of the sailors towards their female companion is extremely sceptical, not least as she does not comply with their conventional perception of femininity. Because of her androgynous physique, the men call her 'Jella', or boy, and they attempt to bring her closer to the traditional feminine ideal by fattening her up and giving her beauty tips: '"You can't meet your fella like that," protested Jimmy. "Why the hell not?" "Because you look like a bleeding fella"' (p. 187).

This chapter will consider a number of qualitative differences to be found in women's travelogues. The dedication of a separate chapter to these differences could imply that women's travel writing basically represents a category of its own and that women's texts have little in common with those of their male contemporaries. This is clearly not the case, if only for the reason that, since the eighteenth century, 'masculine' travel writing has always also enjoyed a female readership and was, as early as the eighteenth century, the subject of criticism by female reviewers such as Mary Wollstonecraft.[2] Furthermore, due to the expectations of the 'general' – that is mixed – audience, the travel writing of women could not be so very 'different' from that of men. Ann Radcliffe's account of her travels on the Continent, *A Journey Made in the Summer of 1794*, is directed at such a general readership and is therefore constructed according to typical genre expectations of the time – which had, of course, been moulded by the travel writing of men. One such typical element is the comparison between home and abroad, which Radcliffe explicitly defends in her preface as a useful convention: 'The references to England ... are made because it has seemed that one of the best modes of describing to any class of readers what they may not know, is by comparing it with what they do' (p. vi). Moreover, Radcliffe admits in this preface that observations made by her husband also enter into the text. In particular, remarks concerning matters of politics and economics – a standard element expected in accounts about the contemporary continental tour – are claimed to result from male assistance: 'where the oeconomical and political conditions of countries are touched upon in the following work, the remarks are less her own than elsewhere' (p. v).

A separatist view of women's travel writing, which has been the aim of some orthodox feminist criticism, is in danger of ignoring general generic characteristics and developments, and of reducing the travellers and their texts to the 'typically' feminine. The previous chapters have attempted to do justice to the position of women's travel writing *within* the general tradition of the genre through the inclusion of examples from texts by women whenever the opportunity arose.

As recent research emphasizes, female subjectivity is a question not only of gender but a construct made up of numerous factors within a culture as a whole. Women thus travel not only as representatives of their gender, but also as members of their particular society and culture. If the emphasis in the rest of this chapter is on certain aspects proper to women's travels and travelogues, this is against a background awareness of the general context of these travels and texts. Of course, one must also be wary of casting all women travellers in the same mould. We will see, for example, that the texts of Isabella Bird convey a personality that is notably different from that of Mary Kingsley. The two women also differ significantly in their style and narrative tone, although their travels and their writing coincide for one decade at the end of the last century. That century was the breakthrough once and for all in women's travel and their travel writing.

Conditions of women's travel

In the Victorian age, British women accompanied their husbands and families throughout the Empire. However, they also travelled independently, as explorers, missionaries or simply for pleasure:

> In the nineteenth century, because of the long peace after the Battle of Waterloo and the increasing prosperity of Britain, more and more women found themselves able to travel to Europe even without a male companion. ... But Europe could not long satisfy the adventurous Victorian woman traveller, so she sailed around the world (Lady Brassey), joined a French man-of-war in the South Seas (Constance Gordon-Cummings), rode across Arabia (Lady Anne Blunt), sailed up the Nile (Amelia Edwards and Lucie Duff Gordon), journeyed to America (Fanny Trollope and Harriet Martineau), and even ventured to remote corners of the Orient (Isabella Bird Bishop and Annie Taylor). By the end of the century, handbooks for women travellers boldly asserted that 'nowadays ... a hundred women travel to one who ventured from the security of her roof tree in bygone days' ...   (Stevenson, 1982, p. 2)

Isabella Bird, whose travels took her to all corners of the world, was famous even in her own lifetime. She travelled through North America, the Sandwich Islands, Japan, the Malayan Peninsula, Persia and Kurdistan, as well as Korea and China, and she was the first woman to be accepted into the Royal Geographical Society. Mary Kingsley, whose father was himself well-travelled, trekked through West Africa in the 1890s and financed her journey by collecting biological samples for the British Museum. Like Bird, she was an acknowledged explorer and lectured extensively on her travels. Another big name among women travellers is Gertrude Bell, who, towards the end of the nineteenth century, undertook archaeological surveys in the Middle East and was later to hold a political post there. As well as specialist books, she produced travelogues such as *Safar Nameh: Persian Pictures* (1894) and *The Desert and the Sown* (1907). Thanks to the kind of achievements outlined above, Victorian women provided a model for female travellers of our own century, and they are often paid tribute in the latter's texts. In *Passenger to Teheran* (1926), for example, Vita Sackville-West records a personal meeting with Gertrude Bell;[3] more recently, Dea Birkett's *Jella* retraces Mary Kingsley's steps through Africa (excerpt 4 above).

A fashion for women's travel does not emerge until the nineteenth century; the tradition of female travel, however, is much older. Women have always travelled – as tradeswomen, as companions to husbands and visitors of relatives, or as pilgrims like the famous Margery Kempe. Later, women also travelled for reasons of health; visits to spa towns in Britain and on the Continent became increasingly respectable and popular. Indeed, many accounts reveal that medical reasons often served as an alibi for the journey described. Besides many other justifications of her home tours at the end of the seventeenth century, Celia Fiennes, for example, expressly mentions her health: 'My Journeys ... were begun to regain my health by variety and change of aire and exercise' (p. 32).

The need for women's travels to be more explicitly justified than those of men is, without doubt, one characteristic proper to them. As we have seen in the context of the Grand Tour, men also had to give good reasons for their journeys, and the usefulness of male travel was not uncontested. The travelling of women, however, was even more restricted and debated, not only because travelling could indeed be dangerous. In his *Itinerary* (1617), Fynes Moryson excluded women from educational travel for the sake of their chastity: 'women for suspition [*sic*] of chastity are most vnfit for this course' (Part III, p. 1). According to Annegret Pelz (1988), 'sexualization, moral risk and uncontrolled freedom ... are long-standing moral objections raised against women travelling' (p. 147; my translation).

Improved travelling conditions caused certain prejudices against women travellers to slacken. Lack of comfort and security became less convincing arguments when the stagecoach network was expanded in the course of the eighteenth century. Above all, however, changes in the general conditions of female life, particularly women's access to education and other systems of knowledge, brought about new opportunities for travel. In 1699, the German painter and engraver Maria Sibylla Merian travelled to Surinam in order to observe its natural world; the voyage yielded her renowned work on the *Metamorphosis insectorum surinamensium* (1705). Almost at the same time, Celia Fiennes was touring England with the aim of gathering useful information about her own country. Fiennes, who was unmarried, sometimes travelled with her mother or other female relations, but she was more often accompanied only by a servant. We can surmise, then, that her tours must also have given her a feeling of independence, even if this is never made explicit in her texts. The following extract, however, implies that Fiennes saw travel, at the very least, as a means of escape from the boredom of upper-class domestic life. To Fiennes, the specific benefits of the home tour for women lay in the fact that it involved them in useful activities:

> Nay the Ladies might have matter not unworthy their observation, soe subject for conversation, within their own compass in each county to which they relate; and thence studdy how to be serviceable to their neighbours especially the poor among whome they dwell, which would spare them the uneasye thoughts how to pass away tedious dayes, and tyme would not be a burthen when not at a card or dice table, and the fashions and manners of foreign parts less minded or desired.
>
> (p. 32)

As is well documented in their own writings, educated women started to travel in greater numbers around the time of the French Revolution;[4] the emerging movement for women's emancipation in the wake of the revolution gave women's travel renewed impetus:

> The wave of social and political change which swept through Europe and England following the French Revolution produced a general heightening of aspiration. Women saw the possibility of moving about and witnessing the large events of the world. In this period, middle-class women began to travel. . . .
> But the women travelers were by no means confined to kitchens and market places. They were travelling at a time when the continent of Europe was convulsed by political conflict, and they were drawn into and affected by these events. Their experiences enlarged

their powers of analysis beyond the limitations which traditional women's education had imposed upon them.

(Adickes, 1991, pp. 3, 5)

Among those women who travelled on the Continent in the late eighteenth century and who wrote about their experiences were Ann Radcliffe, Mary Wollstonecraft and Hester Thrale Piozzi.[5]

Distinctive features of women's travel writing

Radcliffe, Wollstonecraft and Piozzi were acknowledged writers whose travelogues were published in their lifetimes. This was unusual even in the late eighteenth century, when the majority of women's travel writing was still private or semi-private and took the form of diaries, journals or letters. If Celia Fiennes wanted to make the accounts of her tours available to the general audience, she never publicly stated so, and her address to the reader in her manuscript opens with the explicit sentence: 'As this was never designed, soe not likely to fall into the hands of any but my near relations, there needs not much to be said to excuse or recommend it' (p. 32).[6] Similarly, the letters which Lady Mary Wortley Montagu wrote between 1716 and 1718 on her travels to Constantinople (where she accompanied her husband) were only circulated in manuscript form. Only shortly before her death did the author prepare them for a printed edition; they were published posthumously as *Letters from the East* in 1763 and are also known today as *The Turkish Embassy Letters*. Dorothy Wordsworth penned numerous journals about her rambles and travels with her brother William, and occasionally with Samuel Taylor Coleridge; these journals were enjoyed by her friends and acquaintances but also remained unpublished until after her death.[7] Just as women had to justify travelling in the first place, they had to justify writing about these travels – in particular when this writing was also made public.

One prejudice directed at women's travel writing has already been mentioned in connection with Ann Radcliffe: in *A Journey Made in the Summer of 1794*, she resorts to the superior knowledge of *Mr* Radcliffe where politics and economics are concerned. Clearly, this was meant as a concession to the common assumption of her time that the female brain was inferior when it came to certain areas of knowledge and experience. Women travel writers continued to be subject to such prejudices even when the female globetrotter had become a fairly familiar figure. This is illustrated by a remark in Anthony Trollope's

North America, in which he refers to his mother Fanny's popular account of America, *Domestic Manners of the Americans* (1832). With all respect towards his mother, Trollope does not hesitate to find her lacking in an understanding of politics:

> Thirty years ago my mother wrote a book about the Americans, to which I believe I may allude as a well known and successful work without being guilty of any undue family conceit. That was essentially a woman's book. She saw with a woman's keen eye, and described with a woman's light but graphic pen, the social defects and absurdities which our near relatives had adopted into their domestic life. All that she told was worth the telling, and the telling, if done successfully, was sure to produce a good result. I am satisfied that it did so. But she did not regard it as a part of her work to dilate on the nature and operation of those political arrangements which had produced the social absurdities which she saw, or to explain that though such absurdities were the natural result of those arrangements in their newness, the defects would certainly pass away, while the political arrangements, if good, would remain. Such a work is fitter for a man than for a woman.   (p. 2)

Lady Anne Blunt went on many travels with her husband Wilfrid; her *Bedouin Tribes of the Euphrates* (1879) accordingly opens in the first-person plural: 'We left England on the 20th of November, 1877, with the intention of visiting Bagdad . . . We had already visited more than one Arabic-speaking country' (p. 1). However, despite all sense of collaboration implied by 'we', this text is also structured according to gender-specific roles. Wilfrid Blunt, who edited his wife's text, added several chapters of an informative nature. In his preface, Blunt gives reasons for this addition and highlights his sole authorship of them: 'These chapters I am alone responsible for. They are an attempt to epitomise the information collected in the Desert' (p. xi). At the end of 'her' section, his wife also points to the change in authorship: 'All is finished but the last few serious chapters, with which Wilfrid proposes to end this book for me' (vol. 2, p. 160). Lady Anne apparently considers herself to lack her husband's 'manly' competence at writing 'seriously' about factual matters.

The result of such prejudices is that a good number of women's texts automatically include apologies and justifications or an emphasis on the 'amateurish' nature of the writing.[8] Such features are even encountered in texts whose authors appear otherwise particularly independent, brave and hungry for knowledge. One of Isabella Bird's first accounts, *A Lady's Life in the Rocky Mountains* (1879), depicts a tour on which the author went purely for pleasure, unlike her later journeys of exploration. In her 'Prefatory Note' for the book edition, Bird stresses that she published her original letters only on the insistence of others: 'They appeared last year in the *Leisure Hour* at the request of its editor, and were so favourably received that I venture to present them to the public in a separate form' (p. vii). Even much later, in her preface to *The Yangtze Valley and Beyond* (1899), she plays down the merits of her book and calls on the goodwill of her readers:

> I am painfully conscious of the many demerits of this volume, but recognising the extreme importance of increasing by every means the knowledge of, and interest in, China and its people, I venture to ask for it from the public the same kindly criticism with which my former records of Asiatic travel have been received, and to hope that it may be accepted as an honest attempt to make a contribution to the data on which public opinion on China and Chinese questions must be formed.   (p. viii)

Bird's apologetic gestures are quite incongruous with the image which her texts otherwise project of her. Self-justifications and affirmations of modesty only barely conceal her enthusiasm for travel and her pride in achievements that were often quite unwomanly. In her youth, Bird suffered from a condition to which many contemporary well-to-do women were prone: backache and insomnia as well as states of depression. Her travels in the Rocky Mountains proved to be the miracle cure for her illness. 'This is another world', is her enthusiastic opening to a letter from the Wild West (p. 73); in another letter, she is equally exuberant: 'This is a glorious region, and the air and life are intoxicating. I live mainly out of doors and on horseback' (p. 119). In the Rocky Mountains, Bird was not required to ride sidesaddle, which was considered becoming of women but was painful for her; instead, she enjoyed the freedom of movement offered by a Mexican saddle designed for men:

> I could not ride any distance in the conventional mode, and was just going to give up this splendid 'ravage', when the man said, 'Ride your own fashion; here, at Truckee, if anywhere in the world, people can do as they like.' Blissful Truckee! ... I strapped my silk skirt on the saddle ... and was safely on the horse's back before his

owner had time to devise any way of mounting me. Neither he nor any of the loafers who had assembled showed the slightest sign of astonishment, but all were as respectful as possible.   (p. 10)

As far as the demands of her later explorations were concerned, the stamina she showed and the dangers she endured, Bird was every bit as impressive as her male counterparts. Even when travelling primarily for her own pleasure, as in her journey through China which she depicts in *The Yangtze Valley*, Bird was never shy of obstacles along the way or of harsh living conditions, and she makes this plain in her text. She embarked on this trip in 1897, at the age of 64, accompanied for the most part only by some local servants. The journey took her down a river with notoriously hazardous rapids; Bird repeatedly describes being soaked to the skin in a half-open boat or writes of her difficulty in protecting herself from vermin at night. Trips inland were associated with attacks by the unwelcoming, anti-European Chinese; Bird relates such attacks in a blow-by-blow account:

> The crowd became dense and noisy; there was much hooting and yelling. I recognised many cries of *Yang kwei-tze!* (foreign devil) and *'Child-eater!'* swelling into a roar; the narrow street became almost impassable; my chair was struck repeatedly with sticks; mud and unsavoury missiles were thrown with excellent aim; a well-dressed man, bolder or more cowardly than the rest, hit me a smart whack across my chest, which left a weal; others from behind hit me across the shoulders; the howling was infernal: it was an angry Chinese mob. There was nothing for it but to sit up stolidly, and not to appear hurt, frightened, or annoyed, though I was all three.
> (pp. 215–16)

A sense of adventure is as striking here as in the travelogues of Richard Burton and other male explorer-heroes of the nineteenth century. Bird's scientific ambition, as that of many other women explorers of her time, was also equal to that of her male counterparts. She made systematic observations related to the natural world, society, economy and anthropology of the regions travelled, and complained (even on her pleasure trip through China) when the scientific apparatus at her disposal proved inadequate:

> Unfortunately, as preventing accurate observations, a year before I had sent home the instruments lent to me by the Royal Geo-

graphical Society; a pony had rolled on my hypsometer, and an aneroid barometer kindly lent to me was not reliable, and I had no means of ascertaining the amount of its unreliability before I left China.   (p. 356)

In the *Yangtze* account, Bird also illustrates her text with many documentary photographs, which she took herself, and includes a substantial appendix of statistical data relating to Chinese trade.

Mary Kingsley's *Travels in West Africa* (1897) similarly emits self-confidence and pride, although the standard apologies are offered in the preface. Kingsley successfully completed her scientific task for the British Museum, performed feats she would never have dreamt of and endured the most dangerous predicaments. Despite the humorous, self-ironic tone with which most of her adventures are played down, Kingsley's achievements are made quite clear:

> Success crowned my efforts, and I can honestly and truly say that there are only two things I am proud of – one is that Doctor Günther has approved of my fishes, and the other is that I can paddle an Ogowé canoe. Pace, style, steering and all, 'All same for one' as if I were an Ogowé African.   (p. 75)

> On one occasion, the last, a mighty Silurian, as *The Daily Telegraph* would call him, chose to get his front paws over the stern of my canoe, and endeavoured to improve our acquaintance. I had to retire to the bows, to keep the balance right, and fetch him a clip on the snout with a paddle, when he withdrew ...   (p. 25)

For women like Bird and Kingsley, travel provided an opportunity to cross the traditional gender boundaries of their own culture.

> For women, travel indeed represented a new awakening, an escape from the life of a 'normal' contemporary woman ... In the case of those women who also wrote of their experiences and impressions and had these accounts published, this awakening was doubly escapist. The journey becomes a writing-space which offers the travelling woman new realms of opportunity: she has the time to reflect, to express opinions on changes she would like to see made, to understand herself more fully and perhaps even to experience a new-found freedom.
> (Frederiksen, 1985, p. 108; my translation)[9]

However, the possibilities for escape and liberation, in most cases, were clearly limited. Travelling women were caught between the conventional expectations of their home societies and a counter-discourse of emancipation. This frequently led to an awareness of gender *ambiguity*: 'As women became able to travel more widely and more independently they had to adopt a position of gender ambiguity, taking on the "masculine" virtues of strength, initiative and decisiveness while retaining the less aggressive qualities considered appropriate to their own sex' (Foster, 1990, p. 11). Thus the travel accounts of these women fluctuate between a confident record of their achievements and an apparent anxiousness not to come across as masculine. A review in the *Times* of the first edition of Isabella Bird's *A Lady's Life in the Rocky Mountains* had drawn attention to her manly travel dress: 'She donned masculine habiliments for greater convenience.' In the second edition of the book, this was categorically denied by Bird, with an illustration as evidence:

> For the benefit of other lady travellers, I wish to explain that my 'Hawaiian riding dress' is the 'American Lady's Mountain Dress', a half-fitting jacket, a skirt reaching to the ankles, and full Turkish trousers gathered into frills which fall over the boots, – a thoroughly serviceable and feminine costume for mountaineering and other rough travelling in any part of the world.   (p. vii)

Similarly, Mary Kingsley insists in her *Travels* that she faced the West African jungle in feminine attire, and even suggests that her life was saved by wearing a skirt when she fell into a pit filled with elephant tusks.

> It is at these times you realise the blessing of a good thick skirt. Had I paid heed to the advice of many people in England ... and adopted masculine garments, I should have been spiked to the bone, and done for. Whereas, save for a good many bruises, here I was with the fulness of my skirt tucked under me, sitting on nine ebony spikes some twelve inches long, in comparative comfort, howling lustily to be hauled out.   (p. 113)

Kingsley's reaction to reports on her travels in the press is another parallel to Isabella Bird. When the *Daily Telegraph* referred to her as a New Woman because of the 'manly' way in which she endured the dangers encountered, she immediately raised objections (Stevenson, 1982, p. 113).[10]

Women were not necessarily more restricted than male travellers in every respect. In certain cases, women could travel more 'aimlessly' and less 'methodically' than men, as Mary Wollstonecraft observes in *A Vindication of the Rights of Woman* (1792): 'A man, when he undertakes a journey, has, in general, the end in view; a woman thinks more of the incidental occurrences, the strange things that may possibly occur on the road' (p. 67). Here, Wollstonecraft presents the aimlessness of women's travelling in a negative light, in keeping with her general criticism in *Vindication* of the uselessness and superficiality of female life. Travelling without a specific end in view can also be positive, however, in its potential for spontaneous and personal observation. This is made very obvious in Wollstonecraft's own *Letters Written During a Short Residence in Sweden, Norway, and Denmark*.[11] Wollstonecraft had been sent on this journey by the father of her illegitimate child (whom she took on her travels along with a nurse), partly on business for him and partly to help her recover after a suicide attempt. The *Letters* were originally addressed to this man and, even in their published version, they contain many observations that are clearly affected by Wollstonecraft's personal predicament at that time of her life. On describing a farmer returning home with his children, for example, Wollstonecraft expresses her own desire for a conventional family life:

> My eyes followed them to the cottage, and an involuntary sigh whispered to my heart, that I envied the mother, much as I dislike cooking, who was preparing their pottage. I was returning to my babe, who may never experience a father's care or tenderness. The bosom that nurtured her, heaved with a pang at the thought which only an unhappy mother could feel. (p. 158)

Wollstonecraft's *Letters* also illustrate another aspect characteristic of women's travel writing, namely a particular attention paid to female living conditions in the countries visited. Although Wollstonecraft reflects on social injustices of all kinds, she is particularly concerned with the position of women in Scandinavia, which she describes from an openly feminist perspective:

> Still harping on the same subject, you will exclaim – How can I avoid it, when most of the struggles of an eventful life have been occasioned by the oppressed state of my sex: we reason deeply, when we forcibly feel. . . .

I have before mentioned that the men are domestic tyrants, considering them as fathers, brothers, or husbands; but there is a kind of interregnum between the reign of the father and husband, which is the only period of freedom and pleasure that the women enjoy. Young people, who are attached to each other, with the consent of their friends, exchange rings, and are permitted to enjoy a degree of liberty together, which I have never noticed in any other country. (pp. 171–2)

The awareness that a female traveller could gain an insight into realms of experience 'other' than those open to men is displayed earlier in the eighteenth century in the letters of Lady Mary Wortley Montagu. Montagu expresses her pride at being the first traveller to write home about *genuine* insights into the strict confinement of women's culture in the Orient,[12] in particular the harems and bathing houses: 'I am sure I have now entertained you with an account of ... what no book of travels could inform you of, as 'tis no less than death for a man to be found in one of these places' (p. 60). In her awareness of her privileged position, Montagu consciously distinguishes between her authentic report and the false accounts by men:

'Tis also very pleasant to observe how tenderly he and all his brethren voyage-writers lament on the miserable confinement of the Turkish ladies, who are, perhaps, freer than any ladies in the universe, and are the only women in the world that lead a life of uninterrupted pleasure, exempt from cares, their whole time being spent in visiting, bathing or the agreeable amusement of spending money and inventing new fashions. ... They go abroad when and where they please. 'Tis true they have no public places but the bagnios, and there can only be seen by their own sex. However, that is a diversion they take great pleasure in. (p. 134)[13]

Montagu is very open to oriental culture, and absolutely fascinated by it. Taking the unusual position of being the aesthetic *subject* in the perception of female beauty, she describes the physical beauty of oriental women in great detail:

I was three days ago at one of the finest [bagnios] in the town and had the opportunity of seeing a Turkish bride received there and all the ceremonies used on that occasion ... All the she-friends, relations and acquaintance of the two families newly allied meet at the bagnio.

Several others go out of curiosity and I believe there was that day at least 200 women. Those that were or had been married placed themselves round the room on the marble sofas, but the virgins very hastily threw off their clothes and appeared without other ornament or covering than their own long hair braided with pearl or ribbon. Two of them met the bride at the door, conducted by her mother and another grave relation. She was a beautiful maid of about seventeen, richly dressed and shining with jewels, but was presently reduced by them to the state of nature. Two others filled silver gilt pots with perfume and begun the procession, the rest following in pairs to the number of thirty. . . . In this order they marched round the three large rooms of the bagnio. 'Tis not easy to represent to you the beauty of this sight, most of them being well proportioned and white skinned, all of them perfectly smooth and polished by the frequent use of bathing. After having made their tour, the bride was again led to every matron round the rooms, who saluted her with a compliment and a present, some of jewels, others pieces of stuff, handkerchiefs, or little gallantries of that nature, which she thanked them for by kissing their hands.   (pp. 134–5)

Elsewhere, Montagu emphasizes that the Turkish women's bodies are not only beautiful, but that their uninhibited attitude towards the body is also healthier and more natural than the European one. This is experienced by Montagu herself as she gives birth to one of her children in Constantinople:

I don't mention this as one of my diverting adventures, though I must own that it is not half so mortifying here as in England, there being as much difference as there is between a little cold in the head, which sometimes happens here, and the consumptive coughs so common in London. Nobody keeps their house a month for lying in, and I am not so fond of any of our customs to retain them when they are not necessary.   (p. 113)

In the foreign culture Montagu recognizes, at least in some respects, alternatives to the female life of her own culture. This vision is by no means shared by all women travellers. Anne Blunt, for example, writes in *Bedouin Tribes of the Euphrates*: 'I was delighted when the moment came for leaving the harém, for the scene was one of squalor and discomfort. The men, uncouth as they are here, have generally something to say, but the women are without ideas, good-natured, but quite uninteresting' (vol. 1, p. 259). Nevertheless, Montagu is not alone in her enthusiasm for 'other' forms of female existence. A parallel is to be found, more than a century later, in Anna Jameson's account of her stay in Upper Canada, *Winter Studies and Summer Rambles* (1838). Jameson moved in literary circles throughout Europe and wrote books on a whole range of subjects. One of these books, still known today, is devoted to Shakespeare's female characters: *Characteristics of Women* (1832), or *Shakespeare's Heroines* as the later version was entitled. Until she married, Jameson earned her living as a governess, and was interested in all matters concerning women. Her marriage was an unhappy one, and Jameson's trip to Canada in 1836 to see her husband, who was Attorney-General there, was motivated by the wish to gain his consent to separation. She spent a miserable winter in York (now Toronto), where she buried herself in her studies of literature, before starting out on her summer rambles into the wilderness. In Sault Ste Marie, Jameson became acquainted with a group of Chippewa Indians, which proved to be a particularly significant experience. She developed an intimate friendship with one of the Indian women, the wife of a white missionary, who introduced Jameson to a non-European way of female life. In her account, Jameson renders this experience as a kind of rebirth; she reaches near ecstasy when canoeing, Indian-style, through the famous local rapids:

The canoe being ready, I went up to the top of the portage, and we launched into the river. ... I reclined on a mat at the bottom, Indian fashion, (there are no seats in a genuine Indian canoe;) in a minute we were within the verge of the rapids, and down we went with a whirl and a splash! – the white surge leaping around me – over me. The Indian with astonishing dexterity kept the head of the canoe to the breakers, and somehow or other we danced through them. I could see, as I looked over the edge of the canoe, that the passage between the rocks was sometimes not more than two feet in width, and we had to turn sharp angles – a touch of which would have sent us to destruction – all this I could see through the transparent eddying waters, but I can truly say, I had not even a momentary sensation of fear, but rather of giddy, breathless, delicious excitement. I could even admire the beautiful attitude of a fisher, past whom we swept as we came to the bottom. The whole affair, from the moment in entered [*sic*] the canoe till I reached the landing place, occupied seven minutes, and the distance is about three quarters of a mile.

My Indians were enchanted, and when I reached *home*, my good friends were not less delighted at my exploit: they told me I was the first European female who had ever performed it, and assuredly I shall not be the last. I recommend it as an exercise before breakfast. Two glasses of champagne could not have made me more tipsy and more self-complacent! As for my Neengai, she laughed, clapped her hands, and embraced me several times. I was declared duly initiated, and adopted into the family by the name of Wah,sah,ge,wah, no,qua. They had already called me among themselves, in reference to my complexion and my travelling propensities[,] O,daw,yaun, gee, *the fair changing moon*, or rather, *the fair moon which changes her place;* but now, in compliment to my successful achievement, Mrs. Johnston bestowed this new appellation, which I much prefer. It signifies *the bright foam*, or more properly, with the feminine adjunct *qua*, *the woman of the bright foam*; and by this name I am henceforth to be known among the Chippewas.   (pp. 134–5)

In this passage, Jameson's initiation into Indian culture is associated with water, the element traditionally identified with birth and the Christian rite of baptism. Significantly, the European woman is also given a new, Indian name. The allusion, in this context, to the birth of Venus, the goddess sprung from the foam of the sea, seems even a little too obvious. A female traveller could hardly have made her sense of rebirth clearer to an early Victorian audience, and Jameson's euphoric description is indeed exceptional in women's travel writing of her time. Even if they are more muted, however, the texts of other women of the nineteenth century also suggest that travel offered them the means to transgress the boundaries of their own society.

The research on women's travel writing frequently claims that women are more willing and able to cross cultural boundaries than male travellers. Indeed, the extracts quoted from the texts of Montagu and Jameson seem to suggest a particular readiness of these women to engage with other cultures and to see their own culture in relative terms. Despite all the patriotism which Montagu shares with the male travellers of her time and despite her prejudices towards Catholics and Africans,[14] her letters contain many observations such as the following: 'Thus you see ..., gallantry and good breeding are as different in different climates as morality and religion. Who have the rightest notions of both we shall never know till the day of judgement' (p. 23). Montagu is also quite conscious of the fact that she appears just as foreign to the Turkish women as they appear to her, and she does not hesitate to even cast herself as the stranger she is to them. To satisfy the curiosity of a Turkish lady, for example, she once dresses in a particularly grand European style:

> I thought I should very little satisfy her curiosity, which I did not doubt was a considerable motive to the invitation, by going in a dress she was used to see, and therefore dressed myself in the court habit of Vienna, which is much more magnificent than ours.

(pp. 86–7)

Mary Kingsley's account of Africa reveals a similar openness in her approach to a foreign culture. Kingsley is thoughtful and friendly in her relations with the Africans who accompany her on her journey. She takes them seriously as fellow human beings and is not frightened of being tactile with them: 'I put out my hand and laid it on Wiki's gun to prevent him from firing, and he, thinking I was going to fire, gripped my wrist' (p. 112). A sense of camaraderie is also expressed in her text through the frequent use of the first-person plural:

> On we go singing elaborately, thinking no evil of nature, when a current ... comes round from behind a point of the bank and catches the nose of our canoe; wringing it well, it sends us scuttling right across the river in spite of our ferocious swoops at the water, upsetting us among a lot of rocks with the water boiling over them; ... We, up to our knees in water that nearly tears our legs off, push and shove the canoe free, and re-embarking return singing across the river, to have it out with that current. We do; and at its head find a rapid, and notice on the mountain-side a village clearing, the first sign of human habitation we have seen to-day.

(p. 65)

Kingsley's repeated criticism of European missionaries for their narrow-mindedness is rooted in her own understanding of the African lifestyle and mentality:

> Polygamy is the institution which above all others governs the daily life of the native; and it is therefore the one which the missionaries who enter into this daily life, and not merely into the mercantile and legal, as do the trader and the government official, are constantly confronted with and hindered by. All the missionaries have set their faces against it and deny Church membership to

those men who practise it; whereby it falls out that many men are excluded from the fold who would make quite as good Christians as those within it. They hesitate about turning off from their homes women who have lived and worked for them for years, and not only for them, but often for their fathers before them.   (p. 81)

Her criticism of the European imperial powers for their short-sightedness is equally explicit:

This labour question out here, a question that increases daily with the development of plantation enterprise, I do not think will ever be solved by importing foreign labour. Nor is it advisable that it should be, for our European Government puts a stop to the action of those causes which used to keep the native population down, intertribal wars, sacrifices, &c., &c.; and to the deportation of surplus population in the form of slaves, and so unless means of support are devised for 'the indigenous ones', . . . Africa will have us to thank for some smart attacks of famine, for the natives, left to their own devices, will never cultivate the soil sufficiently to support a large population, and moreover a vast percentage of the West African soil is very poor, sour stuff, that will grow nothing but equally valueless vegetation.   (pp. 40–1)

Remarks such as the above have been taken to indicate a readiness on the part of Victorian women, as opposed to men, to voice their disapproval of imperialism; this tendency has been attributed to the women's own marginalization and powerlessness in a patriarchal society (Mills, 1991, p. 3). Ultimately, however, female travellers of the nineteenth century remained bound to the dominant discourses of British society, to which practically all of them returned after their travels.[15] A generalized idealization of women travellers as anti-imperialists is, therefore, feminist wishful thinking (Kuczynski, 1993, p. 13). Paradoxically, it was precisely the fact that women travelled as representatives of their imperialist homeland which put them in a position to break free of traditional gender roles abroad. Indeed, they travelled not 'only' as women, but often took on the role of 'white men', as Dea Birkett (1989, p. 140) observes in her study of the Victorian lady explorers:

In claiming a place in the gallery of white male travellers, the women were claiming more than a mere explorer accolade. They were claiming a freedom from the gender restrictions of their home societies, found in the white male status they could assume in the Dark Continent, the Orient, the Savage Lands. This freedom and power was dependent upon their exaggeration and exploitation of differences of race over differences of gender. . . . everything they achieved outside the traditionally feminine they achieved as 'white men'.[16]

The 'otherness' of women's travel writing is, in almost every respect, a relative otherness and requires subtle differentiation. Women's travelogues share many characteristics with those of their male contemporaries. There is, however, a special propensity in travel writing by women to associate journeys with an escape from 'normal' life and to express a counter-discourse to this life. In women's travelogues of the nineteenth century, this propensity manifested itself in a particularly open manner, so that these texts could work as catalysts for the new developments in travel writing that were pointed out in the conclusion to the previous chapter.

7
British Travel Writing in the Twentieth Century

[1] *But Persia had been left as it was before man's advent. Here and there he had scraped a bit of the surface, and scattered a little grain; here and there, in an oasis of poplars and fruit trees outlining a stream, he had raised a village, and his black lambs skipped under the peach-blossom; but for miles there was no sign of him, nothing but the brown plains and the blue or white mountains, and the sense of space. The crowds of Europe suddenly rushed at me, overwhelmed me; I was drowning under the pressure, when they cleared away, and I was left, breathing, with space all round me, and a serenity that looked down from the peaks on to the great bowl of the plain. The motor, as it swept up and down the hills, might have been an eagle swooping . . .*

(Vita Sackville-West, *Passenger to Teheran*, 1926, pp. 49–50)

[2] *'Does anyone want French? Est-ce que personne qui veut moi de parler en Français?' There were no takers. He looked relieved.*

The running commentary was recited rather than spoken, and it had to be continuously adjusted to the changing speed of the bus. At red lights and sudden holdups in the traffic, it slowed to a dead march of isolated words; as we accelerated away it quickened to a polysyllabic stream, like a new fragment of Finnegans Wake.

'Now . . . approaching us . . . on . . . the . . . right . . . we see . . . the . . . National . . . Portrait . . . Gallery . . . where . . . many famous . . . portraits are . . . on . . . view . . . including several of . . . Lady Di. We are now entering Trafalgar Square, with its statues of Lord Nelson, George Washington who never told a lie, and George the Fourth who spent his life telling lies. Fromteninthemorningonwards,youcanbuy aquartpotofcorntofeedthepigeonsfromastallinthesquare –' . . .

> To be in time for the Changing of the Guard, we had to do
> Westminster Abbey in fifteen minutes flat, with our five-foot guide
> rallying us around him by waving his 'growie' umbrella high over his
> head. We piled at speed around the tombs of Queen Elizabeth I and
> Queen Mary, stamped across the tomb of Joseph Addison and raced
> to keep up with the airborne umbrella as it flew off in the direction
> of Poets' Corner.
>
> (Jonathan Raban, *Coasting*, 1986, pp. 231–3)

The end of travel?

Since many forms of travel which inspired earlier accounts have
become virtually impossible, the travel book has often been declared
dead in the twentieth century. Evelyn Waugh laments over this death
in *When the Going Was Good* (1946):

> My own travelling days are over, and I do not expect to see many
> travel books in the future. When I was a reviewer, they used, I
> remember, to appear in batches of four or five a week, cram-full of
> charm and wit and enlarged Leica snapshots. There is no room for
> tourists in a world of 'displaced persons.' Never again, I suppose,
> shall we land on foreign soil with a letter of credit and passport
> (itself the first faint shadow of the great cloud that envelops us) and
> feel the world wide open before us.   (p. 11)

To Paul Fussell (1980), one of the few critics who have devoted themselves to modern travel writing, the interwar years were 'the final age of
travel' (p. vii), and in *Tristes Tropiques* (1977), Claude Lévi-Strauss
expresses his wish that he 'had lived in the days of *real* journeys, when
it was still possible to see the full splendour of a spectacle that had not
yet been blighted, polluted and spoilt' (p. 33). Somewhat less pessimistic, others speak merely of a 'contemporary dilemma' of travel,
such as Colin Thubron (1986, p. 173) who is, of course, a successful
travel writer himself.

   This fundamental watershed in the history of travel is commonly
attributed to the rapid acceleration of the transport revolution in the
twentieth century. Motor cars and aeroplanes complemented the railway and steamship as modern, technological means of transport, and
the plane even outsped the train. 'It's easy to talk blithely about casting
oneself adrift in the world; not quite so easy to do it in practice, when

most methods of transport turn the would-be traveller into a human bullet', remarks Jonathan Raban (1987, p. 249) on the effect of new means of travel for the travel writer. As early as 1930, in *Labels*, Evelyn Waugh portrayed a flight across the Channel; as the following extract suggests, the traveller's interest shifts significantly from the experience of the space travelled – or rather covered – to the mode of transport and its peculiarities:

> The only movement of which I was conscious was the sudden dropping into air pockets, and this was sensible to the stomach rather than the eye. ... The things which amused me most were (1) the spectacle of a completely horizontal rain storm, and (2) of the pilot telephoning our positions (it seemed extraordinary that they could hear him at Le Bourget when we could scarcely hear him within a few feet), and (3) the look of frightful scorn on the face of the business woman when, soon after we left Le Touquet, I was sick into the little brown paper bag provided for me. One does not feel nearly as ill being air-sick as sea-sick; it is very much more sudden and decisive, but I was acutely embarrassed about my bag. If we had been over the channel it would have been different, but I could not bring myself to throw it out of the window over the countryside. In the end I put it down the little lavatory. As this opened directly into the void the effect was precisely the same, but my conscience was easier in the matter. (pp. 13–14)

At about the same time, Robert Byron's *The Road to Oxiana* (1937) includes an extended reflection on the difference which modern conditions of travel bring to the perception and emotional impact of a place. The place visited is ancient Persepolis, which, for the twentieth-century traveller, has lost much of its archaic magic:

> Patience! In the old days you arrived by horse. You rode up the steps on to the platform. You made a camp there, while the columns and winged beasts kept their solitude beneath the stars, and not a sound or movement disturbed the empty moonlit plain. You thought of Darius and Xerxes and Alexander. You were alone with the ancient world. You saw Asia as the Greeks saw it, and you felt their magic breath stretching out towards China itself. Such emotions left no room for the aesthetic question, or for any question.
>
> Today you step out of a motor, while a couple of lorries thunder by in a cloud of dust. You find the approaches defended by walls.

You enter by leave of a porter, and are greeted, on reaching the platform, by a light railway, a neo-German hostel, and a code of academic malice controlled from Chicago. These useful additions clarify the intelligence. You may persuade yourself, in spite of them, into a mood of romance. But the mood they invite is that of a critic at an exhibition. (p. 166)

The impression of the modernity of travel here depends not only on the presence of the light railway or the motor car, but above all on the place being transformed into a fully infrastructured archaeological sight.

As is to be expected in the light of such developments, many twentieth-century travellers adopt a behaviour which we have already encountered as a reaction to nineteenth-century tourism: consciously avoiding modernity, they resort to older and/or unusual forms of travel. Shortly before the Second World War, Patrick Leigh Fermor set off on foot on the journey he describes in *A Time of Gifts* (1977). On his perambulation from Holland to the Black Sea, he is adamant to avoid modern forms of transport and in particular the motor car: 'I despised lifts and I had a clear policy about them: to avoid them rigorously, that is, until walking became literally intolerable; and then, to travel no further than a day's march would cover' (p. 89). Expressly, Fermor compares himself with antiquated types of travellers: 'like a pilgrim or a palmer, an errant scholar, a broken knight or the hero of *The Cloister and the Hearth!*' (p. 20). After the Second World War, in the age of jet travel, many travelogues – for example by Bruce Chatwin, Paul Theroux, Philip Glazebrook or Eric Newby – testify to a nostalgic preference of travellers for the railway. Dervla Murphy, the renowned Irish travel writer, tours even remote countries 'full tilt', with a bicycle. Jonathan Raban has recourse to yet another old-fashioned means of travel – the sailing vessel. As he writes in *For Love and Money* (1987): 'Going about the world by boat like a snail in its shell feels, at least, as close to true and sincere travelling as you can reasonably come in the age of Intercity and Super Shuttle' (p. 253).

In the twentieth century, 'genuine', individualistic travel is habitually set off against 'mere' tourism, especially custom-made mass tourism. 'Tourists are presented as lacking initiative and discrimination. They are unadventurous, unimaginative and insipid. For them, travel experience is akin to grazing – they mechanically consume whatever the tour operator feeds them. ... The traveller is associated with refined values of discernment, respect and taste' (Rojek, 1993,

p. 175). This polarization is also pronounced in many travelogues of the twentieth century. To Evelyn Waugh, for example, tourism was a nightmare – even though he admits in *Labels* that his own travel is not free of tourist elements:

> With the real travel-snobs I have shuddered at the mention of pleasure cruises or circular tours or personally conducted parties, of professional guides and hotels under English management. Every Englishman abroad, until it is proved to the contrary, likes to consider himself a traveller and not a tourist. As I watched my luggage being lifted on to the *Stella* I knew that it was no use keeping up the pretence any longer. My fellow passengers and I were tourists, without any compromise or extenuation ... (p. 44)

Current research into tourism has established that the discrepancy claimed to exist between 'real' travel and tourism is spurious indeed. According to this research, deriding tourist travel is rather an integral strategy of tourism itself:

> The touristic critique of tourism is based on a desire to go beyond the other 'mere' tourists to a more profound appreciation of society and culture, and it is by no means limited to intellectual statements. All tourists desire this deeper involvement with society and culture to some degree; it is a basic component of their motivation to travel.   (MacCannell, 1976, p. 10)[1]

The accusation that tourists, because of their allegedly indiscriminate mode of travel, miss the 'authentic' qualities of the countries they visit is thus a tactic employed by the supposedly 'true' traveller to confirm his or her own experience of authenticity. However, recent tourist research shows that an increasingly positive attitude to tourism is emerging. In so-called post-tourism, the tourist journey is not rejected but rather practised consciously and playfully (Rojek, 1993, pp. 177–8). Nevertheless, the condemnation of tourism as inauthentic travel also persists today, not least in the travelogue. Jonathan Raban's *Coasting* (1986) includes an episode in which the traveller temporarily turns into a London tourist (excerpt 2). At first, the traveller seems to display a post-touristic attitude, to playfully test out the tourist role, but this experience is soon dismissed as merely second-hand: 'The essence of being a good tourist lay in ignoring everything that you actually saw and listening instead to what the guide told you that you should see' (p. 232). In the end, the 'real' traveller deserts the tourist hordes:

> It was three o'clock by the time we made St Paul's, and I was halfway up the steps, following the umbrella, when my nerve snapped. The prospect of more lectures, more tombs, the very carpet on which Lady Di had set her precious feet, let alone of the Tower ravens and the Crown Jewels, opened ahead of me like a course of dental surgery. As I saw the last of our party disappear into the gloom of the cathedral nave for their first lecture, the afternoon ballooned with sudden light and warmth. *Fiesta!* I could walk where I wanted, see what I chose, I was free of the lifeless and pedantic gabble of the bulkhead speakers in the coach.   (p. 237)

(Mass) tourism is not the only factor considered responsible for the decline of 'true' travel. Another reason frequently given for this decline is the progressive monoculturalization of the travellable world in which indigenous cultures are superseded by the global advance of mass-produced, Western consumer culture. The Coca-Cola bottle has become the prime emblem of this worldwide homogenizing process[2] and appears as such, for example, in the preface to Patrick Leigh Fermor's travel book about Greece, *Mani* (1958):

> In the towns and the more accessible plains many sides of life which had remained intact for centuries are being destroyed apace – indeed, a great deal has vanished since my own first visits to Greece. Ancient and celebrated sites are carefully preserved, but, between the butt of a Coca-Cola bottle and the Iron Curtain, much that is precious and venerable, many living mementoes of Greece's past are being hammered to powder.   (pp. x–xi)

A travel essay by Jan Morris, from her volume *Journeys* (1984), compares the uniformity of the modern world to the standardization of culture in an earlier age, that of the Roman Empire. As she writes in 'Not So Far: A European Journey':

> The great motorways which now criss-cross all Europe are only late successors to the high roads of the legions. The gradual weakening of nationality in western Europe, the blurring of frontiers, the mixing of languages, even the universal acceptance of bank and credit cards . . . – all these phenomena of the 1980s are only returns to the imperial conveniences of Rome.   (pp. 76–7)

However, do such swansongs point to the actual 'end' of travel and, consequently, to the obsolescence of travel writing? The contrary is argued by a number of writers, for example Gavin Young, whose travelogues have been greeted with popularity in Britain since the 1980s. As Young writes in *Worlds Apart* (1987):

> It is quite pointless to complain that the world has been quite turned over like an overworked ploughed field – that there's nothing new left under the sun. Or to sneer that trains, ships, buses and cars have made all travel a clangorous purgatory. Beerbohm asks, reasonably, 'To see what one has not seen before, is not that almost as good as to see what no one has ever seen?' Of course it is. (p. 3)

The very fact that most 'obituaries' of travel/writing are found in travelogues themselves proves the 'death' of the genre a misnomer – as does the sheer number of travelogues still being published. The extensive bibliography in Michael Kowalewski's collection of critical essays on the modern literature of travel, *Temperamental Journeys* (1992), lists 500 travelogues by British and Irish writers published between 1900 and 1990, more than half appearing *after* 1945. Travellers seem to have adapted to the changing circumstances of travel – as they did in previous centuries – and the travelogue has proved flexible enough to textualize a wide variety of travel experiences – including the supposed impossibility of travel.

If the rest of this chapter places the emphasis on characteristics of the modern and postmodern travelogue, it should not be forgotten that twentieth-century travel writing also draws on traditional lines of development – not only in the form of meta- or intertextuality.

Lines of continuity in twentieth-century travel writing

The renaissance of the home tour

As far as the continuation of a tradition is concerned, the account of home tours undergoes a notable renaissance in the twentieth century. Social conditions in Britain before and after the Second World War – above all the loss of identity as a world power and the associated economic problems – meant that travel on home territory gained new importance as an exploration of the *condition anglaise*.

Among the best-known texts on travel of this kind which appeared during the 1930s Depression are J.B. Priestley's *English Journey* (1934) and George Orwell's *The Road to Wigan Pier* (1937). Facing his country's economic problems and their social consequences, Priestley came to believe that preserving a traditional, rural England and its values would be an important revitalizing force for Britain's future development.[3] For Orwell, his account of a journey north to Wigan was to be the basis for the justification of British socialism which he delineates in the second half of the book. *The Road to Wigan Pier* explores an England which, for its middle-class author and well-to-do contemporary readers, was foreign territory: the mining regions of Lancashire and Yorkshire, whose working population was hit particularly hard by the economic crisis of the time. In one of the book's most frequently quoted passages, the traveller's view through a train window gives him an insight – even an epiphany – into the inhumanity of the British class system and its lamentable effects:

> The train bore me away, through the monstrous scenery of slag-heaps, chimneys, piled scrap-iron, foul canals, paths of cindery mud criss-crossed by the prints of clogs. This was March, but the weather had been horribly cold and everywhere there were mounds of black-ened snow. As we moved slowly through the outskirts of the town we passed row after row of little grey slum houses running at right angles to the embankment. At the back of one of the houses a young woman was kneeling on the stones, poking a stick up the leaden waste-pipe which ran from the sink inside and which I suppose was blocked. I had time to see everything about her – her sacking apron, her clumsy clogs, her arms reddened by the cold. She looked up as the train passed, and I was almost near enough to catch her eye. She had a round pale face, the usual exhausted face of the slum girl who is twenty-five and looks forty, thanks to miscarriages and drudgery; and it wore, for the second in which I saw it, the most desolate, hopeless expression I have ever seen. It struck me then that we are mistaken when we say that 'It isn't the same for them as it would be for us', and that people bred in the slums can imagine nothing but the slums. For what I saw in her face was not the ignorant suffering of an animal. She knew well enough what was happening to her – understood as well as I did how dreadful a destiny it was to be kneeling there in the bitter cold, on the slimy stones of a slum backyard, poking a stick up a foul drain-pipe.   (pp. 14–15)

In the 1980s, the predicament in Thatcherite Britain – with the harsh social results of Thatcher's policy of economic individualism, the controversies about the Falklands War (1982) and the miners' strike (1984–5) – unleashed a new wave of travelogues about domestic journeys. As its title suggests, Beryl Bainbridge's *English Journey, or, The Road to Milton Keynes* (1984) was inspired by the home tours of the 1930s. Specifically, Bainbridge travelled in the footsteps of J.B. Priestley, to celebrate the fiftieth anniversary of the publication of his *English Journey* for a BBC documentary. The social and political concern of the 1930s' home tourist is clearly echoed in Bainbridge's own account about what she and her film crew 'saw and heard in the towns and villages of England during the summer of 1983' (p. 7). Sailing alone around the British Isles, Jonathan Raban explored British identity at roughly the same time. As depicted in *Coasting*, his trip was both a search for the essence of his 'fatherland' and the traveller's quest for his own personal identity – an identity in large measure defined by the relationship with his father: 'It was five years later that I learned to ... parse *pater* and *patria*, father and fatherland. It was one of the few things in Latin that I ever understood, the intimate connection between those two words. For England really was my father's land, not mine' (p. 17). The impression that, in our postmodern age of uncertain identities, national and personal identities are increasingly difficult to negotiate and can at best be conceptualized retrospectively, by recourse to earlier generations, is also expressed in an essay from Jan Morris's *Journeys*. To find the spirit of Englishness, the author here looks back even further than Raban – to the nineteenth century. 'A Visit to Barchester' is a report of Morris's search, in the early 1980s, for a 'good old' England as portrayed in Anthony Trollope's Barsetshire novels. In Wells, the model for Trollope's fictitious cathedral town of Barchester, however, nostalgic England is nowhere to be found – despite the restoration of Victorian values under the Thatcher regime:

> It was when I reached the Bishopric at last that I felt my pilgrimage had failed. Faith I had certainly found in Wells, diligence, loyalty, pride: but the sense of authority, of an established order unbreakable and supreme, which is essential to the Romantic view of England, is lost with the winds of social change and historical necessity. In Trollope's allegories that old discipline was represented if not by the person, at least by the office of the Bishop, splendidly identified by his accoutrements, his circumstances and his privileges; but the Anglican Bishop of tradition, gloriously fortified by material well-being and spiritual complacency – that grand

figure of fancy has long gone the way of the Empire-builder and the top-hatted Station Master.   (p. 42)

Although the tone and interest of the home tour today is quite different from its heyday in the eighteenth century, accounts of domestic travel are thriving again. However, they are less self-assured, more elusive, unable to arrive at a coherent image of the nation.

> Where the writers have been in pursuit of what they saw as truth, a 'grand narrative' of nationhood, they discover only a conflict of various moods and attitudes. In Raymond Williams's terms, they have been able to identify the dominant or hegemonic structure of feeling ... but they are also confronted by a competing range of residual and emergent ideologies.   (Bell, 1995, p. 25)

Another line of travel writing continued – and transformed – in the twentieth century is the account of explorer journeys.

Adventurers and explorers in the twentieth century

Modern-day adventurers still cross oceans on rafts or the Antarctic by foot and publish successful books about such expeditions – even if many of these books are not noted for their literary quality. However, the enterprises of contemporary explorers no longer hold the cultural and political significance attributed to those of their Victorian predecessors. The end of 'classic', adventurous exploration was already bemoaned in the first half of this century. '[A]dventure ... is obsolete', Peter Fleming writes in *Brazilian Adventure* (1933), 'the age of geographical discovery has gone' (p. 31). He readily seized the opportunity, however, to participate in the search expedition – described in his account – for a colonel known to be missing in South America. Other travellers of the time also sought out remaining territory for exploration. Freya Stark turned to Luristan, an area which she proclaims in *The Valleys of the Assassins* (1936) to be 'still a country for the explorer' (p. 13). Harry St John Philby and Wilfred Thesiger ventured into a dangerous and largely unknown part of the Arabian desert, the so-called 'Empty Quarter'. Thesiger's *Arabian Sands* (1959) depicts the journeys he made in and around this area from 1945 to 1950:

> It was strange to think that even fifty years earlier a great part of Africa had been unexplored. But since then travellers, missionaries, traders, and administrators had penetrated nearly everywhere. This

was one of the last corners that remained unknown. Below me was a square plain about thirty miles across. (p. 29)

Modern explorers still pursue scientific aims. However, many are also – or primarily – driven by personal interest. Thus Thesiger emphasizes in *Arabian Sands* that '[t]o return to the Empty Quarter would be to answer a challenge, and to remain there for long would be to test myself to the limit' (p. 18). In the results he brought back from his travels and his stamina, Thesiger certainly continues in the vein of the great Victorian explorers, but one element of his account is much more clearly marked: the urge to escape Western civilization. Here Thesiger continues a line of travel writing which we have seen emerging in the late nineteenth century, in the work of Stevenson and Cunninghame Graham. In *Arabian Sands*, the traveller feels a deeper bond with the Bedu in whose company he crosses the desert than with his countrymen, whom he observes in a Royal Air Force camp:

They belonged to an age of machines; they were fascinated by cars and aeroplanes, and found their relaxation in the cinema and the wireless. I knew that I stood apart from them and would never find contentment among them, whereas I could find it among these Bedu, although I should never be one of them. (p. 184)

Unfortunately, as the text stresses repeatedly, the life of the Bedu is doomed to vanish under the progress of European civilization:

I realized that traditions, customs, and rites, long cherished and revered, were soon to be discarded; that the colour and variety which distinguished this scene were to disappear from the land for ever. Already there were a few cars in the streets, harbingers of change. (p. 21)

In his critique of the expansion of Western civilization, Thesiger strikes a note frequently heard in European travel writing of the first half of the century. In excerpt 1 from Vita Sackville-West's *Passenger to Teheran* (1926), the traveller appears virtually suffocated by the idea that Europe is expanding all over the world: 'The crowds of Europe suddenly rushed at me, overwhelmed me; I was drowning under the pressure.' Her own journey by motor car, however, is also itself part of the onslaught of European civilization on a Persia as yet 'untouched' by it.

Between the world wars: travel writing as a critique of civilization

Following the First World War and the experience of radical disconti-
nuity which it entailed, the urge to escape from a civilization at home
whose values were increasingly called into question becomes a dominant theme in British travel writing.[4] The Great War reinforced and
accelerated an open critique of the state of Western culture which had
arisen with the new century and was directed in particular against the
progressive industrialization and mechanization of this culture. Thus
D.H. Lawrence writes in his early travel book, *Twilight in Italy* (1916):
'There was London and the industrial counties spreading like a black-
ness over all the world, horrible, in the end destructive. ... And
England was conquering the world with her machines and her
horrible destruction of natural life' (p. 61).

Many British travellers before the First World War still felt rooted in
their home country and loyal to its values. Between the world wars,
however, many travellers, including a high proportion of writers,
consciously sought escape from their home society. D.H. Lawrence
was almost obsessive in his urge to travel abroad; the most important
of his travel books were written in the 1920s: *Sea and Sardinia* (1923),
Mornings in Mexico (1927) and *Etruscan Places* (1927). Sardinia attracted
Lawrence precisely because of its relative freedom from the touch of
modern progress:

> Where then? Spain or Sardinia. Spain or Sardinia. Sardinia, which
> is like nowhere. Sardinia which has no history, no date, no race, no
> offering. Let it be Sardinia. They say neither Romans nor
> Phoenicians, Greeks nor Arabs ever subdued Sardinia. It lies
> outside; outside the circuit of civilization. Like the Basque lands.
> Sure enough, it is Italian now, with its railways and its motor
> omnibuses. But there is an uncaptured Sardinia still. It lies within
> the net of this European civilization, but it isn't landed yet. And the
> net is getting old and tattered. A good many fish are slipping
> through the net of the old European civilization. Like that great
> whale of Russia. And probably even Sardinia. Sardinia then. Let it
> be Sardinia.   (*Sea and Sardinia*, p. 9)

In all of his travel books, Lawrence took pains to impart the rejuve-
nating sense of energy and freedom which he derived from his
journeys. Travel for Lawrence could become a euphoric experience – a

euphoria also reflected in the style of his accounts. Occasionally, his use of expressive devices such as apostrophe and alliteration, exclamation marks and dashes, even verges on the excess. At the opening of *Sea and Sardinia*, the position of the verb at the very beginning of the sentence further contributes to an impression of urgency in style, which corresponds with the traveller's 'absolute necessity to move':

> Comes over one an absolute necessity to move. And what is more, to move in some particular direction. A double necessity then: to get on the move, and to know whither.
>
> Why can't one sit still? Here in Sicily it is so pleasant: the sunny Ionian sea, the changing jewel of Calabria, like a fire-opal moved in the light; Italy and the panorama of Christmas clouds, night with the dog-star laying a long luminous gleam across the sea, as if baying at us, Orion marching above; how the dog-star Sirius looks at one, looks at one! he is the hound of heaven, green, glamorous and fierce! – and then, oh, regal evening star, hung westward flaring over the jagged dark precipices of tall Sicily: then Etna, that wicked witch, resting her thick white snow under heaven, and slowly, slowly rolling her orange-coloured smoke. . . .
>
> Perhaps it is she one must flee from. At any rate, one must go: and at once. After having come back only at the end of October, already one must dash away. And it is only the third of January. And one cannot afford to move. Yet there you are: at the Etna bidding one goes. (pp. 7–9)

In the 1930s, travel writing became one of the most important genres next to poetry, lending a congenial mode of expression to the great number of writers who virtually fled from Britain or European civilization in general: W.H. Auden, Louis MacNeice, Christopher Isherwood, Evelyn Waugh and Graham Greene, to name but a few. While these writers also worked in the more established literary forms, other authors of this decade are remembered chiefly for their travel writing, such as Peter Fleming or Robert Byron. For Samuel Hynes (1976), travel was the 'basic trope' of a whole generation: 'journeys in the 'thirties were often *symbolic* journeys, . . . self-conscious crossings of the frontier between the known and the unknown, in search of some reality not visible at home' (p. 288).

The account of a journey not only provided writers with an opportunity to depict a literal flight from home society, but the openness of the genre also gave them room to include explicit critique of this society which, in some texts, extends to considerable length. The objects of such critique were not only the concrete social ills of Britain during the Depression, but also an intellectual climate that had become oppressive and narrowing. Paul Fussell (1980) summarizes the circumstances in Britain which provoked so many writers of the 1930s to turn abroad:

> The main loss in England was a loss of amplitude, a decay of imaginative and intellectual possibility corresponding to the literal loss of physical freedom. The very theater of thought and feeling contracted; the horizons closed in. . . . The tone of England turned stuffy, complacent, cruel, bullying, and small-minded.   (p. 10)

In *Labels*, Evelyn Waugh is quite outspoken in his discontent with this kind of England:

> However, I did succeed in getting away from England, and that was all I really cared about. In February 1929 almost every cause was present which can contribute to human discomfort. London was lifeless and numb, seeming to take its temper from Westminster, where the Government, conscious of failure, was dragging out the weeks of its last session.   (pp. 10–11)

Travellers looked abroad for alternatives to the lifelessness and constriction of their own country. Graham Greene's *Journey Without Maps* (1936) depicts a journey to Liberia, which during these years was still unmapped in some of its regions and – as Greene believed – untainted by European imperialism and Western civilization: 'The Republic is almost entirely covered by forest, and has never been properly mapped, mapped that is to say even to the rough extent of the French colonies which lie on two sides of it' (p. 45). It is the marked absence of Europe and the seeming preservation of African 'darkness' which attracts Greene to Liberia: 'It is not then *any* part of Africa which acts so strongly on this unconscious mind; certainly no part where the white settler has been most successful in reproducing the conditions of his country, its morals and its popular art. A quality of darkness is needed, of the inexplicable' (p. 20).[5] The darkness which the traveller hopes to find on Liberian terrain signifies for him a primeval and 'uncorrupted' state both of human culture and of his self. Referring to Freud, Greene's text makes this parallel between outward journey and inner journey into the subconscious explicit:

'Freud has made us conscious as we have never been before of those ancestral threads which still exist in our unconscious minds to lead us back' (p. 248).[6] In the text, this psychological dimension of Greene's journey – his exploration of his own heart of darkness – is also established in numerous digressions into dreams and childhood memories. His actual journey through space turns out to be just as unpredictable as these dreams and memories; from the outset, *Journey Without Maps* significantly accentuates the motif of disorientation: 'and later sitting before a hut in French Guinea, where I never meant to find myself, I remembered this first going astray' (p. 15).[7] For the traveller who strives to escape from the mapped realms of European civilization and who ventures into the unfamiliar interior of his mind, there is no question of a 'method' of travel – or of travel writing.

Many travel books of the twentieth century reveal relatively little formal innovation in comparison with their nineteenth-century predecessors. The travel writing, for example, of Freya Stark, Wilfred Thesiger or Patrick Leigh Fermor is fairly conventional in its manner of reporting as well as the amount of topographical and anthropological description it includes. At the same time, however, its formal flexibility makes the travelogue a particularly suitable genre for the development of modernist modes of expression. Thus Robert Byron's *The Road to Oxiana* has been called 'the *Ulysses* or *The Waste Land* of modern travel books':

> One reason this can be said is that its method is theirs: as if obsessed with frontiers and fragmentations, it juxtaposes into a sort of collage the widest variety of rhetorical materials: news clippings, public signs and notices, letters, bureaucratic documents like *fiches*, diary entries, learned dissertations in art history, essays on current politics, and, most winningly, at least 20 comic dialogues.
>
> (Fussell, 1980, p. 108)

The following example, because of its relative brevity, gives only an approximate impression of Byron's virtuoso *omnium-gatherum*; the lines of space between the short sections are original:

> *Isfahan, 13 February* There is a lot of missionary effort here, of the muscular, wicked-to-smoke-or-drink type. Men in spectacles, tweed coats, and flannel trousers go striding down the Char Bagh accompanied by small boys and bearing the unmistakable imprint of the British schoolmaster; their behinds stick out as if their spines were too righteous to bend. ...

A more humane exponent of English ethics was Archdeacon Garland, who lived here thirty years. During that time, he used to say, he made one convert. She was an old woman, who was ostracized for her apostasy, so that on her deathbed the Archdeacon was the only friend she could send for. She had one last request, she told him.

'What is it?' asked the Archdeacon, anxious to ease his protégée's last moments.

'Please summon a mullah.'

He did so, and repeated the story afterwards.

The pleasure of a walk in the rain this afternoon was completed by the clutch of a corpse. It was passing on a stretcher, the road was a bog, and we collided; the hands and feet, escaping from a check tablecloth, beckoned convulsively.

There is an Armenian cathedral at Julfa across the river, which resembles a Mohammadan shrine of the seventeenth century. Inside, the walls are covered with oil paintings in the Italian tradition of that date. Attached to it is a museum, but the treasures are of historic rather than artistic interest.   (p. 137)

Byron may well be an extreme example, but an emphasis on the heterogeneous, in both experience rendered and modes of expression, characterizes a whole range of twentieth-century travelogues: fragments of narrative are mixed freely with descriptions, sketches, dialogues, scenes, passages of reflection, short essays – or even poetry, as in *Letters from Iceland* (1937) by W.H. Auden and Louis MacNeice.

The break in travel writing with the Second World War is less radical than some critics have suggested. Bruce Chatwin, for example, was an admirer of Robert Byron, and the loosely assembled structural units of *The Road to Oxiana* reappear in Chatwin's texts. Lines of continuity between the earlier and later twentieth century also emerge thanks to travel writers like Patrick Leigh Fermor and Lawrence Durrell, whose work spans the pre- and postwar years.[8] Contemporary travel writing which is close to reportage or documentary tends to be generally traditional in its modes of presentation, such as the essays of Jan Morris (which all appeared initially in magazines) or books like *The Big Red Train Ride* (1978) by Eric Newby, who, for many years, was Travel Editor of the *Observer*.

The more conventional accounts of travel still attract a large audience – despite the fact that television brings the foreign world into our living rooms, that travel abroad has become a common leisure activity, that our homelands themselves are becoming multi-cultural and, last but not least, that the Internet will soon perfect the possibilities for virtual travel.[9] One might argue that travel writing of a traditional kind finds its readership precisely *because* of these developments: the foreign at home – in the form of 'ethnic' restaurants, music and so on – is not, of course, a perfect surrogate for travel abroad, and even television and other electronic media typically only give an impression of '[b]eing there and not being there' (Rojek, 1993, p. 201). Travelogues at least offer their readers the chance to participate in a travel experience which another person has actually lived – in a mode of reception which is more intensive and involving than watching television or surfing the Internet, especially where the texts are also aesthetically challenging. It is possible, then, that in a period of hyper-realities and virtual worlds, the written travelogue in its more traditional forms offers readers the reassurance that a reality exists which can still be authentically experienced.

Nevertheless, even though a large proportion of contemporary travel writing fits conventional moulds, postmodernism has also left its mark and recent decades have seen a range of travel books with a distinctly postmodern orientation.[10] Jacinta Matos (1992) sketches the broader context of this development:

Recent developments in literary theory, in linguistics, in historiography and in all the human sciences have ... put into question the relation between the individual observer and the external world, and between language and reality. ... We no longer hold a positivistic view of a nonfictional text as a neutral, objective reproduction of a prelinguistic reality or meaning capable of affording us a value-free knowledge. We no longer write, read, or travel with the unselfconsciousness of our predecessors, for our sense of crisis and endings is, indeed, an integral part of our world view and of our experience of travel. (p. 216)

Again, certain generic features of travel writing make it particularly open to postmodernization: the account of travel, by definition of its theme, always raises the issue of the relation between a subject and the external world; it is marked by a special tension between fact and fiction, and it has the potential to gather within a single text elements of a quite disparate nature. Above all, travel writing seems to be a congenial genre for an age of exploded, world-wide mobility, an age essentially characterized by nomadism, migration, displacement, deterritorialization and related phenomena considered typical of the postmodern condition.[11] One of the most important recent thrusts of generic development is thus found in travel texts which participate in a postmodern world-view and aesthetics.

Postmodern elements in contemporary travel writing

One of the most striking features of postmodern-orientated travel writing is the openness with which it draws attention to the mediation of the travelled world. It is mediated not only through the perception of the travelling subject, but also through the act of reporting or textualizing the journey. Postmodern travel writing emphasizes, particularly through inter- and metatextual reference, that 'all experience essentially involves patterns of perception and experiential dispositions that have always already been textualized' (Pfister, 1993, p. 111; my translation). With such an emphasis, the world actually travelled is frequently of subordinate importance and, in extreme cases, becomes merely a backdrop for the traveller's very personal concern: how he or she can confront and make sense of the world at all, if and how the journey can become a meaningful experience, and how the subject constitutes itself through and as a result of the journey. If the journey is found to be significant, this often happens not during the act of travelling itself, but rather at the moment when the journey is textualized. Meaningful travelling experience, for many postmodern travellers, will only emerge with the act of travel *writing*.

This supposition manifests itself, for example, in the two seminal travel books by Bruce Chatwin, *In Patagonia* (1977) and *The Songlines* (1987). Both texts are dominated by the traveller's and writer's urge to explain his own travel mania. '[W]hat is, for me, the question of questions: the nature of human restlessness', Chatwin writes in *The Songlines* (p. 181). In both books, Chatwin explores not only the regions he travels – Patagonia and Australia – but above all his fascination with uprootedness, a state he considers the essence of his own existence. This focus on a subjective interest leads Chatwin to begin both texts with childhood memories in which he localizes the origins of the journeys depicted in the respective books. As the first sentence of *In Patagonia* famously claims, Chatwin's interest in Patagonia was evoked by a small piece of skin which he saw, when still 'too young to read', in a cabinet in his grandmother's dining-room. It is not a piece of Patagonian brontosaurus, as he is first made to believe, and the skin eventually gets lost, but '[m]y interest in Patagonia survived the loss of the skin' (p. 6). The title of *The Songlines* refers to the aboriginals' ancient and sacred invisible pathways across Australia, the knowledge about which is preserved in indigenous songs. In this book, Chatwin's motivation for travelling to the Antipodes is also rooted in his childhood:

> In my childhood I never heard the word 'Australia' without calling to mind the fumes of the eucalyptus inhaler and an incessant red country populated by sheep.
>
> My father loved to tell, and we to hear, the story of the Australian sheep-millionaire who strolled into a Rolls-Royce showroom in London; scorned all the smaller models; chose an enormous limousine with a plate-glass panel between the chauffeur and passengers, and added, cockily, as he counted out the cash, 'That'll stop the sheep from breathing down my neck.'
>
> I also knew, from my great-aunt Ruth, that Australia was the country of the Upside-downers. A hole, bored straight through the earth from England, would burst out under their feet.
>
> 'Why don't they fall off?' I asked.
>
> 'Gravity,' she whispered.
>
> She had in her library a book about the continent, and I would gaze in wonder at pictures of the koala and kookaburra, the platypus and Tasmanian bush-devil, Old Man Kangaroo and Yellow Dog Dingo, and Sydney Harbour Bridge.
>
> But the picture I liked best showed an Aboriginal family on the move. They were lean, angular people and they went about naked. Their skin was very black, not the glitterblack of negroes but matt black, as if the sun had sucked away all possibility of reflection. The man had a long forked beard and carried a spear or two, and a spear-thrower. The woman carried a dilly-bag and a baby at her breast. A small boy strolled beside her – I identified myself with him. (pp. 6–7)

Just as the future traveller here is fascinated by nomads even as a child, the grown-up traveller is preoccupied with all phenomena of mobility and migration, and he regards nomadism as a universal of human behaviour. *In Patagonia* presents a whole kaleidoscope of exiles, emigrants and fugitives who have ended up in the country and whom the traveller either meets himself or whose stories he retraces, as in the case of Butch Cassidy and the Sundance Kid. In *The Songlines*, Chatwin's travel companion and expert on the aboriginal pathways, Arkady, is of Russian extraction, a man with 'footloose forebears' (p. 1) and a 'tireless bushwalker' (p. 2).

The motif of human restlessness holds the patchwork of Chatwin's travel books together – his mélange of travel account, portraits, reflections and memories. For any significance constructed from *The Songlines*, the plot of the actual journey is less important than the theme of travel *per se*. Indeed, the plot is interrupted again and again; lengthy passages of the text digress entirely from the Australia trip to quote from Chatwin's numerous notebooks about other journeys.

The collection of extracts from these notebooks implies the intimate relation between travel and writing, and the text also states explicitly that travel and writing go hand in hand: 'To lose a passport was the least of one's worries: to lose a notebook was a catastrophe' (p. 180). Not until the journey is textualized does it become an experience; only as text does the journey gain significance for the traveller. This nexus of travel and writing has also been emphasized by other contemporary writers. According to Michel Butor (1974), 'to travel, at least in a certain manner, is to write (first of all because to travel is to read), and to write is to travel' (p. 2). Charles Grivel (1994) makes a similar claim: 'My traveling is an event of the pen. Is it something other than the story I make of it? . . . Traveling means placing the body into a *state of writing*' (p. 243).

To Butor, reading is as much a part of travel as is writing, and for Chatwin, too, the significance of a journey is constituted not only in its own textualization, but essentially also through other texts. Texts read during the journey contribute in large measure to the travelling experience, as they mediate the travelled world for the traveller; the experience of travel is thus fundamentally intertextual. The various intertexts may be purely fictional, but they are frequently travelogues themselves. *In Patagonia*, for example, refers to Darwin's account of the *Beagle* voyage, W.H. Hudson's *Idle Days in Patagonia*, as well as Edgar Allan Poe's *Narrative of Arthur Gordon Pym*. The traveller in Chatwin's text thus observes Patagonia not only through his 'own' eyes, but also through these and other texts. Reading while travelling is, of course, not a new phenomenon, and books specially designed for the traveller's pocket emerged long before postmodern times.

Jonathan Cape began publishing the [*Travellers' Library*] series in 1926, and by 1932 it included 180 titles with over a million copies in print. ... By 1929 the Travelers' Library list included so many travel books that we must suppose that reading about someone else's travel while traveling oneself was an action widely practiced. It was assumed, indeed, to constitute a large part of what traveling was, which is to say that traveling was considered to be, *ipso facto*, literary traveling.   (Fussell, 1980, p. 59)[12]

We thus find avidly reading travellers in both earlier travelogues of the twentieth century and in contemporary travel writing of a more conventional kind, such as Fermor's *A Time of Gifts* or Newby's *The Big Red Train Ride*. The literariness and intertextuality in postmodern travel writing is, however, much more than a concomitant of travel: it communicates the central concern of these travel books that the meaning of travel is ultimately only constituted through texts.[13]

Intertextuality in contemporary travel writing is most conspicuous in texts about journeys in which the traveller follows in the footsteps of earlier travellers and their accounts. Philip Glazebrook's *Journey to Kars* grew out of a trip through modern-day Turkey and adjacent countries, in which Glazebrook retraced the adventurous journeys of Victorian travellers through the Ottoman Empire (see Chapter 1, p. 10). His prime motive for the journey was his fascination with the heroic image which the earlier travellers projected of themselves in their accounts; Glazebrook wants to test his ideas about these traveller-heroes 'against experience of lands they had travelled through' (p. 9). The traveller of the 1980s is not blind to the reality of the countries he visits, but he travels principally 'in the company of ghosts' (p. 9) – that is, accompanied by the Victorian travellers whose books he has taken along with him. How these texts about past experience repeatedly eclipse the traveller's present experience is particularly striking in episodes where Glazebrook becomes so immersed in his reading that he forgets about the circumstances of his own trip. Thus he does not notice when his train changes direction; not until he looks for his luggage at the wrong end of the train and believes that it is lost is he brought back to reality: 'Whilst I had been sitting thinking of Edmund Spencer's description of Nyssa in 1850, instead of attending to Nis in 1980, had the train perhaps come out of the station backwards as they sometimes do?' (p. 19). Where texts about travel become more important than authentic travelling experience, Glazebrook's conclusion, at the end of his account, is hardly surprising – that he need not have set off on the journey at all to fulfil his purpose, 'except to travel to the London Library' (p. 240).

In *Coasting*, Jonathan Raban also makes explicit reference to the writing traditions in which his own text is located.[14] Earlier accounts of boat trips around Britain are reviewed in detail, and Raban further quotes from other travelogues, including Defoe's *Tour through the Whole Island of Great Britain*, probably the most famous of earlier home tour accounts. However, travel writing forms only a part of the extensive library which Raban has taken with him on his boat: 'Books went aboard in boxfuls, and my predecessors began to look increasingly ill at ease in the company they were keeping' (p. 46). These boxes of books include the works of Laurence Sterne, which are flung through the cabin in rough seas:

> In an unscheduled gale off the coast of Sussex, the collected works of Laurence Sterne took flight in the saloon and flapped about like doves escaping from a magician's hat: hellfire sermons colliding in mid-air with three panic-stricken volumes of *Tristram Shandy*, and *A Sentimental Journey* making a break for it through the galley and up into the wheelhouse. Clinging on to the wheel, too busy trying to angle the bow of the boat into the next wave to be frightened, I thought coldly that death looked as if it was definitely on the cards. ... But this voyage goes on. So long as the book continues to be written, the helmsman's still alive. However, for those who insist on travelling in a more orderly sequence and demand a strict and conventional economy of literary means, here goes –
>
> I got drunk in Torquay, had a fit of memoirs in Portsmouth, turned lyrical in Brighton and philosophical off Beachy Head, was affronted in Dover, ill in Harwich, happy in Grimsby, maudlin in Bridlington, was pleased with myself on Holy Island, got drunk again in Leith, was superior in Inverness, fell in love in Oban and out of love by Stranraer, was at my wits' end in Dublin, said some very clever things in Fishguard, lost my temper off Land's End and summed things up pretty neatly in Falmouth. *The End.*   (pp. 49–50)

Raban's metafictional game here is a complex one. As protagonist in the plot of his account, Raban is at the helm of his storm-beset boat. As the helmsman of his account, he has to steer through the problems of structuring the text, of giving his voyage a narrative order: 'The difficulty with a circular voyage is that, once you have gone on past your original point of departure ..., it has no destination and no ending' (p. 50). Raban attacks this problem in the manner of a literary model explicitly referred to in the passage above – Laurence Sterne, whose metafictional techniques anticipated postmodern writing, and whose *Sentimental Journey*, as we have seen, had a considerable impact on travel writing. Just as Sterne turned narrative conventions upside down, Raban parodies traditional modes of travel writing. For example, he denies his readers an orderly, chronological travel plot. Readers who expect this kind of plot are only granted a mock gratification – a cursory and banal listing of events which would end the book immediately, after only one sixth of the text: '*The End*' (p. 50).

Those who read on will discover that for Raban, too, the journey does not have a meaning until it is textualized. Consequently, *Coasting* closes with a report of the act of travel *writing*. From his desk, the writer catches sight of two ships: 'The masts and deckworks of two coasters showed over the line of the seawall, moving almost imperceptibly from left to right, more slowly, even, than words' (p. 299). In this sentence, a comparison is drawn between coasting and writing/ reading, the *tertium comparationis* consisting in the movement from left to right, that is, the usual direction of writing and reading in Western culture. Ships, a means of travel, and words, the stuff of texts, are made to merge. However, the act of writing does not bring Raban's travel to a definitive end; textualizing his voyage only causes him to yearn for further travel and the quest for meaning it entails: 'I had thought that I might well cure this coaster's itch by writing about it, but the condition seems to have worsened, if anything, during the writing' (p. 300).

Travel books with this kind of inter- and metatextual emphasis foreground the literariness of the genre and reveal that travel writing is always the creative reconstruction of travel experience. Above all, their meta- and intertextuality proves that an understanding of travel writing as a genre of its own – and a genre with a tradition – has established itself over the centuries. The final chapter of this book will be devoted to a variety of twentieth-century travel writing which has added another facet to the genre and which is of particular pertinence to the English-speaking world: with vastly increasing numbers of texts published per year, travelogues by 'postcolonial' writers are currently emerging as one of the genre's most fertile and successful branches.

8
Postcolonial Travel Writing in the Twentieth Century

[1] *When more than twenty years ago I began to travel as a writer, I was uneasy and uncertain. . . . I was glamoured by the idea of the long journey, but I had no idea how I might set about looking at a place in a way that would be of value to other people. . . .*

When it came to the writing, I was uncertain about the value I should give to the traveller's 'I'. . . . In 1960 I was still a colonial, travelling to far-off places that were still colonies, in a world still more or less ruled by colonial ideas. In Surinam in 1961, in a banana plantation . . . the Indian official who – with a Dutch technical expert in attendance – was showing me around broke off to say in a semi-conspiratorial way, 'You are the first one of us to come out on a mission like this.'

To travel was glamorous. But travel also made unsuspected demands on me as a man and a writer, and perhaps for that reason it soon became a necessary stimulus for me. It broadened my world view; it showed me a changing world and took me out of my own colonial shell; it became the substitute for the mature social experience – the deepening knowledge of a society – which my background and the nature of my life denied me. . . . And I learned to look in my own way.

(V. S. Naipaul, *Finding the Centre*, 1984, pp. 10–11)

[2] *As I was coming out of Canterbury Cathedral I observed a little English boy of about six sitting on the grass and looking at me with an intense gaze, like a lion cub watching a distant zebra. When I came near him he began to rise slowly on his knees, and while still half kneeling raised his arm, pointed a finger at me, and cried out in his sharp treble, 'You're from Africa!' . . . I shouted back, 'No, from*

150

India!' *The boy dropped on the grass and kept his eye fixed on it. I
thought he had been abashed, but when I met him in another part of
the close the mischievous little fellow again piped out, 'You're from
Africa!' He clearly felt that he had succeeded in teasing me.*
(Nirad Chaudhuri, *A Passage to England*, 1959, pp. 125–6)

[3] *The Sikh did not know that 'British citizens of Asian origin' needed
a visa to enter Kenya.*

*'Always visa. Wherever I go it's visa this and visa that. What is a
man to do?' He wrung his hands. 'What is wrong with my passport?
A British citizen is a British citizen.'*

*The Immigration Officer remained unmoved. 'Stand aside, bwana.
You're holding up the queue.'*

*The two English girls were next in line. He glanced cursorily at
their passports. They were stamped and returned with a smile. 'Enjoy
your stay and welcome to Kenya.' . . .*

*It was my turn. I did not need a visa, being a citizen not of the
United Kingdom but of Trinidad and Tobago. He worked through my
passport carefully, page by page. 'Where's your visa?'*

*I said the Kenya High Commission in London had told me that I
would not need one.*

*'They told you that, did they?' He squinted at me. 'Is Trinidad and
Tobago a member of the Commonwealth?'*

'It is.'

*Again he squinted at me. He consulted a booklet. 'You're right,' he
said, as if surprised to confirm the truth of what I had told him. He
studied me. 'You were born there?'*

'I was.'
(Shiva Naipaul, *North of South*, 1978, pp. 28–9)

[4] *The Imam turned away and laughed scornfully. 'He's lying,' he said
to the crowd. 'They don't burn their dead in the West. They're not an
ignorant people. They're advanced, they're educated, they have
science, they have guns and tanks and bombs.'*

*Suddenly something seemed to boil over in my head, dilemmas and
arguments I could no longer contain within myself.*

*'We have them too!' I shouted back at him. 'In my country [India]
we have all those things too; we have guns and tanks and bombs.
And they're better than anything you've got in Egypt – we're a long
way ahead of you.' . . .*

> *It was about then, I think, that Khamees appeared at my side and led me away, or else we would probably have stood there a good while longer, the Imam and I: delegates from two superseded civilizations, vying with each other to establish a prior claim to the technology of modern violence.*
>
> *At that moment, despite the vast gap that lay between us, we understood each other perfectly. We were both travelling, he and I: we were travelling in the West. The only difference was that I had actually been there, in person: I could have told him a great deal about it, seen at first hand, its libraries, its museums, its theatres, but it wouldn't have mattered. We would have known, both of us, that all that was mere fluff: in the end, for millions and millions of people on the landmasses around us, the West meant only this – science and tanks and guns and bombs.*
>
> (Amitav Ghosh, *In an Antique Land*, 1992, pp. 235–6)

Mapping postcolonial travel writing

The postcolonial world has been affected by travel in many respects: the countries in question were 'discovered', explored, conquered or settled by people who came to them from Europe. Displacement is an experience particularly associated with the postcolonial condition, which, for many individuals, entails a history of transportation, migration, expatriation, diaspora or exile. If travel is of special pertinence to Britain's former colonies, the travel *writing* produced in these parts of the world has been practically ignored by scholars until recently – with the prominent exception of V S Naipaul. The number of travel writers from the 'Commonwealth' seems small indeed if compared to the mass of travel writers from the British Isles. Nevertheless, the colonial world formerly travelled by Britons *is* increasingly travelling itself, and its modes of travel writing deserve to be examined in their own right.

When this chapter devotes itself to the 'postcolonial' travelogue, it makes use of a concept – for lack of a more satisfactory one – that continues to be criticized for its origins in Western thinking, as well as its relative imprecision.[1] As an umbrella term, 'postcolonialism' blurs important distinctions between former colonies: those between settled and conquered colonies, between colonies that became independent early or late in the twentieth century, or between postcolonial cultures now located in the so-called Third and those in the First World. The term also disguises the problematic relationship between dominant and subaltern groups within postcolonial societies themselves, notably that between European settlers and indigenous populations. Moreover, as David Spurr (1993) points out, the 'post-colonial' cannot be clearly demarcated from the 'colonial':

> I shall refer to the postcolonial in two ways: as an historical situation marked by the dismantling of traditional institutions of colonial power, and as a search for alternatives to the discourses of the colonial era. ... in neither the historical nor the cultural sense does the postcolonial mark a clean break with the colonial: the relations of colonizer to colonized have neither remained the same nor have they disappeared. (pp. 6–7)

The intricacies of the postcolonial world pose considerable problems for a definition of postcolonial travel writing. The question even arises whether truly postcolonial travel writing is possible at all. In fact, some scholars consider the travelogue an essentially imperialist mode of representation. Jim Philip (1993), for example, concludes that travel writing

> is most practiced and most read among those peoples who, for the longest time, have exercised commercial or political power over others and whose cultural relations have therefore been most wide-spread and most problematical. In this sense, it might be argued, travel writing is European and has been involved in one way or another with the history of colonialism. (p. 242)[2]

Intertextually, this involvement emerges in many references which postcolonial travel writers make – more or less critically – to imperial travelogues. V. S. Naipaul, for example, in *The Middle Passage* (1962), quotes from James Anthony Froude's notoriously racist *The English in the West Indies* (1887); his brother Shiva Naipaul, in *North of South* (1978), repeatedly mentions Mungo Park, and Christopher Ondaatje's *Sindh Revisited* (1995) depicts a journey 'in the Footsteps of Captain Sir Richard Francis Burton'.

For this chapter, 'postcolonial' travel writing will be considered with the following understanding: it comprises travelogues by writers originating from former British colonies (apart from the United States). For reasons of scope, it will not encompass the intricate situation of (post)colonialism within the British Isles themselves, that is, in (Northern) Ireland, Scotland and Wales. It will include, however, the travelogues produced within Britain by writers who migrated there from former colonies overseas – predominantly India, Pakistan and the West Indies. As far as its time range is concerned, the chapter concentrates on travel writing produced since the Second World War, that is in a period when decolonization was achieved or in progress in most parts of the former Empire.[3] However, as the borderline between the colonial and the postcolonial condition is fluid, a few texts of the early twentieth century will also be taken into account.[4]

Even within such fairly straight criteria, the postcolonial travelogue is difficult to map because of the many strands in which it appears. The *Encyclopedia of Postcolonial Literatures in English* proposes the following subcategories: postcolonial travel writing can be about 'inter-commonwealth travel', in which 'a traveler/writer from one country or region visits and offers commentary upon another'; about 'return travel' (of a migrant to his or her 'native' post/colony); and about 'within-the-country travel', where the traveller explores his or her own national community (Benson and Conolly, 1994, pp. 1586–7). These divisions suggest that travellers from former colonies prefer to travel in regions which have a particular affinity to their own postcolonial condition. As V. S. Naipaul writes in *Finding the Centre* (1984): 'I go to places which, however alien, connect in some way with what I already know' (p. 87). However, this is a preference which can hardly be generalized for all travellers, and another variety of postcolonial travel writing should therefore be added: accounts of travel to countries outside the former Empire.

Grouping travelogues by destinations of travel provides a certain measure of orientation, but it also tends to disguise the broad cultural spectrum in which postcolonial travel writing manifests itself. The attitudes of the travellers/writers range from allegiance to the old mother country to open critique of imperialism and its consequences, or, most recently, even to a globalized perspective. The different cultures from which postcolonial travellers emerge all have their own special outlooks and traditions of travel. The conditions of post-colonial travel change significantly even within a single country. Aus-tralian travel to Europe, for example, was essentially transformed by 'the greater economic accessibility of overseas jet travel in the 1960s', and 'expatriatism became a less common option or necessity as Australians became more satisfied with their own culture and more confident about it' (Hergenhan and Petersson, 1994, p. xv). The differences which now exist between former 'sister' colonies are specifically noted by some inter-commonwealth travellers, as in the account which the Canadian novelist, Jack Hodgins, wrote about his trip to Australia, *Over 40 in Broken Hill* (1992). Everywhere in Australia, the Canadian is aware of differences rather than affinities, and even the allegedly common language causes problems in intercultural communication:

> 'You don't have panel beaters in Canada?'
> 'Not to my knowledge.'
> It was too silly to say this out loud. I wondered if panels might possibly be an Australian word for carpet – surely carpets and tapestries were made up of panels – so that a 'panel beaters' shop might be full of people slamming tennis racquets against hanging rugs. . . .
> 'It's where you'd take your car after a collision – to have the dents taken out. What do they call a place like that in Canada?'
> 'A body shop. You'd take your car to a body shop.'
> 'Body shop? Body shop?' Roger laughed. It seemed to me that he took a sort of contemptuous delight in this bit of news. 'Sounds like a chain of cosmetic merchandisers to me!'   (pp. 23–4)

In fact, the former British colonies differ in the extent to which they have produced accounts of travel at all. The former settled colonies like Canada and Australia have contributed prolifically to the genre, but travel writing is comparatively uncommon – as yet – in the Indian subcontinent, Black Africa and the West Indies,[5] while writers of Caribbean origin in the British diaspora have recently produced quite a few travelogues. One plausible reason for this uneven distribution is that cultures differ in the opportunity to travel, as well as in the ways in which travel experience is customarily expressed. Almost all cultures have traditions of military and hunting expeditions, nomadism, pilgrimage or travel for purposes of trade. They have also found various means of textualizing such experiences. In Australia, for example, nomadic experience was captured in the aboriginals' songlines by which a European travel writer, Bruce Chatwin, was so deeply fascinated. The travel account, however, as understood in the present volume, appears to be a textual tradition which, in the English-speaking world, is strongly associated with a Western tradition of travel and travel writing. The entry about South African travel writing in the *Encyclopedia of Postcolonial Literatures* points out that there appears to be a significant difference between European (Western) and non-European (non-Western) traditions of travel and textualizing travel experience:

Though oral tradition in Southern Africa commemorates crucial movements of peoples, such as communal migrations and military expeditions, the literature of travel, understood as individually recorded journeying, is virtually by definition an exogenous form in the region. ... For the majority of South Africans, individual travel for the sake of observation and reflection has scarcely been an option in the face of material deprivation and legislative restriction. Not surprisingly, western conventions of travelogue have not been adopted by black South African writers. A different journey paradigm has produced writing such as the tales of Mtutuzeli Matshoba ... or Miriam Tlali ...: crossing the land as listener rather than observer, transmitting the stories of the community of township commuters and labour migrants on the train and bus routes.

(Benson and Conolly, 1994, pp. 1595, 1598)[6]

The majority of British travelogues discussed in the chapters above has, since the eighteenth century, been rooted in travel as an individual experience that requires leisure and a certain amount of material means. In Europe and other First World cultures, this mode of travelling thus used to be a privilege until the emergence of modern mass tourism. In the developing postcolonial societies, it still is the privilege of an elite, as Doris Lessing remarks in *African Laughter* (1992): 'If it is hard for most of the white people to leave Zimbabwe, then for nearly all the black people it is impossible, and the world outside Southern Africa hardly exists' (p. 273).

Generally speaking, then, the travelogue seems to have been adopted primarily by English-speaking writers who travel and write in modes which developed in Europe over the last centuries.[7] As will be shown, these modes can be modified or inverted, but on the whole postcolonial travellers and travel writers, just as their colonial predecessors, appear not to stray very far from the established, Western paths.

An early travelogue of the twentieth century shows exemplarily how the colonial subject writing a travelogue was deeply enmeshed in the colonizer's language and form – even though this particular text was not originally written in English, nor for an audience in Britain. *Sir Apolo Kagwa Discovers Britain* is Ham Mukasa's report of his visit, in the company of Sir Apolo, to Britain in 1902, where the two Ugandans were their country's official representatives at the coronation of Edward VII. This account was originally written in Luganda, the language of the Baganda people, but the text itself suggests that a *written* account was not the most natural way of representation for Mukasa's original audience back home. When Mukasa and Sir Apolo return to Uganda, a crowd is waiting for them to *tell* about their adventures. From its Luganda original, the text was translated into English by the same minister who had shepherded the two Africans during their tour, and, in 1904, it was published as *Uganda's Katikiro in England*. The English translator clearly manipulated the text as well, and, as the Ugandan editor of the cited edition suggests, he also 'seems to have influenced the two grandees with his prejudices' (p. v). At the same time, the translator tried to retain the 'native' flair of the language, as this enhanced – to a British audience – the childlikeness of the colonial visitors. The English text is marked, for example, by features of oral narrative, such as the direct address of the audience, interspersed proverbs, exclamations and questions. The translator also retained the Luganda paraphrases for various English achievements, again with the obvious intent of highlighting the Ugandans' naive admiration: Mukasa and Apolo use 'the room which takes people to the upper floors' (a lift, p. 41) and visit a 'house of remembrance' (a museum, p. 38). Clearly, the text was doctored to suit imperialist ideology. It also implies that writing a travelogue in the first place should be considered a tradition of the imperial centre rather than the colonial periphery: several individuals whom Sir Apolo and Mukasa visit in England because of their involvement in Uganda have written accounts about their travels in Africa, such as Henry Morton Stanley, or they are avid readers of travel writing, such as King Edward himself. Furthermore, that Mukasa's account should be made available to readers in the mother country is presented as an idea suggested by a high colonial administrator in London, Sir Clement Hill: '"The book which you are going to write telling about your travels, should be put into English, as a great many people will want to hear about all you have seen; the Baganda and a great many English people, too, will be glad to read it"' (p. 140). Even when the African audience is addressed directly, the text thus is always double-voiced. To a British readership at the beginning of the twentieth century, the following sentences, for example, would have signalled that their colonials were obedient and grateful and that the colonial scheme accordingly deserved to be continued:

> Well, my friends, you should read this book very carefully and attentively, that you may understand what other and wiser lands are like; and though we call these lands wise, you should remember that wisdom does not come to a lazy and weak man, but one who works hard and thinks daily about his work. (p. 159)

With its textual history, Ham Mukasa's account is a special case, but the ties of colonial and postcolonial travel writing to the (former) imperial centre are of a general nature. Since a great number of travelogues by writers from (former) colonies used to be published by companies in Britain, it is often difficult to make out who a text's primary audience was: a readership in the writer's own country, one in the (former) mother country, or both. V. S. Naipaul's *The Middle Passage*, for example, was originally suggested by the Premier of Naipaul's native Trinidad. The book was published, however, by a London company, Andre Deutsch, which also brought out all of Naipaul's other travel books

> and so, arguably, Trinidadian sponsorship was supplanted by the constraint of metropolitan publication. Certainly there is ample evidence to suggest that Naipaul is writing with British readers in mind: refusing to play the part of the 'innocent' travel writer, he frequently places his remarks in context by alluding to British travellers' accounts of the West Indies and provides basic information about the Caribbean situation, presumably for the benefit of such readers.   (Thieme, 1982, p. 141)

A few years before *The Middle Passage*, on the eve of independence of his native British Guyana, Edgar Mittelholzer wrote *With a Carib Eye* (1958). Mittelholzer, the son of a Swiss-German father and a mother of African descent, migrated to England in 1948. His travel book about the Caribbean is, as his title emphasizes, written from the perspective of 'one born and bred in the region' (p 8) At the same time, however, Mittelholzer is writing for an audience in Britain and with a somewhat defensive attitude. It is for British readers that he constantly emphasizes how the Caribbean has been misrepresented in accounts by 'Northerners' and for whom he wishes to correct this view: 'The strange and the "exotic" have always been high-lighted, and rarely has a balanced, authentic picture of the region been presented' (p. 7). At about the same time, Peter Abrahams, a Black South African living in Britain, composed his *Jamaica: An Island Mosaic* (1957) for the Corona Library, that is a 'series of illustrated volumes under the sponsorship of the Colonial Office dealing with the United Kingdom's dependent territories' (n.p.), and Nirad Chaudhuri first wrote his *Passage to England* (1959) for another British institution, the BBC Overseas Service.

With increasing opportunities for many – though not all – postcolonial travel writers to publish their books independently of the

British book market, the question of the writers' double-voicedness becomes less pertinent. Contemporary accounts of Canadian home tours, for example, are primarily addressed at a Canadian readership, while other recent postcolonial travel writing is as openly directed at an international audience. Perhaps this latter development can be seen as a marker of the genre's progressive 'decolonization' – though not its de-Westernization, which seems hard to achieve considering the genre's history in the English-speaking world. V. S. Naipaul has been frequently knocked for his alleged inability to free himself from Western moulds of travel writing:

> It is not as if the genre of travel writing could not have been inflected in a way that could have caught the deeper contours of culture guiding the lives of third-world people. By resorting to pastiche, collage, juxtapositions, irony, playfulness, and so forth Naipaul could have initiated a contestory movement of thought and subverted the authority of the travel writing genre from within.
>
> (Dissanayake and Wickramagamage, 1993, p. 156)

> [B]ecause he soon adjusted himself to a predominantly metropolitan perspective, he has contributed little to the tradition of inverted travelogues produced by Third Worlders or colonial subjects who have sought to write up the foreign peculiarities of Britain and the United States.   (Nixon, 1992, p. 56)

Proclaiming a *tradition* of inflected or inverted travelogues seems to be wishful thinking. To date, no postcolonial travel writer has established an entirely new line of the travel account. Nevertheless, postcolonial travellers – like women travellers – have certainly developed 'other' *perspectives* which turn their texts, in the words of Mary Louise Pratt (1992), into vehicles for 'transculturation' from the colonies to the metropolis. In a few instances, writers have also consciously reversed canonized patterns of travel.

Inverted patterns of travel

Reversing the colonizer's direction of travel (from imperial centre to colonial periphery) is a travel pattern encountered long before the emergence of postcolonialism. From the nineteenth until the mid-twentieth century, it was customary for well-to-do British settlers to travel 'back' to the mother country. Although this kind of journey was undertaken with an increasingly independent perspective, most of these travellers still felt loyal to Britain, which they considered an ancestral home and a place for culture worship. To colonials of non-European origin, Britain was also a country familiar through its culture export, though without family ties.[8] More or less consciously, these travellers in reverse returned the gaze of the British imperial travellers. At the same time, however, they were unable to escape the imperialist gaze while in the mother country itself – especially when they were visibly foreign. Ham Mukasa, who travelled Britain at the beginning of the twentieth century, records in his account how he is continually stared at. The good colonial that he is, however, he manages to develop some understanding for this situation and even makes it easier for a curious old man to have a good look at him because, 'since he had become an old man he had never seen a black man, or perhaps he might have seen one at a distance, but never so close as I was' (p. 44). Being gazed at – being treated as a 'sight' – used to be a common experience of non-European travellers in Western countries before the advent of multi-ethnic societies. Nirad Chaudhuri, in *A Passage to England*, also refers to this gaze – and to being teased – by a little boy in Canterbury (excerpt 2). The same experience is reported in another Indian's account of his journey west. In *My Dateless Diary* (1964), R.K. Narayan renders his first visit to the United States in the late 1950s, on an invitation by the Rockefeller Foundation. Although he is frequently treated as an exotic 'showpiece' (p. 19), Narayan enjoys America. More poignantly than Chaudhuri, however, he also holds a satirical mirror up to the West. Measured against the attitudes and values of the East, the United States and its inhabitants often appear in a ridiculous light, as in the following passage, which turns the notion of Western 'progressive' civilization upside down:

> Some [women] wore hats which had the aesthetic finish of the lid of a marmalade can, some of the women's hats produced the same visual impression as Christy's feltcap of ancient times. ... At the turn of the century, Christy's caps, [*sic*] were considered in South India at any rate, as the acme of men's fashion. ... With the advancing standards of civilized appearance this scheme was given up, and after losing sight of it for years in India, I noticed it now in New York ...; and even the skirts and jackets had a resemblance to the *dhoti* that South Indians wear. I was taken aback to see the

abandoned masculine fashion of India adopted by the women of
New York as the latest.   (p. 15)

In this observation, a typical pattern of imperialist travel writing is
clearly inverted: 'One way of domesticating the primitives that
inhabit the worlds that Western travel writers visit is by placing them
on an evolutionary ladder – that is, by seeing them as living in a stage
of human development that the West has experienced centuries ago'
(Dissanayake and Wickramagamage, 1993, p. 13).

   A younger generation of postcolonial writers tends to reverse traditional travel patterns more systematically and with the outspoken aim
of foregrounding the traveller's postcoloniality. Interestingly, both of
the following examples are by writers of Caribbean origin living in
Britain, that is in a situation which constantly reminds them of their
postcolonial condition. In 1984, Caryl Phillips, an Afro-Caribbean
born in St Kitts but brought to Britain as a baby, undertook a journey
through Europe; *The European Tribe* (1987) is the collection of his
essays about this trip. As a person both Black and British, Phillips feels
ethnically marginalized and culturally confused. Europe is part of his
cultural inheritance ('the European Academy that had shaped my
mind', p. 9), but at the same time, it denies him full participation in
its culture, and the prime motive for Phillips's journey thus is to trace
the racism 'in the soul of Europe' (p. viii). As the title of his book
suggests, this journey is, on one level, a reversal of imperialist expeditions: the *European* tribe – 'primitive' in its blind racism – and not the
native tribes of another continent, is the object of 'exploration'. At the
same time, Phillips mimics the pattern of the Grand Tour: the traveller
embarks on his journey at the end of his university years and comes
back 'enlightened' – if not in the sense intended for the original tour.
Even in the classical stops of his trip, Phillips encounters not a Europe
of civilization, learning and art, but one of a racist past. Venice, for
example, a canonized highlight of continental travel, arouses
thoughts of Shakespeare's Othello and Shylock, the old Jewish ghetto
and anti-semitism in general. The Black Briton's 'grand' tour reveals
the 'high price' of racism which Europe paid for its cultural heritage,
its 'churches, art galleries, and architecture' (p. 128). The final
sentence of *The European Tribe* alludes once more to imperialist travel,
explicitly rejecting the nineteenth-century missionary pose. Black
people in Europe, Phillips claims, could teach Europe a lesson – but
they will not act as missionaries for the European tribe; the reversal of
roles has its limits:

Europe must begin to restructure the tissue of lies that continues to be taught and digested at school and at home for we, black people, are an inextricable part of this small continent. And Europeans must learn to understand this for themselves, for there are among us few who are here as missionaries.   (p. 129)

Ferdinand Dennis, in *Behind the Frontlines* (1988), rewrites another traditional type of travelogue: that of the home tour. A classic of this variety, Priestley's *English Journey*, is mentioned (pp. 58–9), but Dennis's Britain is quite different from Priestley's. Like Caryl Phillips, Dennis is a Black Briton born in the West Indies (Jamaica) and transplanted to Britain at a young age. His 'journey into Afro-Britain', undertaken in 1987 after the outburst of race riots in Thatcherite Britain, leads him through cities familiar from other accounts of domestic tourism, but these cities are depicted in aspects normally unperceived by the white traveller. London, Liverpool, Sheffield, Birmingham, Cardiff, Bristol and Bath are represented as locations where people of African descent have settled for centuries and, in the 1980s, live under postcolonial conditions within the former mother country. Dennis explores the history of the places and people as well as their present condition, but also ethnic conflict between different immigrant groups, Afro-Britons and Asians in particular. Like Phillips, Dennis accentuates the migrant's identity problem in a dominant racist culture: 'Occasionally, you see the Rasta colours next to the Union Jack, signifying, perhaps, a dual allegiance, an emergent sense of being both black and British, with all the contradiction and tensions that go with such an identity' (p. 99).

Such rewritings of canonized types of travelogues are comparatively rare. Consistently, however, postcolonial travel writing displays perspectives deviating from those familiarly exhibited by British or American travellers and thus shedding a new light even on regions which appear to have been travelled exhaustively.

Postcolonial viewpoints

Nirad Chaudhuri, in his *Passage to England*, draws attention to the fact that he views Britain with Indian eyes: 'I saw things there in doublets – there were the things which were positively English, but there were also their shadows cast in a dark mass under the light from India' (p. 3). When Christopher Hope, a white South African who settled in London in 1975, travelled the Soviet Union in the late 1980s, his special background made for some unusual – and cynical – parallels in *Moscow! Moscow!* (1990):

> I was reminded of the place I knew best, South Africa. The resemblance was shadowy and in many ways incorrect, yet there were reminders and recognitions so instructive, so comforting and terrible, that I fell into an hypnotic state of resigned relaxation, almost of enjoyment, rather like a sleepy child who fears he will be woken by nightmares but in a curious way welcomes them because he knows them, they are *his* bad dreams, his very own familiar horrors. ... There were even in the Soviet Union 'homelands', governed from Moscow but called sovereign republics. (p. 2)

Naturally, the outlook of postcolonial travellers is affected by whether their country is now situated in the First or in the Third World. Nevertheless, all postcolonial travellers seem to display a special sensitivity for the colonial history of the countries they visit. In *An Innocent in Ireland* (1995), for example, the Canadian poet David McFadden records how Britain's oldest colony constantly reminded him of its long history of occupation and also invited many comparisons to the colonial past of his own country. Even when they travel outside the former British Empire, postcolonial travellers are particularly aware of relics of colonialism. Thus in V.S. Naipaul's *Among the Believers* (1981), the account of his travels in the Islamic East, traces of Muslim imperialism are explicitly related to imperialism in the New World:

> This desert town ... was the pattern of small towns I had seen far away in Spanish America ... Spain had been the vehicle: conquered by the Arabs between AD 710 and 720, just eighty years after Persia, and incorporated into the great medieval Muslim world, the great universal civilization of the time. Spain, before it had spread to the Americas, had rejected that Muslim world, and gained vigour and its own fanaticism from that rejection. But here in Iran, five hundred years on, that world still existed, with vague ideas of its former greatness, but ignorant ... of the contributions it had once made, and of the remote continent whose fate it had indirectly influenced. (pp. 53–4)

A particularly prominent historical dimension marks Amitav Ghosh's *In an Antique Land* (1992), a book of travel in time as much as in space. Ghosh, an Indian who came to England with a student scholarship, retraces the history of an Indian slave whose name is mentioned in a twelfth-century manuscript – a letter to a Jewish-Egyptian merchant living in Mangalore. This ancient relationship between the Middle East and India came about through trade, and Ghosh accordingly evokes the great non-European tradition of travel in the East:

> The fortunes of each of these men were founded on the trade between India and the Middle East but their part in it was that of brokers and financiers rather than travelling merchants. ... There was no lack of travellers in their circle, however: at least two of Madmun's friends deserve to be counted amongst the most well-travelled men of the Middle Ages, perhaps of any age before the twentieth century.   (p. 157)

The old Eastern world linked by travel was destroyed and appropriated by European imperialism. The manuscript mentioning the Indian slave, for example, originally preserved in a Cairo synagogue, was brought to England (where Ghosh read it) as an item of stolen history, robbed from Egypt for the benefit of Western scholarship. How severely ancient ties of friendship between the cultures of the East were disrupted by the West becomes obvious to the traveller when he quarrels with an Imam about whether India or Egypt is now the more 'progressive', that is Westernized, country (excerpt 4).

Contemporary travel writers from Britain and the United States are also frequently aware of the sins of imperialism, the dichotomies of East and West, or First and Third World. Travel writers with a post-colonial background, however, are often more keenly and personally concerned with these phenomena. Thus Margaret Laurence, in *The Prophet's Camel Bell* (1963), criticizes 'the sahib-type English' (p. 205) still to be found in the British protectorate of Somaliland. Although the Canadian novelist would like to despise these people, she cannot, because she realizes that her presence in Africa is also implicated in colonialism: Laurence's husband has found a job as engineer in the developing country, and Laurence herself, as a writer grown up in the European tradition, exploits the 'darkness' and 'primitivity' of Africa imaginatively: 'This was something of an irony for me, to have started out in righteous disapproval of the empire-builders, and to have been forced at last to recognize that I, too, had been of that company' (p. 228). Ronald Wright is a Canadian travel writer with a special interest in South America. Most of his texts display a strong sympathy with the plights of developing countries that have suffered from European colonialism in the past and are now subjected to the neo-imperialism of the United States – a powerful country by which first-world Canadians also feel dominated. However, Wright also exemplifies the guilt which many travellers from former settled colonies now tend to feel towards the indigenous population of the countries they travel – whether foreign or their own. As the cultural inheritors of European settlers, they have a paradoxical history of being both colonial subjects to Britain and colonizers of indigenous people within the colony. In *Home and Away* (1993), Wright thus comments on the situation of the native population in his own country Canada: 'I'd criticized Latin republics such as Peru and Guatemala for their repression of indigenous societies. But here, strewn across one of the world's wealthiest and supposedly most liberal countries, was social wreckage of an extremity I'd seldom seen in the Third World' (p. 152).[9]

Even though some travel writers, in a situation of forthcoming or immediate decolonization, used to claim that their view was consciously apolitical,[10] the postcolonial condition arouses in many travellers a strong political interest and a special sensitivity to the mechanisms of power. In other contexts, too, travel writing has long been overtly or implicitly political. Although this potential of the genre was not emphasized in the chapters above, it should have become apparent to what extent accounts about Grand Tours and home tours, the imperialist travelogue or the travel writing of women have, for centuries, implied or even proclaimed their authors' political convictions. Postcolonial travellers, however, tend to make their political statements in a particularly outspoken manner. Thus all studies on V. S. Naipaul, although usually critical of his 'colonial' attitude and British affiliations, concede that he is a writer of political commitment. Naipaul himself, when asked to compare himself to the British travel writers of the 1930s, has also made this point: 'The primary difference between my travel and theirs is that while they travel for the picturesque, I'm *desperately* concerned about the countries I'm in.'[11] The specific nature of the postcolonial traveller's concern is determined by his or her individual cultural background. The Naipaul brothers, for example, were both shaped by their status as members of the East Indian diaspora in Trinidad's predominantly Afro-Caribbean culture. When Shiva Naipaul depicts his travels in Africa, he thus devotes special attention to a relic of British imperial rule of which many European travellers in Africa are unaware: the situation of the Indian diaspora in African countries (excerpt 3). The British Empire transplanted Indians to its African colonies as a workforce, just as it did in the Caribbean, but 'Africanized' Africa tries to extradite Asians who refuse to adopt African passports.

Salman Rushdie's *The Jaguar Smile* (1987) records his visit to Nicaragua in 1986 when the political conflict there was at its height. Everywhere, the traveller is aware of the traces of American neo-imperialism, sympathizing – though not uncritically – with the Sandinistas. Like Shiva Naipaul, Rushdie travels with a different sensitivity than the average Western traveller – from the Indian subcontinent, he is accustomed to Third World problems: 'In my first hours in the city streets [of Managua], I saw a number of sights that were familiar to eyes trained in India and Pakistan' (p. 17). It is this special perspective which makes him particularly alert to US American imperialism in Central America:

> When the Reagan administration began its war against Nicaragua, I recognized a deeper affinity with that small country in a continent ... upon which I had never set foot. I grew daily more interested in its affairs, because, after all, I was myself the child of a successful revolt against a great power, my consciousness the product of the Indian revolution. It was perhaps also true that those of us who did not have our origins in the countries of the mighty West, or North, had something in common – not, certainly, anything as simplistic as a unified 'third world' outlook, but at least some knowledge of what weakness was like, some awareness of the view from underneath, and of how it felt to be there, on the bottom, looking up at the descending heel.   (p. 12)

Neo-imperialism is usually associated, as in this example, with the United States. However, postcolonial travellers are also sensitive to neocolonial tendencies within the postcolonial world itself. When Ronald Wright travelled to Australia, for example, he perceived the country as an economic power which means the same to the South Pacific as the United States do to America: 'Australia is the United States of the South Pacific: an economic powerhouse; a neo-colonial presence. The tiny island countries hear her breathing over the horizon: Australian accents on the airwaves, Australian electrical sockets, fragments of dialect, and great trading firms ... with a branch everywhere you go' (*Home and Away*, p. 183).

A phenomenon frequently associated with First World neo-imperialism is tourism, on which many former colonies now depend economically. As has been shown in the preceding chapter (see pp. 130–2), travel writers in general tend to be critical of mass tourism. Many postcolonial travel writers, however, are outspokenly political in their critique of tourism, especially where tourism in developing countries is concerned. This is obvious as early as in V. S. Naipaul's *The Middle Passage*, where the Caribbean societies themselves, however, are also attacked for succumbing to the lures of tourism: 'Every poor country accepts tourism as an unavoidable degradation. None has gone as far as some of these West Indian islands, which, in the name of tourism, are selling themselves into a new slavery' (p. 210). To Pico Iyer, in *Video Nights in Kathmandu* (1988), tourists are 'the great foot soldiers of the new invasion; . . . the terrorists of cultural expansionism, what Sartre once called "the cool invaders". . . . anyone with a credit card could become a lay colonialist' (p. 13).

Pico Iyer belongs to a younger generation of postcolonial travellers who were born in the decades following the Second World War. Born of Indian parents in England, Iyer grew up in Britain and California and currently lives in California and Japan. As in his comments on tourism, Iyer has much in common with the older generation of postcolonial travel writers. However, as he is 'a British subject, and American resident and an Indian citizen' (p. 34), his perspective is also internationalized, transcultural, nomadic and distinctly deracinated. This kind of perspective – shared with other travel writers of the postmodern age (see Chapter 7, p. 144) – emerges in much recent writing by travellers with a postcolonial background. In a critical article, Revathi Krishnaswamy (1995) identifies – with faultfinding overtones – a new type of postcolonial writer who has become deterritorialized:

A new type of 'Third World' intellectual, cross-pollinated by postmodernism and postcolonialism, has arrived: a migrant who, having dispensed with territorial affiliations, travels unencumbered through the cultures of the world bearing only the burden of a unique yet representative sensibility that refracts the fragmented and contingent condition of both postmodernity and postcoloniality. Journeying from the 'peripheries' to the metropolitan 'centre', this itinerant intellectual becomes an international figure who at once feels at home nowhere and everywhere. No longer disempowered by cultural schizophrenia or confined within collectivities such as race, class, or nation, the nomadic postcolonial intellectual is said to 'write back' to the empire in the name of all displaced and dispossessed peoples, denouncing both colonialism and nationalism as equally coercive constructs. (p. 125)[12]

Pico Iyer is a traveller of the global village who can make his home(s) both in the West and in the East and who travels in many roles – including that of the tourist: 'In one country I found myself an American journalist, in another a former British schoolboy, in yet another a homecoming Indian relative and in a fourth a plain tourist' (p. 36). When he travelled Asia in 1985, Iyer's primary intent therefore was not to reterritorialize himself, as other postcolonial writers, also of his own generation, still attempt to do (see next section). Rather, Iyer wished to explore the spread of Western (pop-)culture in the East: 'I wanted to see what kind of resistance had been put up against the Coca-Colonizing forces and what kind of counter-strategies were planned' (p. 11). In the course of his travels, however, Iyer arrived at a more placatory, syncretic view of the cultural processes observed: 'On a grand collective level, the encounters between East and West might well be interpreted as a battle; but on the human level, the meeting more closely resembled a mating dance' (p. 30). *Video Nights in Kathmandu* accordingly ends with observations on how the East is increasingly leaving its impact on the West:

> En route from Bombay to L.A., I happened to stop off for three days in London. There I found West Indian sitcoms crowding the airwaves and *samosas* filling the sandwich bars. Culturally, the talk of the town was a new movie written by a twenty-nine-year-old Pakistani, *My Beautiful Laundrette*. . . .
> Thus the colonials were effectively staging their own take-over, erecting tandoori palaces in their former rulers' home, introducing their own pungent terms into the mainstream, even seizing control of much of the nation's culture. . . . The empire had struck back.
>
> (pp. 410–11)

Another writer of Iyer's generation, Vikram Seth, displays a similarly globalized perspective. Seth was born in Calcutta, studied in Britain and in the United States, and returned to live in India in 1987. *From Heaven Lake* (1983) is the account of his travels from China, where he was spending a two-year turn of studies, to Tibet and across the border to Nepal and India. Like Iyer, Seth is a traveller of an itinerant age. When he ends the first part of his journey, together with his international fellow students from Nanjing university, the farewell party, celebrated with Californian red wine bought in a Friendship store, makes him reflect on his inherent restlessness in a Chatwinesque mood: 'I recall drinking sherry in California and dreaming of my earlier student days in England, where I ate *dalmoth* and dreamed of Delhi. What is the purpose, I wonder, of all this restlessness? I sometimes seem to myself to wander around the world merely accumulating material for future nostalgia' (p. 35). To Seth, food and drink are exemplary symbols of a world turned multi- or transcultural. To celebrate his safe arrival in Nepal after an exhausting stay in isolated Tibet, he indulges in the global fast-food that Kathmandu, an icon of cultural syncretism, has to offer – next to other attractions from East and West:

> Kathmandu is vivid, mercenary, religious . . .; shops selling Western cosmetics, film rolls and chocolate; or copper utensils and Nepalese antiques. Film songs blare out from the radios, car horns sound, bicycle bells ring . . . I indulge myself mindlessly: buy a bar of Tobler marzipan, a corn-on-the-cob . . .; a couple of love story comics, and even a *Reader's Digest*. All this I wash down with Coca Cola and a nauseating orange drink, and feel much the better for it.   (p. 175)

Tahir Shah, born in the 1960s into an Afghan family but now based in Britain, is also a cosmopolitan traveller; characteristically, one of his travel books, *Beyond the Devil's Teeth* (1995), depicts a journey grown out of a truly intercontinental interest: the question of whether connections still exist between the regions that once formed the ancient supercontinent of Gondwanaland – India and Pakistan, Africa and South America. The mobility of the postmodern traveller appears almost persiflated when Shah, globe-jetting, is once chased around half the world within a few hours:

> The journey from the borderlands of Pakistan's north-west frontier, to West Africa, had been anything but simple. A travel agent in one of Peshawar's darker backstreets had sold me a cut-price ticket. Although somehow the fare was extremely convenient, the route was not. Having diced with death by taking the 'Flying Bus' from Peshawar to Islamabad, I first flew to Damascus. From there, I jetted on to Aden in Yemen, before taking an evening cargo flight to Moscow – then I was hustled on board an indirect flight to Paris. And, it was from there – as my internal clock was spinning out of control – that I ventured on by air to Dakar.   (pp. 139–40)

An internationalized view, which emphasizes transculturality, cultural hybridity and syncretism, is certainly gaining ground in the postcolonial travelogue. At the same time, however, a great number of texts are still preoccupied with questions of origin, belonging, identity, nationality, etc., which have long been prime themes of postcolonial writing. The urge to find one's 'roots' may even arise in postcolonial travellers who otherwise appear quite comfortable with a cosmopolitan identity. Ferdinand Dennis, for example, born in Jamaica and living in London, felt, when travelling Africa, that he would like to determine the exact origin of his African forebears. As he writes in *Back to Africa* (1992):

> The girl's words echoed in my exhausted mind: 'I thought you were a Yoruba. You look so much like a Yoruba.'
>
> Not for the first time I wondered which of the African tribes I originated from. Who were my gods? What were my myths? ...
>
> It was a discomforting end to what had been an enjoyable night of music and laughter. ... Before that Lagos morning, I regarded Africans or Europeans who were aggressively assertive in their tribalism or nationalism with the quiet disdain of a person who, lacking such emotional ties, believed himself to be a superior being, tomorrow's man. But that morning made me aware that I have in the past hungered for an identity more concrete than 'world citizen', that I wear a mask which sometimes slips. Perhaps if I had arrived at this rootlessness, this lack of belonging, by a less violent route than the middle passage, the slave plantations of the Caribbean and migration as a child, I would never hunger for roots, which I know, in my composed moments, are irrevocably lost. (p. 170)

To many postcolonial travellers, then, the question of defining one's home still seems to be more urgent than for other travellers, and the search for a home may even be their primary motive for travel.

Postcolonial home touring

As shown in Chapter 4, domestic travel with the purpose of discovering a country of one's own is a tradition in Britain that dates back to the sixteenth century. The British settled colonies, too, have an early tradition of 'interior' travel, which overlaps with exploration as long as there is still much left to discover in the respective regions. At first, much settlers' writing about their colony was directed at readers back in the country from which they or their parents had emigrated. Increasingly, however, domestic travel and travelogues became a means of familiarizing the colonials themselves with their new country – even long after decolonization had set in. As late as 1937, the Australian journalist Ernestine Hill published *The Great Australian Loneliness* to make her countrymen familiar with a country 'still a stranger to the world and to its own people' (p. 8). At about the same time, Stephen Leacock felt that the Canadian West was still an area to be discovered. Throughout the twentieth century, in fact, Anglo-Canadian travelogues impart their writers' frustration that a country as vast as Canada is difficult to know. Bruce Hutchison's *Canada: Tomorrow's Giant* (1957) was intended to make Canadian readers acquainted with a country which the author believed would soon become a world power: 'Fifteen years ago I wrote a book about Canada and called it *The Unknown Country*. Today that country is still largely unknown to its natives and almost totally unknown to the world in which it is destined to be a leading power not long hence' (preface). A decade later, when the issue of a national identity was vehemently discussed in Canada, Edward McCourt attempted to evoke a sense of unity by depicting a journey along the road that had recently been built to connect the country. As he wrote in *The Road Across Canada* (1965), '[i]t is still the hope of all Canadians to whom national unity is a passionately desired end that a trans-Canada highway should draw closer together all parts of the nation and help us, if not to love, at least to understand one another' (p. 196). In the 1980s and 1990s, home touring gained new vigour in Canada thanks to an identity debate rekindled, among other factors, by Quebec separatism. Now the tone of the travelogues becomes considerably more doubtful concerning the possibility of a unified national identity. Thus Kildare Dobbs's *Ribbon of Highway: By Bus Along the Trans-Canada* (1992), sets in with a distinctly pessimistic note:

> In the summer of 1991, ... I began to feel unbearably anxious about the state of Canada, the country I had chosen as my own and in which I had invested nearly forty years of my life. ... And now the country I believed I had made my own appeared to be disintegrating for lack of imagination.   (p. 7)[13]

We have seen in relation to Jonathan Raban's *Coasting* (p. 135) that a Briton's sense of home may also be insecure in a postmodern age of uncertain (national) identities. To many postcolonial travel writers, however, the issue of belonging is still a matter of personal concern, and insecurities about this sense of belonging are not easily discarded in the name of postmodernism or cosmopolitanism. The Canadian travelogues of the 1980s and 1990s are certainly doubtful about the precise nature of Canadianness. Nevertheless, they still convey the idea that a clear Canadian identity would be desirable, and they leave their readers with the impression that the respective travellers identify Canada as home.[14]

For yet another kind of postcolonial traveller, however, the question of belonging and of conducting 'home' tours is extremely complicated owing to the complexity of the postcolonial world. The processes of journeying which have brought this world into being have caused a situation in which many individuals have more than one homeland to travel. Home may be a place where a person no longer lives – for reasons of expatriation, exile or migration – and the return journey is therefore an important postcolonial variety of the home tour. In *Down Home: Revisiting Tasmania* (1988), Peter Conrad, who now lives in London, acknowledges a lasting allegiance to his earlier home: 'Tasmania had set the terms of my life. The home you cannot return to you carry off with you: it lies down there at the bottom of the world, and of the sleeping, imagining mind' (p. 232).

Immediately following the Second World War, Laurens van der Post was the best-known travel writer from a Commonwealth country other than Britain. Born in South Africa of a Dutch father still mentally rooted in Europe and feeling 'exiled' in Africa, van der Post was raised between cultures: the Dutch of his father, the Euro-African of his English settler mother, but also Black Africa, by which he was fascinated even as a young child. After his service in the war, van der Post returned in 1949 to an Africa from which he had been absent for many years. The first of his travelogues about South and Central Africa, *Venture to the Interior*, appeared in 1957. The venture depicted here, like van der Post's travels in general, was devoted not only to geographical exploration (in the service of the British government), but also to his personal quest for his emotional home. He attempted to relocalize himself, or at least part of himself, in Africa, which was associated with the 'unconscious, female, feminine, mother', while Europe was linked with the 'conscious, male, masculine, father' (p. 10). At the end of his journey, van der Post felt reconciled to the African side of his identity. Yet he decided to mentally take this maternal home away with him to England, which he intended to make his country of residence: 'I felt that I was not leaving [Africa], but taking it with me. I might even be able to give some of it to Europe, to the Britain that had given me so much' (p. 238).

For political reasons, Africa continues to be a region with which return journeys are frequently associated. Doris Lessing, who spent the greater part of her childhood in Rhodesia, today Zimbabwe, left her country to live in London in 1949. In 1956, when still a member of the Communist Party, she first returned to Rhodesia to write a series of articles which were published in book form under the title *Going Home* (1957). Decades later, Lessing wrote *African Laughter*, the account of several journeys back to Zimbabwe since 1982, after her long years of exile. This exile was first voluntary (because she wanted to live in London rather than provincial Rhodesia), but later enforced because Lessing was considered a Prohibited Immigrant:

> I was already a Prohibited Immigrant in 1956 but did not know it. It never crossed my mind I could be: the impossibility was a psychological fact, nothing to do with daylight realities. You cannot be forbidden the land you grew up in, so says the web of sensations, memories, experience, that binds you to that landscape. (p. 11)

Lessing's travels back to the land she grew up in were strongly shaped by a then/now mode of perception – not only regarding her personal memories, but also, in a broader political perspective, regarding the country itself: the relics of colonial Rhodesia, and the development of independent Zimbabwe. At the end of the last visit reported in her book, Lessing felt that it was 'time to go home, from home' (p. 426); she had re(dis)covered the home territory of her youth, but she also had another home to return to.

The problem of identifying with an earlier homeland that has become decidedly unhomelike characterizes the return travels of South African exiles, whose accounts usually strike a determined and often a passionate political note. Christopher Hope, in *White Boy Running* (1988), reports a trip back to South Africa which he conducted at a moment chosen for its particular political significance – the election of 1987:

> Why come for an election? Why come at all? Because the place is a fever, an infection, a lingering childhood disease I simply cannot get over. Perhaps part of it is due to the fact that I am of that generation which knew no other way of life but that of the crusading segregation which came to be called apartheid. My generation are the children of apartheid. (p. 16)

The journalist Rian Malan stems from an Afrikaner family that has, for centuries, played a dominant role in the history of apartheid. *My Traitor's Heart* (1990) is both a travel book and an exploration of Malan's feelings of guilt and responsibility for his family's political sins. Frustrated with apartheid and his inability to oppose it effectively, Malan, the leftist 'renegade', went to live in the United States for a couple of years. He then decided to return and work against apartheid from within a home country he could not identify with but could equally not live without: 'I was going home to be a crime reporter again, to seek a resolution of the paradox of my South African life in tales of the way we killed one another' (p. 103). A sense of paradox also pervades Breyten Breytenbach's *Return to Paradise* (1993), the account of his journey in 1991 back from his French exile to a South Africa in which he had been imprisoned for several years because of his resistance to apartheid but which, in the liberal mood of the early 1990s, awarded the former 'terrorist' with a literary prize.[15] During his years of expatriation, South Africa has become foreign to Breytenbach: 'Why did I come back? ... Why will I not return to stay? Too late now. Foreigner here. ... No roots. Attachment too painful. Deathwish' (p. 162). Even this estrangement from a former home, however, raises the issue of belonging: 'It's true, I think of myself as a cosmopolitan. Now I'm scratching for my Afrikaner roots again' (p. 80).

While Breytenbach ultimately rejects the country of his birth, other postcolonials travel with the explicit motive to regain a former home. From immigrant countries such as Canada, for instance, travellers often return to the country of their origin. In *Days and Nights in Calcutta* (1977), a travel book co-written by Bharati Mukherjee and Clark Blaise, the perspective of the Indian returning home stands out clearly in comparison with the view of her Euro-Canadian husband, who visits India not as a homeland but as an exotic country. To Mukherjee, by contrast, India is the country she grew up in and where she hopes that she can recover the self-assurance which she has lost as an immigrant in Canada:

> I knew the rules in India (I hoped I still remembered them); there, I felt, it would be possible to control my destiny better. In Canada I was helpless and self-absorbed. ... I was going because I had discovered that while changing citizenship is easy, swapping cultures is not. ... In Canada I am both too visible and too invisible. (pp. 168–9)

At the end of Mukherjee's stay in her old world, however, this expectation has not been fulfilled; migration has estranged her from an earlier home without giving her a new one: 'The India that I had carried as a talisman against icy Canada had not survived my accidental testings' (p. 285).

Mukherjee travelled back as a member of a visible minority who feels marginalized in Canadian society. Christopher Ondaatje, by contrast, went back to his native Sri Lanka as an established Toronto businessman. Nevertheless, his *The Man-Eater of Punanai* (1992) also conveys the importance which his homeland still holds for him even after four decades' absence. To Ondaatje, Sri Lanka is the country of his personal history, especially the relationship to his father, and travelling through space thus becomes 'an emotional journey' (p. 12) into submerged feelings and the sources that have shaped his personality. Unlike Mukherjee, Ondaatje does not travel back to compensate for a lack he feels in his new home country, but because rediscovering his roots will enrich his life in Canada: 'I wanted to realize the past again, capture it, and bring it back to my family and my life in Canada' (ibid.).

Mukherjee and Ondaatje are first-generation migrants who travel back to countries in which they themselves have actually lived. For other travellers with 'hyphenated' identities, countries to which they 'return' are only ancestral homes, places of which they have no lived experience or personal remembrance. Their connection with the old homeland is founded merely on the collective memory of their immigrant community – on folklore and legend. For such return travellers, 'memory' and the actuality of travel can be hard to reconcile. Myrna Kostash, for example, is a Canadian with Ukrainian forebears, who considers this extraction an important source of her identity, as she writes in *Bloodlines* (1993): 'I explain that I am Ukrainian-Canadian and that the hyphen is essential – the juncture of sources' (p. 152). *Bloodlines* is the account of Kostash's trips, in the 1980s, into Ukraine and other parts of the former Eastern bloc. Since cold-war politics made it impossible to maintain close family ties, Kostash did not see the country from which her grandmother had emigrated until she was an adult. To the woman grown up in multi-cultural Canada, Ukraine was a kind of home through customs and storytelling only: 'The only story that had mattered in my childhood was the story of the arrival of my Ukrainian grandparents in Canada: everything that preceded it was a folktale, and everything that happened in Galicia after *they* had abandoned the place was hearsay' (p. 121). Kostash's return journey was therefore a paradoxical experience: 'How do you go back to where you've never been?' (p. 162). She was even afraid of this journey because the real-life experience could have disturbed her image of the ancestors' home. In a similar manner, the clash between a home 'remembered' and the country actually visited is addressed in Thomas Keneally's *Now and in Time to Be* (1991). When the Australian novelist travelled to Ireland, he returned to a country from which his grandparents had emigrated and which he knew through stories and customs preserved in the antipodes. Accordingly, his trip led him through a country both familiar and foreign: 'and we see a place like Ballycotton, and recognise it straight away as a never but always known place' (p. 4).

Travelling 'home' seems nowhere to be more intricate than for people with a Caribbean background now living in Britain. Their cultural background is built not only on the historical middle passage from Africa to the New World, but also the more recent, postwar migration from the Caribbean to Britain. Amryl Johnson, in *Sequins for a Ragged Hem* (1988), depicts her journey back from Britain to her native Trinidad and other islands in the West Indies. On this visit, she first felt deeply estranged and did not even – for a brief moment – recognize her own mother: 'A woman strangely familiar. A stranger yet not a stranger. Familiar. Totally' (p. 11). A homecomer and yet a stranger who had to (re)discover the cultures of the West Indies, Johnson at times even travelled as a tourist or was mistaken for one. Gradually, however, she overcame her foreignness and was reinitiated into her region of origin: 'Before long I would be baptised in the waters of six islands' (p. 33).

Another type of return journey encountered among Afro-Caribbean writers is the journey back to African roots, that is the kind of travel which the success of Alex Haley's *Roots* (1976) popularized for African Americans. In 1990, Ferdinand Dennis, whose account of a home tour through Britain was considered above (p. 162), also undertook a journey to his ancestral 'home' of Africa, originally for a BBC radio series. *Back to Africa* pays particular attention to those regions of the continent which are of historical importance as places of remigration for African slaves from the West Indies and the United States, namely Sierra Leone and Liberia. Dennis also goes on a quest for his own African heritage, but, as has already been shown above (p. 170), there is no specific region to which he might trace his African identity – the history of transportation and diaspora endured by his people has made it impossible to locate the exact place from where his ancestors were deracinated. Although Dennis feels a certain affinity with Africa, his journey therefore concludes with his insight that there is no real possibility of his return: 'I began to realise then that I had no home to which I could return, no place to which I belonged. . . . I felt relieved that I would soon be leaving this Africa which so often and with such intensity made me feel like an orphan of history' (p. 189).

The East Indian population in the Caribbean has not experienced the collective trauma of the middle passage and slavery, although it also lives in a diaspora. The most famous case of confusions about belonging in a postcolonial traveller is V.S. Naipaul, who, meanwhile, seems to have solved his enigma of arrival and found his home in England. As early as 1962, in *The Middle Passage*, Naipaul wrote about the Caribbean from the Eurocentric and 'anglicized' perspective for which he has been under severe attack ever since. However, his difficulties in identifying the Carribean as a homeland are due not only to his affiliation with England, but also because, in his native Trinidad, he was the member of a minority within an Afro-Caribbean majority.[16] To Naipaul in the early 1960s, the British West Indies had failed to develop when British rule slackened: 'For nothing was created in the British West Indies, no civilization as in Spanish America, no great revolution as in Haiti or the American colonies' (p. 27). Above all, the islands did not succeed in creating an identity of their own because of their ethnic composition:

We were of various races, religions, sets and cliques; and we had somehow found ourselves on the same small island. Nothing bound us together except this common residence. There was no nationalist feeling; there could be none. . . . indeed, it was only our Britishness, our belonging to the British Empire, which gave us any identity. (p. 45)

The Middle Passage conveys the image of a traveller who is clearly distanced from his native country. About two decades later, Naipaul's *Finding the Centre* (1984) suggests another attitude. Naipaul now acknowledges that his relationship to the Caribbean has been important for his personal development and his development as a writer: 'To become a writer, that noble thing, I had thought it necessary to leave. Actually to write, it was necessary to go back. It was the beginning of self-knowledge' (p. 40). But going 'back', to Naipaul, also entails 'returning' to India, which proves to be just as difficult as his return to the Caribbean. Coming to terms with this ancestral country took Naipaul many years and several trips. He has been attacked for his unsympathetic portrayal of India in his first book about this region, *An Area of Darkness* (1964). The country of his forebears is here presented as paralysed by its colonial history – not only British rule but also the Muslim conquest that happened centuries earlier. Post-independence India is thus incapable of coping with the challenge of a new age and continues to be parasitic on other cultures. The title of Naipaul's second travel book of the region indicates that Naipaul still sees India as a country severely handicapped by its colonial past: *India: A Wounded Civilization* (1977). This account, however, already betrays a higher degree of understanding, although India, to Naipaul, is still 'a difficult country. It isn't my home and cannot be my home; and yet I cannot reject it or be indifferent to it' (p. 8).

It seems appropriate to end this chapter with these remarks on V. S. Naipaul, who still takes first place as the most prominent – and also the most controversial – postcolonial travel writer. Typically, Naipaul's travel books express the urgent concern with belonging which induces many postcolonials to travel and which is arguably one of the most salient characteristics of postcolonial travel writing. As we have seen, this writing is still firmly rooted in traditions of travel and travel writing which have evolved in Europe – specifically England – over the last five centuries. However, even if travel writers from Britain's former colonies have, on the whole, not subverted the traditional generic patterns, they have certainly added a range of 'other' sensitivities, perspectives and attitudes which enrich the genre and make a significant contribution to keeping it alive.

Conclusion

The same things every day slowly kill us off. To crave anew, the
pleasure of travel helps us to do this.

(Ernst Bloch, 1986, p. 370)

The present volume has achieved one of its aims if it has managed to
awaken an enthusiasm not only for travel, but also for accounts of it.
With its limited scope, the book was restricted to introducing and
illustrating English travel writing in only some of its most important
forms. The great variety in which this writing manifests itself can, in
part, be attributed to the numerous kinds of journey that have formed
its theme and content matter over the centuries: the pilgrimage,
mercantile travel, exploration, the Grand Tour, the home tour, the
tourist trip, travel to escape from civilization, journeys into the self or
journeys for the sake of writing – to name only a few.

Just as the modes of travel have changed throughout the centuries,
so the reporting about it displays a rich history, as we have seen in the
chronological chapters. Even within the same period, travelogues are
composed with very different proportions of narrative, descriptive and
expository modes of presentation. Their emphasis on the travelling
subject or the object of travel is just as varied as is their intention to
instruct and/or entertain. A writer's preference for certain textual
strategies depends not only on their suitability for rendering a particular travel experience, but is also determined by the general cultural
and aesthetic discourses in which the respective text participates.

Although the travel account has been described as a hybrid genre,
owing to its particular flexibility and openness to other forms of text,
it has developed a characteristic set of features which allow us to
consider it as a distinct class of writing. Thus a travel account always

179

has a narrative core; it narrates an authentic journey conducted by the autobiographical subject of the text. As a re-creation of this journey, the travelogue has an element of fictionality despite the fact that it normally claims to be and is read as a 'true' account. As early as the eighteenth century, metatextual comment in accounts themselves as well as treatises on travel writing have testified to a certain generic consciousness and tradition, which also shows itself in the high degree of intertextuality that characterizes the postmodern travelogue in particular. It is precisely the pronounced literariness of the latter which suggests that travel writing deserves the attention of literary studies as much as that of geography, history or the currently popular discipline of cultural studies. In the scope of the present volume, it has not been possible to do full justice to the research conducted on travel and travel writing to date. Alongside cited materials, the bibliography thus includes a selection of further material useful to a more in-depth study of the English travelogue.

As Chapter 8 has suggested, the evolving branch of postcolonial travel writing should be a particularly interesting area for further research as far as the English-speaking world is concerned. However, even if this relatively new line of travel writing is an especially vital one, other lines are by no means dead. As we have seen, feminism and postmodernism have also contributed to a significant rejuvenation of the genre, and even traditional forms of travel writing continue and remain popular. Thanks to the genre's adaptability, new facets of travel writing are continually being developed. To come back to our opening quotation: 'The literature of travel is gigantic; it has a thousand forms and faces.'

Notes

Introduction

1. In this book, the terms 'travel account', 'travelogue' and 'travel writing' will generally be used as synonyms, although, in a narrower understanding, 'travelogue' is sometimes reserved for accounts that are composed retrospectively, that is after a journey has been completed – in contrast to accounts in the form of journals, diaries or letters which are normally written (or at least drafted) while a journey is still in progress.

2. An important line of non-European travel writing is that of the great Muslim travellers of the Middle Ages, the foremost being Ibn Battuta (1304–77). East Asia also has ancient traditions of travel and travel writing which, in China, date back to the fourth century; for an anthology with texts by Chinese travellers see Mirsky (1964). A study of more recent accounts of travel in China by the Japanese is Fogel (1996).

3. For all extracts from travel accounts, page numbers refer to the editions listed in the bibliography.

4. For geographers, historians and anthropologists, by contrast, travelogues have long represented a recognized source material. See, for example, the bibliography listed by Cole (1981). The first issue of a specialized, multi-disciplinary journal, *Studies in Travel Writing*, appeared in 1997.

5. Works of English literature inspired by travel writing range from Thomas More's *Utopia* and Shakespeare's *The Tempest*, through Daniel Defoe's *Robinson Crusoe*, to S.T. Coleridge's 'Kubla Khan' and 'The Rime of the Ancient Mariner'. On the influence of travel writing on particular areas of English literature, see the monographs of Lowes (1927), Cawley (1951, 1966, 1967), Coe (1979) and Maquerlot and Willems (1996). For studies that consider travelogues in the broader context of travel literature, see Batten (1978) and Adams (1983), as well as the German monograph by Possin (1972).

Chapter 1 Charting the genre

1. See Kohl (1990 and 1993) and Kowalewski (1992, p. 7).

2. On the 'plotting' of exploration accounts, see also MacLulich (1979).

3. Thus the condemnation of travel writing as a lie, which is as old as this literary form itself (see Adams, 1962), is supported at least in part by the element of fictionality inherent in the genre itself. For a more in-depth discussion of 'travel fact' and 'travel fiction' see also the volume edited by von Martels (1994).

4. See also John Tallmadge, in the quotation above (p. 9), on Darwin's *Voyage of the Beagle*.

5. A more recent example of parallel reporting is provided by Jonathan Raban's *Coasting* (1986) and Paul Theroux's *Kingdom By the Sea* (1983).

Raban sailed around his native Britain at around the same time as the American, Paul Theroux, explored England by land. Their paths crossed in Brighton, but when Raban later read the Brighton episode in Theroux's *Kingdom*, he found that '[t]here wasn't a single start of recognition for me in his two pages: what he described was not at all what I remembered. But then memory, as Paul had demonstrated with his forearm lying flat on the table at Wheeler's, is a great maker of fictions' (*Coasting*, p. 199).

6. See also Possin (1972, p. 18) and Segeberg (1983, pp. 20–1) on subject orientation as a prime criterion to assess the literariness of travel writing.

7. See the introduction in the cited edition, p. 3.

8. For an inventory of older texts, see the long list in *The Cambridge Bibliography of English Literature*, and, for the twentieth century, the extensive bibliography in Kowalewski (1992).

Chapter 2   Paths to the real world

1. Said's groundbreaking study of 'orientalism' (1978) significantly refers to many classics of European travel writing. Constructions of the Orient in English travelogues are investigated from a double perspective of English and Oriental studies in a German volume edited by Christoph Bode (1997). On the role of travel writing in constructing the idea of the South Seas see Rennie (1995).

2. Despite its special relevance to the travelogue, it is impossible here to summarize the extensive and multi-disciplinary debate surrounding the notion of 'otherness'. A selection of relevant titles is included in the bibliography; see, in particular, Said (1978), Todorov (1984), Hartog (1988), Kristeva (1991), Clifford (1992), the German-language study by Bitterli (1991), as well as Bitterli (1989).

3. For a survey of the travel and travel writing of antiquity see Casson (1974). Adams (1983, pp. 38–80) provides a concise overview of travel writing up to 1800.

4. Sollius' *Collectanea rerum memorabilium* were inspired by Pliny.

5. For a more detailed discussion of medieval travel and travel writing see the selection of titles listed in the bibliography.

6. Even today, there remain over 250 manuscripts in several languages; moreover, *Mandeville's Travels* was one of the first texts to be printed. The cited edition is based on three early English versions which are closest to the original text.

7. On the sources of *Mandeville's Travels* see the detailed study by Bennett (1954).

8. See also Howard (1980, pp. 27–30), who demonstrates this curiosity for the itinerary of William of Boldensele.

9. However, reference to them is sometimes swiftly followed by a remark that the traveller did not actually see the fabulous creatures *himself*, as, for example, in William of Rubruck's account of his journey to the realm of the Great Khan between 1253 and 1255. This account became so popular that, as late as the seventeenth century, it was included in Samuel Purchas's extensive travel compendium, *Hakluytus Posthumus*. As far as the

monstrous races are concerned, William insists that he has never seen any, and indeed doubts their existence:

> Towards the north there are numerous other tribes besides who are not well off and who spread as far as they can, given the cold: . . . I enquired about the monsters or human freaks who are described by Isidore and Solinus, but was told that such things had never been sighted, which makes us very much doubt whether [the story] is true.
>
> (p. 201)

10. By contrast, see the precise distances given for the route from Bethlehem to Jerusalem, p. 27 above.
11. As is well known, Columbus, after his first voyage across the Atlantic, still believed that he had landed in the Old World, near Japan, that is Marco Polo's Cipangu. He thus encountered America – at least to some extent – with a mind-set shaped by both the classical and the medieval tradition about the fabulous East and the old conception of earthly paradise. '[T]he result of all these mixtures is a Caribbean that belongs as much to the Other World of medieval geographic fantasy as it does to the map Columbus helped realize' (Campbell, 1988, p. 10).
12. Mary C. Fuller (1995) points out the crucial role which written records of the Elizabethan and Jacobean voyages to the New World played in the colonial and commercial enterprises of the time: 'The imperative for travelers to write promised both to stimulate observation and to organize it. If sailors had always had to be observant, the requirements of the new overseas trading companies enforced attention in new directions and at a new level of intensity' (p. 7).
13. Penrose (1952) is still a valuable source on European voyages of discovery between 1420 and 1620.
14. See the German study by Böhme (1904) for a detailed description of the most important of these compilations.
15. On the cabinet of curiosities see Impey and MacGregor (1985).
16. See, for example, Greenblatt (1991, pp. 111, 121–2) on the kidnapping and displaying of Native Americans in Europe.
17. These texts on the so-called Virginia Colonies are cited from the edition by A.L. Rowse which is listed in the bibliography. Reference will be made to the following accounts: Edward Hayes, 'Sir Humphrey Gilbert's Newfoundland Voyage, 1583', Silvester Wyet, 'The Newfoundland Voyage of the *Grace*, 1594', Philip Amadas and Arthur Barlow, 'The First Virginia Voyage, 1584', Ralph Lane, 'The First Virginia Colony, 1585–6', as well as Thomas Hariot, 'Brief and True Report of the New Found Land of Virginia'. One of the most famous Elizabethan explorer accounts, Sir Walter Raleigh's *The Discovery of the Large, Rich, and Beautiful Empire of Guiana* (1596), is discussed extensively by Campbell (1988). Charles Nicholl's *The Creature in the Map* (1995) is a fascinating piece of scholarship-cum-travelogue which retraces Raleigh's expedition in quest of El Dorado and its contemporary background, including alchemy.
18. It is not possible here to discuss the representation of indigenous populations in the Early Modern texts with the differentiation that it deserves.

For a more detailed discussion see, for example, Bitterli (1989 and 1991) and Greenblatt (1991).

19. See also Kalb (1983): 'Generally speaking, English travel literature can be regarded as a practical complement to the empirical line in the history of ideas in England. Travel offered an ideal field for the application of empirical thinking in the investigation of the real world . . .' (p. 409; my translation).

20. Frantz (1934) includes the travel instructions of the Royal Society. The cited edition of Darwin's *Voyage of the Beagle* quotes the 'Admiralty Instructions for the *Beagle* Voyage' (pp. 378–99).

21. Stafford provides an extensive study of the illustrated accounts of scentific travels. See also the richly illustrated volume by Jacobs (1995), who emphasizes the artists' scientific mission: 'they were employed to make an objective record of the peoples, landscapes, animals, flora and fauna of the countries they visited or explored' (p. 9).

Chapter 3 Paths to the self

1. The term 'Grand Tour' does not, however, appear until the seventeenth century: 'In 1670, Richard Lassels uses the term "Grand Tour" for the first time in an English book for travellers: "The Grand Tour of France and the Giro of Italy"' (Howard, 1914, p. 145). Among the numerous publications on the Grand Tour, Hibbert's richly illustrated volume (1987) is particularly useful; further publications are listed in the bibliography.

2. See James Boswell, *Life of Johnson* (1791), p. 742.

3. See Masello (1985) on Thomas Hoby's *A Booke of the Travaile and Lief [sic] of Me Thomas Hoby, with Diverse Thinges Woorth the Notinge, 1547–1564*, for an analysis of a typical Grand Tour with these aims in mind. Howard (1914), Stoye (1952) and Bates (1987) provide other informative studies on the early Grand Tour and its objectives.

4. Black (1985) devotes an entire chapter to the distractions of 'Love, Sex, Gambling and Drinking' for the eighteenth-century tourist. Chloe Chard (1989) considers the frequent criticism in tour accounts of the travelled countries as a psychological strategy to come to terms with their tempting otherness:

> Extremes of sensuality and extremes of religious devotion, are usually defined as the two forms of excessiveness most often encountered by the traveller in Italy: lust and 'superstition' are classified as equivalent, interchangeable, and equally culpable outlets for the inclination towards immoderacy which travellers observe in the inhabitants of the various Italian cities, or of Italy as a whole. (pp. 7–8)

5. See also Richard Hurd's 'Dialogues on the Uses of Foreign Travel: Between Lord Shaftesbury and Mr. Locke' (1763) for an extensive treatment of the benefits and dangers of eighteenth-century travel. The text presents an imaginary dialogue in which Shaftesbury supports travel for education against Locke's protestations.

6. An extensive list of apodemic writing appears in Howard (1914, pp. 205–9). For secondary materials on this kind of writing see, in particular, the studies of Justin Stagl listed in the bibliography.
7. Cited after Hibbert (1987, p. 241), who also gives many similar examples (pp. 235–42).
8. Yorick is particularly careful to distinguish himself from travel writers who only see the negative in a foreign country. The traveller *Smelfungus*, who can do nothing but complain, is probably a caricature of Smollett.
9. See also Kalb (1981, p. 65). Kalb devotes particular attention to Sterne's moral concern, a concern which also characterizes many other accounts of the eighteenth century.
10. This strategy of separating the subject-orientated and the object-orientated parts of a travelogue is also evident in other eighteenth-century writers: 'Dividing *Travels in France* in this manner, Young did not invent, despite what he implies, a new way of writing travel books. James Boswell had composed his *Account of Corsica* in 1768 using the same format but reversing the order so that his autobiographical section came last' (Batten, 1978, p. 34). It was precisely this autobiographical section, the travel account in the strict sense, which drew Dr Johnson's praise: '"Your history was copied from books; your journal rose out of your own experience and observation. You express images which operated strongly upon yourself, and you have impressed them with great force upon your readers"' (ibid.).
11. See, for a similar example, the 'Advertisement' to Mary Wollstonecraft's *Letters Written during a Short Residence in Sweden, Norway, and Denmark*:

> In writing these desultory letters, I found I could not avoid being continually the first person – 'the little hero of each tale.' I tried to correct this fault, if it be one . . .; but in proportion as I arranged my thoughts, my letter, I found, became stiff and affected: I, therefore, determined to let my remarks and reflections flow unrestrained, as I perceived that I could not give a just description of what I saw, but by relating the effect different objects had produced on my mind and feelings, whilst the impression was still fresh. (p. 62)

12. On Forster, see also the German article by Hentschel (1992).
13. See also, in this context, the example from Darwin's account discussed in Chapter 1 (p. 16).

Chapter 4 The home tour

1. The tradition of English domestic journeys and of accounts about them has been retraced in more detail by Esther Moir (1964), Richard Trench (1990) and Ian Ousby (1990), as well as in a German study by Ria Omasreiter (1982).
2. The 1630 edition of Taylor's works which is cited here includes, alongside the *Pennyles Pilgrimage*, the following pieces of travel writing: *A Discovery by Sea, from London to Salisbury*; *Taylors Travels: Three Weekes, three Dayes, and three Houres Observations, from London to Hamburgh in Germanie*; *Taylors*

Travels to Prague in Bohemia. For a more detailed analysis of Taylor's travel pamphlets, in particular his later work, see also Wooden (1983).

3. On the unguided nature of domestic travel see also Moir (1964, p. 34).

4. In Kemp's text, however, the sensational nature of the enterprise is absolutely at the fore. Of the places 'visited', his readers learn little more than their names.

5. 'By means of a travel narrative, Defoe sought to turn the geographical phenomenon of an island into the political phenomenon of a nation, and the sense of national identity conferred upon citizens was wholly identified with their role in the successful management of a cohesive market economy' (Bell, 1995, p.10).

6. See, in particular, the following passage from Sprat's *History of the Royal Society* (1667): 'They have exacted from all their members, a close, naked, natural way of speaking; positive expressions; clear senses; a native easiness: bringing all things as near the Mathematical plainness, as they can: and preferring the language of Artizans, Countrymen, and Merchants, before that, of Wits, or Scholars' (p. 113).

7. On the artful 'design' of Defoe's *Tour* see, in great detail, Rogers (1997).

8. In respect of this 'exoticism', see the opening of Boswell's *Journal of a Tour to the Hebrides*:

> Dr Johnson had for many years given me hopes that we should go together, and visit the Hebrides. Martin's *Account* of those islands had impressed us with a notion that we might there contemplate a system of life almost totally different from what we had been accustomed to see; and, to find simplicity and wildness, and all the circumstances of remote time or place, so near to our native great island, was an object within the reach of reasonable curiosity. ... When I was at Ferney, in 1764, I mentioned our design to Voltaire. He looked at me, as if I had talked of going to the North Pole. (p. 161)

9. For extensive coverage of this kind of journey, see Andrews (1989), who also provides a select bibliography of tour accounts. Incidentally, the fashion of scenic travel overlapped with a popularization of pedestrian travel among the middle and upper classes. On this type of travel see Wallace (1993) and Jarvis (1997), who emphasizes the element of autonomy associated with this mode of travel: 'Walking affirmed a desired freedom from context, however partial, temporary or illusory that freedom might be' (p. 28).

10. Gray's account of his walk through the Lake District in 1769 was published as *Journal in the Lakes* (1775). On Gray's use of the Claude glass (or 'the mirror', as he called it himself) see also Manwaring (1925, p. 182).

11. Other titles include *Observations on the River Wye and several Parts of South Wales* (1782); *Observations ... on Several Parts of England; particularly the Mountains and Lakes of Cumberland and Westmoreland* (1786); *Observations on Several Parts of Great Britain, particularly the High-lands of Scotland* (1789); *Observations on the Western Parts of England* (1798).

12. This year relates to the fifth edition of Wordsworth's book. An earlier version of the text, *Select Views in Cumberland, Westmoreland, and*

Lancashire (1810), was written to accompany a volume of engravings by Joseph Wilkinson. Wordsworth later expanded the text and published it in several variously titled editions; the fifth edition was originally entitled *Guide through the District of the Lakes in the North of England*.

13. This originally appeared in Rudolph Ackermann's *Poetical Magazine*. In book form, *Dr Syntax* was published in 1812.

14. See, however, Bohls (1995), who claims that this aesthetic disinterested-ness characterizes male rather than female travelogues. To Bohls, travel writing as one of the genres 'more accessible to women' (p. 3) became a means for women writers of the eighteenth century (such as Lady Mary Wortley Montagu, Mary Wollstonecraft, Dorothy Wordsworth or Ann Radcliffe) to develop an aesthetics of their own in which the aesthetic subject is not a distanced viewer but remains rooted in – and concerned with – the material conditions of everyday life.

Chapter 5 Travel writing in the nineteenth century

1. The *Sketches* were originally written in 1865 for the *Pall Mall Gazette*.

2. See Edgeworth's letter of 14 September 1820 in the cited edition of her letters, p. 237.

3. For the origin of this development in capitalism, see Enzensberger (1990):

> The new ruling class, the bourgeoisie, organized industrial labour and the world market which depended on it. These processes did not lead immediately to social, but to spatial homogeneity. Technological progress, in particular the invention of the railway and the steamboat, allowed capitalism to develop the network of transport necessary to this homogenization of space.　　　　(pp. 70–1; my translation)

4. For a detailed study of tourism and its relationship with literature, see Buzard (1993).

5. On Cook see, for example, Pudney (1953) and Swinglehurst (1974).

6. Hyde (1988) is an excellent introduction to the forms and history of panoramic entertainments. On the history of the panorama, see also the German-language study of Oettermann (1980), as well as the catalogue to a German exhibition, *Sehsucht* (1993).

7. See, in particular, this famous passage from the book:

> I would have run to him, only I was a coward in the presence of such a mob – would have embraced him, only, he being an Englishman, I did not know how he would receive me; so I did what cowardice and false pride suggested was the best thing – walked deliberately to him, took off my hat, and said: 'Dr. Livingstone, I presume?' 'YES,' said he, with a kind smile, lifting his cap slightly. I replace my hat on my head, and he puts on his cap, and we both grasp hands, and I then say aloud: 'I thank God, Doctor, I have been permitted to see you.' He answered, 'I feel thankful that I am here to welcome you.'　　　　(pp. 411–12)

8. For a more detailed discussion of this aspect, see Breitinger (1981, pp. 19–20).
9. Since antiquity, cannibalism has served as a marker of utter foreignness. Thus many of the fabulous creatures in *Mandeville's Travels* are anthropophagi ('Men and women of that isle have heads like dogs, and they are called Cynocephales. . . . If they capture any man in battle, they eat him', p. 134), and many accounts of sixteenth-century explorers also claim that the inhabitants of the New World are man-eaters, as, for example, in a text about Martin Frobisher's second journey into the Polar Sea. Here, Inuits are recognized as human beings, but are nevertheless believed to practise cannibalism: 'I think them rather anthropophagi, or devourers of man's flesh than otherwise' (Hakluyt, 1972, p. 194).
10. See Loomis (1978) and Stone (1987).
11. However, a more differentiating view is required here. Not all explorers of the Victorian period were uncritical champions of imperialism. Some had a rather ambivalent attitude to the culture of their home country or even attempted to break free from it. At the same time, the complexity of the question of imperialist ideology in the travelogue is also apparent in the fact that the discourse of the Empire includes texts by writers who, in other respects, were clearly opposed to the values of their home culture. Richard Burton is a famous case in point: as a translator of oriental erotic literature, and with the sexually explicit essays which accompanied his famous translation of the *Arabian Nights* (1885–8), Burton clearly overstepped the bounds of Victorian propriety. On the multiple identities of Burton, see also Bishop (1957).
12. Other important studies on travel writing and Empire include Spurr (1993) and Youngs (1994). Gikandi (1996, chapter 3) investigates the complex relation 'between English identity, theories of alterity, and imperial travel' (p. 87), with special reference to travel books about the West Indies.
13. A related strategy is observed by Ashton Nichols (1982, p. 1) – the silencing of the indigenous population in the text:

> Like the stereotypical Victorian attitude towards sexuality, nineteenth-century attitudes toward the native population of Africa produced interpretations centered on the verbal silencing of a potential source of power, the discrediting of any language use that might threaten a dominant authority, and the marginalization of silenced individuals because of their supposed lack of verbal sophistication.

14. See for detail Sternberger (1981), in particular chapter 2 ('Über Land und Meer'), as well as Schivelbusch (1986) to whom Schiffer also refers. According to Schivelbusch,

> Panoramic perception, in contrast to traditional perception, no longer belonged to the same space as the perceived objects: the traveler saw the objects, landscapes, etc. *through* the apparatus which moved him through the world. That machine and the motion it created became integrated into his visual perception: thus he could only see things in motion. That mobility of vision – for a traditionally orientated

sensorium, such as Ruskin's, an agent for the dissolution of reality –
became a prerequisite for the 'normality' of panoramic vision. This
vision no longer experienced evanescence: evanescent reality had
become the new reality. (p. 64)

15. See also Jan Morris in her 'Introduction' to the cited edition: 'There was
never a travel book more intensely subjective and selective, more immune
to the orthodox demands of descriptive reportage' (p. ix).
16. A journey undertaken by Hilaire Belloc at the beginning of the twentieth
century appears more eccentric still: he attempted a pilgrimage from
Northern France to Rome in the straightest possible line, which caused
him considerable difficulties, particularly in mountainous regions. His
difficulties are humorously captured, in text and illustrations, in *The Path
to Rome* (1902).
17. The title translates as 'The Far West'.
18. See the 'Introduction' of the cited edition, p. xi.

Chapter 6 Women's travel writing

1. This material is, however, often only analysed from a biographical or soci-
ological perspective. For bibliographies of travel writing by women up to
and including the twentieth century see Russell (1986), Tinling (1989, pp.
313–42) and Robinson (1990). A selection of monographs on women's
travel writing is included in the bibliography.
2. See the introduction to the cited edition of Wollstonecraft, p. 38.
3. 'I had known her first in Constantinople, where she had arrived straight
out of the desert, with all the evening dresses and cutlery and napery that
she insisted on taking with her on her wanderings; and then in England;
but here she was in her right place, in Iraq, in her own house, with her
office in the city, and her white pony in a corner of the garden, and her
Arab servants, and her English books, and her Babylonian shards on the
mantelpiece, and her long thin nose, and her irrepressible vitality. I felt all
my loneliness and despair lifted from me in a second' (p. 41).
4. Blondel (1983/84) provides a general overview of travel writing by women
of this period. Bohls (1995) investigates how eighteenth-century women
writers used the genre to develop a feminine aesthetics (see also Chapter 4
in the present volume, note 14).
5. Piozzi's *Observations and Reflections Made in the Course of a Journey through
France, Italy and Germany* was published in 1789.
6. See, however, the comment of her editor in the cited edition:

But ... why did she take such pains to state that various persons
mentioned were 'cousins' or 'relations of mine' and sometimes to
explain in detail how they were related? Besides, she calls it specifically
a 'book' and there is something about the remarks she addresses to her
countrymen and to her sex in general which suggests that she may have
had in mind a wider public. (p. 17)

7. See *The Alfoxden Journal* (written 1798), of which only some sections remain, *The Grasmere Journal* (1800–3), *Recollections of a Tour Made in Scotland 1803* (1805) and the *Journal of a Tour on the Continent 1820*. Dorothy's records of walks in the Lake District, *An Excursion on the Banks of Ullswater 1805* and *An Excursion up Scawfell Pike 1818*, were used by William Wordsworth for his *Guide to the Lakes* and were the inspiration for certain poems by Wordsworth and Coleridge. Dorothy Wordsworth's editor, Ernest de Selincourt, writes in the preface to her published *Journals*: 'Dorothy Wordsworth is probably the most remarkable and the most distinguished of English writers who never wrote a line for the general public' (vol. 1, p. v).

8. It was observed in Chapter 3 that such gestures of apology are also to be found in the travel writing of men. Arthur Young, for example, felt obliged to justify the degree of subjectivity in his *Travels in France and Italy* (see p. 57). Here, however, the apology is related to only one aspect of the text; it is not an apology for writing the text at all, as is often the case in women's travel writing.

9. Thus, in many travelogues by nineteenth-century women, there is a sense of grief, or at least nostalgia, about the end of the journey, as for example in Isabella Bird's Rocky Mountains account:

> Mr. Fodder rattled so amusingly as we drove away that I never realised that my Rocky Mountain life was at an end, not even when I saw 'Mountain Jim,' with his golden hair yellow in the sunshine, slowly leading the beautiful mare over the snowy plains back to Estes Park, equipped with the saddle on which I had ridden 800 miles! A drive of several hours over the plains brought us to Greeley, and a few hours later, in the far blue distance, the Rocky Mountains, and all that they enclose, went down below the prairie sea.   (p. 296)

See also Amelia Edwards in *Untrodden Peaks*·

> And now, arriving at Botzen [*sic*], we arrive also at the end of our mid-summer ramble. For a week we linger on in this quaint old mediaeval town – for a week the pinnacles of the Schlern and the grand façade of the Rosengarten yet look down upon us from the heights beyond the Eisack. As long as we can stroll out every evening to the old bridge down behind the Cathedral and see the sunset crimsoning those mighty precipices, we feel that we have not yet parted from them wholly. They are our last Dolomites; and from that bridge we bid them farewell.   (pp. 356–7)

10. See also the following extract from Amelia Edwards's *Untrodden Peaks*. The author was an active suffragette, and indeed laid great importance on the unconventional nature of her tour of the Dolomites. However, when she meets another female hiker in over-manly dress, this woman is described as a ridiculous 'phenomenon':

> It wears highlows, a battered straw hat, and a brown garment which may be described either as a long kilt or the briefest of petticoats. Its hair is

sandy; its complexion crimson; its age anything between forty-five and sixty. It carries a knapsack on its back, and an alpenstock in its hand. The voice is the voice of a man; the face, tanned and travelstained as it is, is the face of a woman. (pp. 333–4)

11. For a detailed discussion of this text, see Lawrence (1994), chapter 2.
12. For a detailed study of how female travellers of the *nineteenth* century perceived and represented 'oriental' women's culture, see Ghose (1998).
13. See also the following comments Montagu makes of men's travel writing:

> You will perhaps be surprised at an account so different from what you have been entertained with by the common voyage writers, who are very fond of speaking of what they don't know. (p. 85)

> Your whole letter is full of mistakes from one end to the other. I see you have taken your ideas of Turkey from that worthy author Dumont, who has writ with equal ignorance and confidence. 'Tis a particular pleasure to me here to read the voyages to the Levant, which are generally so far removed from truth and so full of absurdities I am very well diverted with them. (p. 104)

14. In a letter from Nuremberg, for example, she speaks of 'the farce of relics with which I have been entertained in all Roman churches' (p. 9), and, in another letter, Montagu compares North African women with apes: 'their own country people, the baboons' (p. 151).
15. Mary Kingsley's 'ambiguous status in relation to the dominant culture's imperial ethos' and her complex relationship with West African culture is discussed in detail by Lawrence (1994, chapter 3; quoted passage on p. 129). See also Gikandi (1996, pp. 143–56), to whom 'Kingsley's narrative is a different kind of imperial discourse, one underwritten by irony, parody, and reversal. It is, nevertheless, a discourse underwritten also by a certain investment in imperialism and its mission' (p. 146). To Gikandi,

> Kingsley's modernized imperial discourse seeks to clear a cultural space for the engenderment of the domestic female subject but to sustain as well the larger ideologies that enable its engagement with Africa. Engendered in the space of the other, the imprisoned European woman cannot but have some affinity with the natives whose lives she chronicles; but she can be in this space only because it is under European control. (Ibid., p. 152)

16. Birkett here refers to a phrase in Mary Kingsley's *Travels in West Africa*: 'I had behind me the prestige of a set of white men' (p. 118).

Chapter 7 British travel writing in the twentieth century

1. See also Culler (1988).
2. See chapter 10 in Cocker (1992, pp. 243–60) on travel in the 'Coca-Cola Age'.

3. A companion piece to Priestley's account was Edwin Muir's *Scottish Journey* (1935). Muir records the economic problems of recession-hit industrialized Scotland, but, at a time of revived Scottish nationalist feeling, his prime interest is to explore the nature of Scottish identity, with a rather pessimistic conclusion: 'that Scotland is gradually being emptied of its population, its spirit, its wealth, industry, art, intellect, and innate character' (p. 3).

4. On British travel writing between the wars, see in particular Dodd (1982) and Fussell (1980).

5. As an 'undiscovered' part of the world, Guiana held a similar attraction for Evelyn Waugh. As he writes in *Ninety-Two Days* (1934): 'And so gradually a vague, general idea began to take shape in my mind of a large empty territory stretching up three great rivers and their tributaries to shadowy, undefined boundaries; most of it was undeveloped and unsurveyed, large areas quite unexplored' (p. 13).

6. Dennis Porter (1991) observes this psychological dimension for the travel writing of D.H. Lawrence: 'As frequently with Freud, travel is associated with archeology, the journey in geographic space with a voyage back in historical time in search of more archaic forms of consciousness' (p. 203).

7. In *Ninety-Two Days*, Waugh similarly emphasizes the lack of method to his journey: 'and took my ticket to Georgetown, with two small suitcases, a camera, a letter of credit and no clear plan of what my procedure would be when I arrived' (p. 14). See also the opening of Evelyn Waugh's *Labels*: 'I did not really know where I was going.'

8. Durrell's best-known travel books are *Prospero's Cell* (1945) and *Bitter Lemons* (1957).

9. On virtual travel, see, for example, an article in *Time* magazine by Tom Dworetzky (1997), who predicts that, very soon, '[t]his brave new virtual world will let us visit many places that inaccessibility, inconvenience and danger have heretofore made remote – even exotic. Zoom to the top of Everest, plunge to the bottom of the sea. Someday soon it will be all too real' (p. 85).

10. On this 'postmodernization' see also Pfister (1996b), who concentrates in particular on Bruce Chatwin's *In Patagonia*. On this book, see also Bode (1994).

11. See, for example, Clifford (1992), Carter, Donald and Squires (1993) and Wolff (1993). It is not surprising, then, that travel and related concepts (like borders, exile, migration and so on) have become favourite metaphors in postmodern critical discourses, as Kaplan (1996) points out.

12. See also Schivelbusch (1986), to whom the phenomenon of reading while travelling emerges with modern means of speedy transport and the new modes of perception associated with them (see Chapter 5 of the present volume, pp. 94–5):

> While the railroad caused the foreground to disappear, it also replaced looking at the landscape with a new practice that had not existed previously. Reading while traveling became almost obligatory. The dissolution of reality and its resurrection as panorama thus became agents for the total emancipation from the traversed landscape ...   (p. 64)

13. On intertextuality in contemporary travel writing see also Pfister (1993), as well as Glaser (1989) and Caesar (1990) on Paul Theroux, Estes (1991) on Chatwin, Henderson (1991) and Kohl (1993) on Glazebrook.
14. For a discussion of *Coasting*, see also Hudson-Ettle (1992) and Kohl (1993).

Chapter 8 Postcolonial travel writing in the twentieth century

1. For this criticism see Appiah (1991) and, in particular, Shohat (1992).
2. For similar views, see Pratt (1992, p. 23), Nixon (1992, p. 56) and Dissanayake and Wickramagamage (1993, p. 15).
3. Even when (quasi-)independence was achieved before the Second World War, many travel writers from former colonies before the mid-century still have a strong sense of dual allegiances – a loyalty both to the old mother country and to the colonial world. See, for example, Whitlock (1993) on an Australian travel writer of the 1930s, Mary Gaunt.
4. It should also be remembered that long before the first moves towards decolonization, colonized people wrote about their travel experiences, both enforced and voluntary. Excerpts from eighteenth-century accounts of enslaved Africans from the Caribbean are collected in Edwards and Dabydeen (1991). The most famous of these accounts, by Olaudah Equiano, is also available in a separate edition, as is the well-known book of a Black Victorian traveller, Mary Seacole. Seacole's *Wonderful Adventures* (1857) is discussed by Gikandi (1996, pp. 125–43), who emphasizes Seacole's attempt to inscribe herself, as a black woman from the West Indies, into the dominant discourse of Englishness.
5. Indigenous writers in the former settled colonies also appear to be hesitant in adopting the genre.
6. For a similar view, see MacLaren (1990): 'Travel literature is largely a Western genre. There is not yet, therefore, an extensive body of travel literature by, for example, Black Africans' (p. 6). One of the few travelogues by Black African writers which I managed to trace is *Songs to an African Sunset* (1997), by the Zimbabwean Sekai Nzenza-Shand. Having lived in Australia for years, Nzenza-Shand decided to travel back to the country of her birth in order 'to reclaim something of myself that I had lost during years of living in the West' (p. 25). That she writes a travelogue about this experience could, however, be seen as an indication of how deeply she has been Westernized.
7. Even though non-Western traditions of travel writing (see Introduction, note 2) are not, in general, part of the collective memory of the former British Empire, they are occasionally evoked by postcolonial writers. When Idries Shah, a writer of Afghan origin, reverses the conventions of the imperialist exploration account in his *Adventures, Facts and Fantasy in Darkest England* (1987), he explicitly refers to a non-Western heritage of travel and travel writing. His title, of course, alludes to Stanley's *In Darkest Africa*, but the tradition with which he aligns himself is clearly another one: 'I take my inspiration from such as Ibn Battutah of Tangier, the extraordinary fourteenth-century globetrotter who still holds the record as the

greatest traveller of all time' (p. 8).

8. See, for example, Kröller (1987) on the Canadian and Pesman (1996) on the Australian tradition of travelling 'back' to Europe. Döring (1997) discusses a number of travellers to Britain from a variety of colonial and postcolonial contexts, including Mukasa and Chaudhuri. The difference among colonial travellers to Britain is stressed in Chaudhuri's *A Passage to England*:

> We cannot say as an Australian, New Zealander, or even American can say to his son, 'Go and see that manor or farm, for that is where your ancestors came from.' It is not for us to say that blood is thicker than water. The only ties felt in the heart that we can have with England are those created by things of the mind. (p. 16)

9. For Australian travel books which similarly emphasize the injustice to the aboriginals, see Robyn Davidson's *Tracks* (1980), or Barry Hill's *The Rock* (1994).

10. Mittelholzer remarks in *With a Carib Eye* that 'politics bore me stiff' (p. 181), and Chaudhuri opens *A Passage to England* with the announcement that 'politics . . . are going to be excluded from the book' (p. 1).

11. Nixon (1992, p. 55), quoting from Charles Michener, 'The Dark Visions of V. S. Naipaul', *Newsweek*, 16 November 1981, pp. 104–15.

12. However, as Krishnaswamy also points out in this article, postcolonial cultures vary in the degree to which a deterritorialized consciousness can take root: 'The views of Indian immigrant writers such as Naipaul and Rushdie depart from the positions taken by many African writers who, in the wake of colonialism, have sought to re-territorialize rather than de-territorialize themselves' (p. 139).

13. For other contemporary accounts of domestic travel in Canada see, for example, David McFadden's *Trips Around the Great Lakes* (1980–8), George Galt's *Whistlestop: A Journey Across Canada* (1987), Marian Botsworth Fraser's *Walking the Line* (1989) and Stuart McLean's *Welcome Home* (1992).

14. A relatively secure sense of belonging marks domestic travel writing from India, such as Narayan's *The Emerald Route* (1977) or, more recently, Royina Grewal's *In Rajasthan* (1997) – even though the vastness of India also leaves much to discover for its home tourists.

15. Breytenbach's account of a return visit to South Africa before his imprisonment, *A Season in Paradise*, was originally written in Afrikaans and published in an English translation in 1980. Other accounts of return travels to South Africa with a strong political interest are David Robbins's *The 29th Parallel* (1986) and Justin Cartwright's *Not Yet Home* (1996). Dan Jacobson's *The Electronic Elephant: A Southern African Journey* (1994), by contrast, is less focused on contemporary politics as on the region's colonial history.

16. Naipaul's criticism – even dislike – of Afro-Caribbeans and Africans can also be attributed to this ethnic background; his brother Shiva, in *North of South*, is similarly critical of Africans.

Bibliography

Travel writing

Abrahams, Peter (1957) *Jamaica: An Island Mosaic*. London: Her Majesty's Stationery Office.

Addison, Joseph (1914) *Remarks on Several Parts of Italy*. In: *The Miscellaneous Works of Joseph Addison*, vol. 3. London: Bell (first published 1705).

Arnim, Elizabeth von (1990) *The Adventures of Elizabeth in Rügen*. London: Virago (first published 1904).

Auden, W.H. and MacNeice, Louis (1973) *Letters from Iceland*. London: Faber (first published 1937).

Bainbridge, Beryl (1984) *English Journey or The Road to Milton Keynes*. New York: Braziller.

Beckford, William (1928) *The Travel-Diaries of William Beckford of Fonthill*. Cambridge: Constable (first published 1782).

Bell, Gertrude (1928) *Safar Nameh: Persian Pictures. A Book of Travel*. London: Ernest Benn (first published 1894).

—— (1985) *The Desert and the Sown*. London: Virago (first published 1907).

Belloc, Hilaire (n.y.) *The Path to Rome*. London: Thomas Nelson & Sons (first published 1902).

Bird, Isabella (1982) *A Lady's Life in the Rocky Mountains*. London: Virago (first published 1879).

—— (1985) *The Yangtze Valley and Beyond: An Account of Journeys in China, Chiefly in the Province of Sze Chuan and Among the Man-Tze of the Somo Territory*. London: Virago (first published 1899).

Birkett, Dea (1994) *Jella: From Lagos to Liverpool. A Woman at Sea in a Man's World*. London: Gollancz (first published 1992).

Blaise, Clark and Mukherjee, Bharati (1977) *Days and Nights in Calcutta*. Garden City, NY: Doubleday.

Blunt, Anne (1968) *Bedouin Tribes of the Euphrates*, edited, with a Preface and some Accounts of the Arabs and their Horses by W.S. Blunt, 2 vols. London: Cass (first published 1879).

Boswell, James (1955) *Boswell on the Grand Tour: Italy, Corsica, and France 1765–1766*, Yale Edition of the Private Papers of James Boswell. London: Heinemann.

—— (1984) *The Journal of a Tour to the Hebrides*. In: Samuel Johnson and James Boswell, *A Journey to the Western Islands of Scotland* and *The Journal of a Tour to the Hebrides*. Harmondsworth: Penguin, pp. 153–411 (first published 1786).

—— (1996) *The Journal of a Tour to Corsica*. Brighton: In Print (first published 1768).

Breytenbach, Breyten (1980) *A Season in Paradise*. New York: Persea Books.

—— (1993) *Return to Paradise*. London: Faber.

Brydone, Patrick (1773) *A Tour through Sicily and Malta: In a Series of Letters to*

William Beckford, 2 vols. London: W. Strahan & T. Cadell.

Burton, Richard Francis (1964) *Personal Narrative of a Pilgrimage to Al-Madinah & Meccah,* 2 vols. New York: Dover (first published 1855–6).

—— (1987) *First Footsteps in East Africa or, An Exploration of Harar.* New York: Dover (first published 1856).

—— (1995) *The Lake Regions of Central Africa.* New York: Dover (first published 1860).

Byron, Robert (1981) *The Road to Oxiana.* London: Picador (first published 1937).

Cartwright, Justin (1997) *Not Yet Home.* London: Fourth Estate (first published 1996).

Chatwin, Bruce (1979) *In Patagonia.* London: Picador (first published 1977).

—— (1988) *The Songlines.* London: Picador (first published 1987).

Chaudhuri, Nirad C. (1959) *A Passage to England.* London: Macmillan.

Cobbett, William (1985) *Rural Rides.* Harmondsworth: Penguin (first published 1830).

Combe, William (1903) *The Tour of Doctor Syntax in Search of the Picturesque: A Poem. With Thirty-One Coloured Illustrations by Thomas Rowlandson.* London: Methuen (first published 1809).

Conrad, Peter (1988) *Down Home: Revisiting Tasmania.* London: Chatto & Windus.

Cook, James (1967) *The Voyage of the 'Resolution' and 'Discovery' 1776–1780,* Part 1. Cambridge: Cambridge University Press (for the Hakluyt Society).

Coryat, Thomas (1905) *Coryat's Crudities: Hastily gobled up in five Moneths travells in France, Savoy, Italy, Rhetia commonly called the Grisons country, Helvetia alias Switzerland, some parts of high Germany and the Netherlands; Newly digested in the hungry aire of Odcombe in the County of Somerset, and now dispersed to the nourishment of the travelling Members of this Kingdome.* 2 vols. Glasgow: James MacLehose (first published 1611).

Cunninghame Graham, Robert Bontine (1988) *Mogreb-el-Acksa.* London: Century (first published 1898).

Dampier, William (1697) *A New Voyage Round the World* 2nd edn corrected. London: For James Knapton.

Darwin, Charles (1989) *Voyage of the Beagle.* Harmondsworth: Penguin (first published 1839).

Davidson, Robyn (1992) *Tracks.* London: Vintage (first published 1980).

Defoe, Daniel (1986) *A Tour through the Whole Island of Great Britain.* Harmondsworth: Penguin (first published 1724–6).

Dennis, Ferdinand (1988) *Behind the Frontlines: Journey into Afro-Britain.* London: Victor Gollancz.

—— (1992) *Back to Africa: A Journey.* London: Sceptre.

Dickens, Charles (1957) *American Notes and Pictures from Italy,* The Oxford Illustrated Dickens. Oxford: Oxford University Press (first published 1842 and 1846 respectively).

Dobbs, Kildare (1992) *Ribbon of Highway: By Bus Along the Trans-Canada.* Toronto: Little, Brown.

Doughty, Charles M. (1926) *Travels in Arabia Deserta,* 2 vols. London: Cape (first published 1888).

Douglas, Norman (1993) *Old Calabria.* Marlboro, VT: Marlboro Press (first published 1915).

Durrell, Lawrence (1945) *Prospero's Cell: A Guide to the Landscape and Manners of the Island of Corcyra*. London: Faber.

—— (1959) *Bitter Lemons*. London: Faber (first published 1957).

Edgeworth, Maria (1979) *Maria Edgeworth in France and Switzerland: Selections from the Edgeworth Family Letters*. Oxford: Clarendon Press.

Edwards, Amelia (1986) *Untrodden Peaks and Unfrequented Valleys: A Midsummer Ramble in the Dolomites*. London: Virago (first published 1873).

Edwards, Paul and Dabydeen, David (eds) (1991) *Black Writers in Britain 1760–1890: An Anthology*. Edinburgh: Edinburgh University Press.

Equiano, Olaudah (1995) *The Interesting Narrative and Other Writings*, ed. Vincent Carretta. Harmondsworth: Penguin.

Evelyn, John (1906) *Diary and Correspondence of John Evelyn*. London: Routledge.

Fermor, Patrick (1979) *A Time of Gifts: On Foot to Constantinople. From the Hook of Holland to the Middle Danube*. Harmondsworth: Penguin (first published 1977).

—— (1984) *Mani: Travels in the Southern Peloponnese*. Harmondsworth: Penguin (first published 1958).

Fielding, Henry (1899) *The Journal of a Voyage to Lisbon*, The Works of Henry Fielding. Westminster: Constable and New York: Scribner's, vol. 12, pp. 215–395 (first published 1755).

Fiennes, Celia (1995) *The Illustrated Journeys of Celia Fiennes 1685–c.1712*, ed. Christopher Morris. Phoenix Mill: Alan Sutton.

Fleming, Peter (1966) *Brazilian Adventure*. London: Cape (first published 1933).

Forster, Georg (1965) *Reise um die Welt*, Georg Forsters Werke. Berlin: Akademie-Verlag (first published 1778–80).

—— (1968) *A Voyage Round the World*, Georg Forsters Werke. Berlin: Akademie-Verlag (first published 1777).

Franklin, John (1969) *Narrative of a Journey to the Shores of the Polar Sea in the Years 1819, 20, 21, and 22*. Edmonton: Hurtig (first published 1823).

Fraser, Marian Botsworth (1989) *Walking the Line*. Toronto: Douglas & McIntyre.

Galt, George (1987) *Whistlestop: A Journey Across Canada*. Toronto: Methuen.

Ghosh, Amitav (1994) *In an Antique Land*. London: Granta and Penguin (first published 1992).

Gilpin, William (1808) *Three Essays: On Picturesque Beauty; On Picturesque Travel; and on Sketching Landscape. With a Poem, on Landscape Painting*. London: Cadell & Davies (first published 1792).

—— (1973) *Observations on the Mountains and Lakes of Cumberland and Westmoreland*. Richmond, Surrey: Richmond Publishing (first published 1786).

—— (1973) *Observations on the Western Parts of England*. Richmond, Surrey: Richmond Publishing (first published 1798).

Glazebrook, Philip (1985) *Journey to Kars*. Harmondsworth: Penguin (first published 1984).

Gray, Thomas (1884) *Journal in France 1739*. In: *The Works of Thomas Gray in Prose and Verse*, ed. Edmund Gosse, vol. 1: *Poems, Journals and Essays*. London: Macmillan, pp. 235–46.

—— (1884) *Journal in the Lakes, 1769*. In: *The Works of Thomas Gray in Prose and Verse*, ed. Edmund Gosse, vol. 1: *Poems, Journals and Essays*. London: Macmillan, pp. 247–81 (first published 1775).

Greene, Graham (1980) *Journey Without Maps*. Harmondsworth: Penguin (first published 1936).

Grewal, Royina (1997) *In Rajasthan*. Melbourne etc.: Lonely Planet Publications.

Hakluyt, Richard (1972) *Voyages and Discoveries: The Principal Navigations, Voyages, Traffiques and Discoveries of the English Nation*, ed. and abridged by Jack Beeching. Harmondsworth: Penguin.

—— (1986) *Voyages to the Virginia Colonies*, ed. A.L. Rowse. London: Century.

Hill, Barry (1994) *The Rock: Travelling to Uluru*. St Leonards, Australia: Rathdowne Book and Allen & Unwin.

Hill, Ernestine (1995) *The Great Australian Loneliness*. Sydney: ETT Imprint (first published 1937).

Hodgins, Jack (1992) *Over 40 in Broken Hill: Unusual Encounters in the Australian Outback*. Toronto: McClelland & Stewart.

Hope, Christopher (1988) *White Boy Running*. London: Secker & Warburg.

—— (1990) *Moscow! Moscow!* London: Minerva.

Hudson, William Henry (1923) *Idle Days in Patagonia*, The Collected Works of W.H. Hudson in Twenty-Four Volumes, vol. 17. London: Dent and New York: Dutton (first published 1893).

Hutchison, Bruce (1957) *Canada: Tomorrow's Giant*. Toronto: Longman's, Green & Co.

Ibn Battūta (1959–94) *The Travels of Ibn Battūta A.D. 1325–1354*, trans. H.A.R. Gibb, 4 vols. London: The Hakluyt Society.

Iyer, Pico (1989) *Video Nights in Kathmandu and Other Reports from the Not-So-Far East*. London: Black Swan (first published 1988).

Jacobson, Dan (1995) *The Electronic Elephant: A Southern African Journey*. Harmondsworth: Penguin (first published 1994).

Jameson, Anna Brownell (1965) *Winter Studies and Summer Rambles in Canada: Selections*. Toronto: McClelland & Stewart (first published 1838).

Johnson, Amryl (1988) *Sequins for a Ragged Hem*. London: Virago.

Johnson, Samuel (1984) *A Journey to the Western Islands of Scotland*. In: Samuel Johnson and James Boswell, *A Journey to the Western Islands of Scotland* and *The Journal of a Tour to the Hebrides*. Harmondsworth: Penguin, pp. 33–151 (first published 1775).

Kemp, William (1966) *Kemps Nine Daies Wonder: Performed in a Daunce from London to Norwich*, Elizabethan and Jacobean Quartos, ed. G.B. Harrison. New York: Barnes & Noble (first published 1600).

Kempe, Margery (1985) *The Book of Margery Kempe*, trans. B.A. Windeatt. Harmondsworth: Penguin.

Keneally, Thomas (1992) *Now and in Time to Be: Ireland and the Irish*. London: Flamingo (first published 1991).

Kinglake, Alexander (1982) *Eothen: Or Traces of Travel Brought Home from the East*. Oxford: Oxford University Press (first published 1844).

Kingsley, Mary (1993) *Travels in West Africa*, abridged edn, Everyman's Library. London: Dent and New York: Dutton (first published 1897).

Kostash, Myrna (1993) *Bloodlines: A Journey into Eastern Europe*. Vancouver and

Toronto: Douglas & McIntyre.

Laurence, Margaret (1963) *The Prophet's Camel Bell*. Toronto: McClelland & Stewart.

Lawrence, D. H. (1944) *Sea and Sardinia*. Harmondsworth: Penguin (first published 1923).

—— (1956) *Etruscan Places*. London: Heinemann (first published 1927).

—— (1960) *Twilight in Italy*. Harmondsworth: Penguin (first published 1916).

—— (1986) *Mornings in Mexico*. Harmondsworth: Penguin (first published 1927).

Leacock, Stephen (1937) *My Discovery of the West: A Discussion of East and West in Canada*. Boston and New York: Hale, Cushman & Flint.

Leland, John (1993) *John Leland's Itinerary: Travels in Tudor England*, ed. John Chandler. Stroud, Glos.: Alan Sutton.

Lessing, Doris (1992) *African Laughter: Four Visits to Zimbabwe*. New York: HarperCollins.

—— (1996) *Going Home*. New York: HarperCollins (first published 1957).

Livingstone, David (1858) *Missionary Travels and Researches in South Africa; including a Sketch of Sixteen Years' Residence in the Interior of Africa*. New York: Harper & Bros (first published 1857).

McCourt, Edward (1965) *The Road Across Canada*. Toronto: Macmillan of Canada.

McFadden, David W. (1980–8) *Trips Around the Great Lakes*, 3 vols. Toronto: Coach House Press.

—— (1995) *An Innocent in Ireland: Curious Rambles and Singular Encounters*. Toronto: McClelland & Stewart.

McLean, Stuart (1994) *Welcome Home: Travels in Smalltown Canada*. Toronto: Penguin Books of Canada (first published 1992).

Malan, Rian (1991) *My Traitor's Heart: Blood and Bad Dreams: A South African Explores the Madness in His Country, His Tribe and Himself*. London: Vintage (first published 1990).

Mirsky, Jeanette (ed.) (1964) *The Great Chinese Travelers: An Anthology*. New York: Pantheon Books.

Mittelholzer, Edgar (1958) *With a Carib Eye*. London: Secker & Warburg.

Montagu, Lady Mary Wortley (1994) *The Turkish Embassy Letters*. London: Virago (first published 1763, written 1716–18).

Morris, Jan (1992) *Journeys*. Oxford: Oxford University Press (first published 1984).

Moryson, Fynes (1971) *An Itinerary*. New York: DaCapo Press and Amsterdam: Theatrum Orbis Terrarum (first published 1617).

Mukasa, Ham (1975) *Sir Apolo Kagwa Discovers Britain*, ed. Taban lo Liyong. London: Heinemann.

Muir, Edwin (1979) *Scottish Journey*. Edinburgh and London: Mainstream Publishing (first published 1935).

Murphy, Dervla (1965) *Full Tilt: Ireland to India with a Bicycle*. London: Murray.

—— (1979) *A Place Apart*. Harmondsworth: Penguin (first published 1978).

Naipaul, Shiva (1980) *North of South: An African Journey*. Harmondsworth: Penguin (first published 1978).

Naipaul, V. S. (1969) *The Middle Passage: Impressions of Five Societies – British, French and Dutch – in the West Indies and South America*. Harmondsworth:

Penguin (first published 1962).
—— (1979) *India: A Wounded Civilization*. Harmondsworth: Penguin (first published 1977).
—— (1982) *Among the Believers: An Islamic Journey*. Harmondsworth: Penguin (first published 1981).
—— (1985) *Finding the Centre: Two Narratives*. Harmondsworth: Penguin (first published 1984).
Narayan, R. K. (1980) *The Emerald Route*. Mysore: Indian Thought Publications (first published 1977).
—— (1988) *My Dateless Diary: An American Journey*. Harmondsworth: Penguin (first published 1964).
Newby, Eric (1989) *The Big Red Train Ride*. London: Picador (first published 1978).
Nicholl, Charles (1996) *The Creature in the Map: Sir Walter Ralegh's Quest for El Dorado*. London: Vintage (first published 1995).
Nzenza-Shand, Sekai (1997) *Songs to an African Sunset: A Zimbabwean Story*. Melbourne etc.: Lonely Planet.
Ondaatje, Christopher (1993) *The Man-Eater of Punanai: A Journey of Discovery to the Jungles of Old Ceylon*. Toronto: HarperPerennial (first published 1992).
—— (1996) *Sindh Revisited: A Journey in the Footsteps of Captain Sir Richard Francis Burton. 1842–1849: The India Years*. Toronto: HarperCollins.
Orwell, George (1989) *The Road to Wigan Pier*. Harmondsworth: Penguin (first published 1937).
Park, Mungo (1983) *Travels into the Interior of Africa*. London: Eland (first published 1799 as *Travels in the Interior Districts of Africa*).
Pausanias (1979) *Guide to Greece*, trans. Peter Levi, 2 vols, rev. edn. Harmondsworth: Penguin (this edition first published 1971).
Philby, H. St J. (1986) *The Empty Quarter*. London: Century (first published 1933).
Phillips, Caryl (1993) *The European Tribe*. London: Picador (first published 1987).
Piozzi, Hester Thrale (1789) *Observations and Reflections Made in the Course of a Journey, through France, Italy and Germany*. London: n.p.
Priestley, J. B. (1994) *English Journey: Being a Rambling but Truthful Account of What One Man Saw and Heard and Felt and Thought during a Journey through England during the Autumn of the Year 1933*. London: Mandarin Paperbacks (first published 1934).
Polo, Marco (1931) *The Travels of Marco Polo*, trans. Aldo Ricci. London: Routledge & Kegan Paul.
Purchas, Samuel (1965) *Hakluytus Posthumus or Purchas His Pilgrimes: Contayning a History of the World in Sea Voyages and Lande Travells by Englishmen and others*, 20 vols. New York: AMS Press.
Raban, Jonathan (1987) *Coasting*. London: Picador (first published 1986).
—— (1987) *For Love & Money: Writing, Reading, Travelling 1969–1987*. London: Collins.
Radcliffe, Ann (1975) *A Journey Made in the Summer of 1794, through Holland and the Western Frontier of Germany*. Hildesheim: Olms (first published 1795).
Ralegh, Sir Walter (n.y.) *The Discovery of Guiana*, The Works of Sir Walter Ralegh. New York: Franklin, vol. 8, pp. 391–476 (first published 1596).

Robbins, David (1990) *The 29th Parallel: A South African Journey.* Harmondsworth: Penguin (first published 1986).

Rushdie, Salman (1987) *The Jaguar Smile: A Nicaraguan Journey.* London: Picador.

Sackville-West, Vita (1991) *Passenger to Teheran.* London: Arrow Books (first published 1926).

Seacole, Mary (1984) *The Wonderful Adventures of Mrs Seacole in Many Lands*, eds Ziggi Alexander and Audrey Dewjee. Bristol: Falling Walls Press.

Seth, Vikram (1983) *From Heaven Lake: Travels through Sinkiang and Tibet.* London: Chatto & Windus.

Shah, Idries (1987) *Adventures, Facts and Fantasy in Darkest England.* London: Octagon Press.

Shah, Tahir (1997) *Beyond the Devil's Teeth.* London: Phoenix (first published 1995).

Smollett, Tobias (1981) *Travels through France and Italy.* Oxford: Oxford University Press (first published 1766).

Southey, Robert (1960) *Journals of a Residence in Portugal 1800–1801 and a Visit to France 1838.* Oxford: Clarendon Press.

Stanley, Henry Morton (1969) *How I Found Livingstone: Travels, Adventures, and Discoveries in Central Africa.* New York: Negro University Press (first published 1872).

—— (1988) *Through the Dark Continent: Or, The Sources of the Nile Around the Great Lakes of Equatorial Africa and Down the Livingstone River to the Atlantic Ocean*, 2 vols. New York: Dover (first published 1878).

Stark, Freya (1983) *Beyond Euphrates.* London: Century (first published 1951).

—— (1991) *The Valleys of the Assassins and Other Persian Travels.* London: Arrow Books (first published 1936).

Sterne, Laurence (1928) *A Sentimental Journey through France and Italy.* London: Oxford University Press (first published 1768).

Stevenson, Robert Louis (1984) *Travels with a Donkey – An Inland Voyage – The Silverado Squatters*, Everyman's Library. London: Dent and New York: Dutton (first published 1879/1878/1883).

Taylor, John (1973) *All the Works of John Taylor the Water Poet*, A Scolar Press Facsimile. Menston and London: Scolar Press (first published 1630).

Theroux, Paul (1980) *The Old Patagonian Express: By Train through the Americas.* Harmondsworth: Penguin (first published 1979).

—— (1984) *The Kingdom by the Sea: A Journey Around the Coast of Great Britain.* Harmondsworth: Penguin (first published 1983).

Thesiger, Wilfred (1991) *Arabian Sands.* Harmondsworth: Penguin (first published 1959).

Thubron, Colin (1987) *Behind the Wall: A Journey through China.* London: Heinemann.

—— (1995) *The Lost Heart of Asia.* Harmondsworth: Penguin (first published 1994).

The Travels of Sir John Mandeville (1983), trans. and ed. C.W.R.D. Moseley. Harmondsworth: Penguin.

Trollope, Anthony (1866) *Travelling Sketches.* London: Chapman & Hall.

—— (1987) *North America*, 2 vols. Gloucester: Alan Sutton and New York: Hippocrene (first published 1862).

Trollope, Fanny [Frances] (1984) *Domestic Manners of the Americans*. Phoenix Mill: Alan Sutton (first published 1832).

van der Post, Laurens (1957) *Venture to the Interior*. Harmondsworth: Penguin (first published 1952).

Wafer, Lionel (1934) *A New Voyage and Description of the Isthmus of America*. Oxford: The Hakluyt Society (first published 1699).

Waugh, Evelyn (1946) *When the Going Was Good*. London: Duckworth.

—— (1974) *Labels: A Mediterranean Journey*. London: Duckworth (first published 1930).

—— (1985) *Ninety-Two Days*. Harmondsworth: Penguin (first published 1934).

Wey, William (1857) *The Itineraries of William Wey, Fellow of Eton College. To Jerusalem, A.D. 1458 and A.D. 1462; and to Saint James of Compostella, A.D. 1456*. London: J.B. Nichols for the Roxburghe Club.

William of Rubruck (1990) *The Mission of Friar William of Rubruck: His Journey to the Court of the Great Khan Möngke 1253–1255*, trans. Peter Jackson. London: The Hakluyt Society.

Wollstonecraft, Mary (1987) *A Short Residence in Sweden, Norway, and Denmark*. Harmondsworth: Penguin (first published 1796).

Woodcock, George (1993) *Letter from the Khyber Pass and Other Travel Writing*, ed. Jim Christy. Vancouver and Toronto: Douglas & McIntyre.

Wordsworth, Dorothy (1952) *Journals of Dorothy Wordsworth*, ed. Ernest de Selincourt, 2 vols. London: Macmillan.

—— (1991) *The Grasmere Journals*, ed. Pamela Woof. Oxford: Oxford University Press.

Wordsworth, William (1977) *Wordsworth's Guide to the Lakes: The Fifth Edition*, ed. Ernest de Selincourt. Oxford: Oxford University Press (fifth edn 1835).

Wright, Ronald (1994) *Home and Away*. Toronto: Vintage Books (first published 1993).

Young, Arthur (n.y.) *Travels in France and Italy: During the Years 1787, 1788 and 1789*, Everyman's Library. London: Dent and New York: Dutton (first published 1792).

Young, Gavin (1987) *Worlds Apart: Travels in War and Peace*. London: Hutchinson.

Select secondary sources on travel and travel writing

Adams, Percy G. (1962) *Travelers and Travel Liars 1660–1800*. Berkeley: University of California Press.

—— (1978) 'Travel Literature of the Seventeenth and Eighteenth Centuries: A Review of Recent Approaches', *Texas Studies in Literature and Language*, XX, 488–515.

—— (1983) *Travel Literature and the Evolution of the Novel*. Lexington, KY: University Press of Kentucky.

Addison, Joseph (1759) 'Essay No. 254, 23 November 1710', *The Tatler*. London: Jacob & Richard Tonson, vol. 4, pp. 363–9.

Adickes, Sandra (1991) *The Social Quest: The Expanded Vision of Four Women Travelers in the Era of the French Revolution*. New York: Lang.

Allen, Alexandra (1980) *Travelling Ladies*. London: Jupiter.

Andrews, Malcolm (1989) *The Search for the Picturesque: Landscape Aesthetics and Tourism in Britain, 1760–1800*. Aldershot: Scolar Press.

Bacon, Francis (1908) 'Of Travels'. In: *The Essays of Francis Bacon*, ed. Mary A. Scott. New York: Scribner's, pp. 79–82.

Barrell, John (1991) 'Death on the Nile: Fantasy and the Literature of Tourism 1840–1860', *Essays in Criticism*, XLI, 97–127.

Bates, E. S. (1987) *Touring in 1600: A Study in the Development of Travel as a Means of Education*. London: Century (first published 1911).

Batten, Charles L. (1978) *Pleasurable Instruction: Form and Convention in 18th-Century Travel Literature*. Berkeley: University of California Press.

Bausinger, Hermann, Beyrer, Klaus and Korff, Gottfried (eds) (1991) *Reisekultur: Von der Pilgerfahrt zum modernen Tourismus*. Munich: Beck.

Bell, Ian A. (1995) 'To See Ourselves: Travel Narratives and National Identity in Contemporary Britain'. In: *Peripheral Visions: Images of Nationhood in Contemporary British Fiction*, ed. Ian A. Bell. Cardiff: University of Wales Press, pp. 6–26.

Bennett, Josephine Waters (1954) *The Rediscovery of Sir John Mandeville*. New York: MLA.

Benson, Eugene and Conolly, Leonard W. (eds) (1994) *Encyclopedia of Post-Colonial Literatures in English*, 2 vols. London and New York: Routledge, vol. 2 (entries on 'Travel Literature': pp. 1586–98).

Bergmann, Klaus and Ockenfuß, Solveig (eds) (1984) *Neue Horizonte: Eine Reise durch das Reisen*. Reinbek: Rowohlt.

Birkett, Dea (1989) *Spinsters Abroad: Victorian Lady Explorers*. Oxford: Blackwell.

Bishop, Jonathan (1957) 'The Identities of Sir Richard Burton: The Explorer as Actor', *Victorian Studies*, I, 119–35.

Black, Jeremy (1985) *The British and the Grand Tour*. London: Croom Helm.

—— (1990) 'Tourism and Cultural Challenge: The Changing Scene of the Eighteenth Century'. In: McVeagh (1990), pp. 185–202.

—— (1991) 'On the Grand Tour in 1771–1773', *Yale University Library Gazette*, October, 33–46.

Bleicher, Thomas (1981) 'Einleitung: Literarisches Reisen als literaturwissenschaftliches Ziel', *Komparatistische Hefte*, 3, 3–10.

Blondel, Madeleine (1983/84) 'Le recit de voyage feminin au XVIIIe siècle'. *Bulletin de la Société d'Etudes Anglo-Américaines des XVIIe et XVIIIe Siècles*, 16/17, 109–27, and 18, 108–23.

Bode, Christoph (1994) 'Beyond/Around/Into One's Own: Reiseliteratur als Paradigma von Welt-Erfahrung', *Poetica*, XXVI, 70–87.

—— (1997) 'Putting the Lake District on the (Mental) Map: William Wordsworth's *Guide to the Lakes*', *Journal for the Study of British Cultures*, IV, 95–111.

—— (ed.) (1997) *West Meets East: Klassiker der britischen Orient-Reiseliteratur*. Heidelberg: Winter.

Boerner, Peter (1982). 'Die großen Reisesammlungen des 18. Jahrhunderts'. In: Mączak and Teuteberg (1982), pp. 65–72.

Bohls, Elizabeth A. (1995) *Women Travel Writers and the Language of Aesthetics 1716–1818*. Cambridge: Cambridge University Press.

Böhme, Max (1904) *Die großen Reisesammlungen des 16. Jahrhunderts und ihre Bedeutung*. Strasbourg: Heitz.

Brantlinger, Patrick (1985) 'Victorians and Africans: The Genealogy of the Myth of the Dark Continent', *Critical Inquiry*, XII, 166–203.

Breitinger, Eckhard (1981) 'Travels into the Interior of Africa: The "Discovery" of a Continent', *Komparatistische Hefte*, 3, 11–27.

Brenner, Peter J. (ed.) (1989) *Der Reisebericht: Die Entwicklung einer Gattung in der deutschen Literatur*. Frankfurt am Main: Suhrkamp.

—— (1990). *Der Reisebericht in der deutschen Literatur: Ein Forschungsüberblick als Vorstudie zu einer Gattungsgeschichte*, Sonderheft Internationales Archiv für Sozialgeschichte der deutschen Literatur, 2. Tübingen: Niemeyer.

Briggs, Asa (1982) 'Trollope the Traveller'. In: *Trollope Centenary Essays*, ed. John Halperin. New York: St. Martin's Press, pp. 24–52.

Brilli, Attilio (1987) *Il viaggio in italia: Storia di una grande tradizione culturale dal XVI al XIX secolo*. Cinisello Balsamo: Silvana Editoriale.

Brothers, Barbara and Gergits, Julia (eds) (1996) *British Travel Writers, 1837–1875*. In: *Dictionary of Literary Biography*. Detroit and London: Gale Research.

—— (1997) *British Travel Writers, 1876–1909*. In: *Dictionary of Literary Biography*. Detroit and London: Gale Research.

—— (1998), *British Travel Writers, 1910–1939*. In: *Dictionary of Literary Biography*. Detroit and London: Gale Research.

—— (1999) *British Travel Writers, 1940–1997*. In: *Dictionary of Literary Biography*. Detroit and London: Gale Research.

Bürgi, Andreas (1989) *Weltvermesser: Die Wandlungen des Reiseberichts in der Spätaufklärung*. Bonn: Bouvier.

Butor, Michel (1974) 'Travel and Writing', *Mosaic*, VIII, 1, 1–16 ('Le voyage et l'écriture', 1972).

Buzard, James (1993) *The Beaten Track: European Tourism, Literature, and the Ways to 'Culture' 1800–1918*. Oxford: Clarendon Press.

Caesar, Terry (1990) 'The Book in the Travel: Paul Theroux's *The Old Patagonian Express*', *Arizona Quarterly*, XLVI, 2, 101–10.

Campbell, Mary B. (1988) *The Witness and the Other World: Exotic European Travel Writing, 400–1600*. Ithaca, NY and London: Cornell University Press.

—— (1991) '"The Object of One's Gaze": Landscape, Writing, and Early Medieval Pilgrimage'. In: *Discovering New Worlds: Essays on Medieval Exploration and Imagination*, ed. Scott D. Westrem. New York: Garland, pp. 3–15.

Casson, Lionel (1974) *Travel in the Ancient World*. London: Allen & Unwin.

Cawley, Robert Ralston (1951) *Milton and the Literature of Travel*. Princeton, NJ: Princeton University Press.

—— (1966) *The Voyagers and Elizabethan Drama*. New York: Kraus (first published 1938).

—— (1967) *Unpathed Waters: Studies in the Influence of the Voyagers on Elizabethan Literature*. New York: Octagon Books (first published 1940).

Chard, Chloe (1989) 'Pleasure and Guilt in Greece and Italy', *Comparative Civilizations Review*, XX, 1–31.

Clifford, James (1992) 'Traveling Cultures'. In: *Cultural Studies*, eds Lawrence Grossberg, Cary Nelson and Paula Trichler. London and New York: Routledge.

Cocker, Mark (1992) *Loneliness and Time: British Travel Writing in the Twentieth*

Century. London: Secker & Warburg.

Coe, Charles Norton (1979) *Wordsworth and the Literature of Travel*. New York: Octagon Books (first published 1953).

Cole, Garold (1981) 'Travel Literature: Recent Articles of Bibliographic Interest, 1949–1978', *Bulletin of Bibliography*, XXXVIII, 3, 109–16, 127.

Cotsell, Michael (ed.) (1990) *1830–1876: Creditable Warriors*. English Literature and the Wider World, vol. 3. London and Atlantic Highlands, NJ: Ashfield Press.

Cox, Edward Godfrey (1935) *A Reference Guide to the Literature of Travel: Including Voyages, Geographical Descriptions, Adventures, Shipwrecks and Expeditions*, 2 vols. Seattle: University of Washington.

Culler, Jonathan (1988) 'The Semiotics of Tourism'. In: *Framing the Sign: Criticism and Its Institutions*. Oxford: Blackwell, pp. 153–67.

Curley, Thomas M. (1976) *Samuel Johnson and the Age of Travel*. Athens: University of Georgia Press.

—— (1990) 'Sterne's *A Sentimental Journey* and the Tradition of Travel Literature'. In: McVeagh (1990), pp. 203–16.

Dischner, Gisela (1972) *Ursprünge der Rheinromantik in England: Zur Geschichte der romantischen Ästhetik*. Frankfurt am Main: Klostermann.

Dissanayake, Wimal and Wickramagamage, Carmen (1993) *Self and Colonial Desire: Travel Writings of V.S. Naipaul*. New York etc.: Lang.

Dodd, Philip (1982) 'The Views of Travellers: Travel Writing in the 1930s'. *Prose Studies*, V, 127–38.

Döring, Tobias (1997) 'Discovering the Mother Country: The Empire Travels Back', *Journal for the Study of British Cultures*, IV, 181–201.

Douglas, Norman (1926) 'Arabia Deserta'. In: *Experiments*. London: Chapman & Hall, pp. 1–25 (first published 1925).

Dworetzky, Tom (1997) 'Next . . . Virtual Vacations', *Time*, 16 June, 84–5.

Elliott, J. H. (1970) *The Old World and The New 1492–1650*. Cambridge: Cambridge University Press.

Enzensberger, Hans Magnus (1990) 'Eine Theorie des Tourismus'. In: *Erstes Allgemeines Nicht-Reise-Buch*, ed. Andrea Wörle and Lutz-W. Wolff. Munich: dtv, pp. 61–85 (first published 1958).

Erker-Sonnabend, Ulrich (1987) *Das Lüften des Schleiers: Die Orienterfahrung britischer Reisender in Ägypten und Arabien. Ein Beitrag zum Reisebericht des 19. Jahrhunderts*. Hildesheim: Olms.

Ertzdorff, Xenia von and Neukirch, Dieter (eds) (1992) *Reisen und Reiseliteratur im Mittelalter und in der Frühen Neuzeit*. Chloe. Beihefte zum Daphnis, 13. Amsterdam and Atlanta, GA: Rodopi.

Estes, David C. (1991) 'Bruce Chatwin's *In Patagonia*: Traveling in Textualized Terrain', *New Orleans Review*, XVIII, 2, 67–77.

Fabricant, Carole (1987) 'The Literature of Domestic Tourism and the Public Consumption of Private Property'. In: *The New Eighteenth Century: Theory, Politics, English Literature*, eds Felicity Nussbaum and Laura Brown. New York: Methuen, pp. 254–75.

Feldmann, Doris (1997) 'Economic and/as Aesthetic Constructions of Britishness in Eighteenth-Century Domestic Travel Writing', *Journal for the Study of British Cultures*, IV, 31–45.

Fogel, Joshua A. (1996) *The Literature of Travel in the Japanese Rediscovery of*

China, 1862–1945. Cambridge: Stanford from Cambridge University Press.

Foster, Shirley (1990) *Across New Worlds: Nineteenth-Century Women Travellers and Their Writings*. New York: Harvester/Wheatsheaf.

Frantz, R.W. (1934) *The English Traveller and the Movement of Ideas 1660–1732*. Lincoln: University of Nebraska Press.

Frederiksen, Elke (1985) 'Der Blick in die Ferne: Zur Reiseliteratur von Frauen'. In: *Frauen Literatur Geschichte: Schreibende Frauen vom Mittelalter bis zur Gegenwart*, eds Hiltrud Gnüg and Renate Möhrmann. Stuttgart: Metzler, pp. 104–22.

Fuller, Mary C. (1995) *Voyages in Print: English Travel to America 1576–1624*. Cambridge: Cambridge University Press.

Fussell, Paul (1980) *Abroad: British Literary Traveling between the Wars*. New York and Oxford: Oxford University Press.

Gatrell, Simon (ed.) (1992) *1876–1918: The Ends of the Earth*, English Literature and the Wider World, vol. 4. London and Atlantic Highlands, NJ: Ashfield Press.

—— (1992) 'Introduction'. In: Gatrell (1992), pp. 1–66.

Ghose, Indira (1998) *Women Travellers in Colonial India: The Power of Female Gaze*. Delhi: Oxford University Press.

Gikandi, Simon (1996) *Maps of Englishness: Writing Identity in the Culture of Colonialism*. New York: Columbia University Press.

Glaser, Elton (1989) 'The Self-Reflexive Traveler: Paul Theroux on the Art of Travel and Travel Writing', *The Centennial Review*, XXXIII, 193–206.

Graue, Frank (1991) *Schönes Land: Verderbtes Volk. Das Spanienbild britischer Reisender zwischen 1710 und 1850*, Grenzüberschreitungen, 2. Trier: Wissenschaftlicher Verlag Trier.

Greenblatt, Stephen (1991) *Marvelous Possessions: The Wonder of the New World*. Oxford: Clarendon Press.

Gregory, Alexis (1991) *The Golden Age of Travel, 1880–1939*. London: Cassell (*L'Age d'or du voyage*, 1990).

Griep, Wolfgang (ed.) (1991) *Sehen und Beschreiben: Europäische Reisen im 18. und frühen 19. Jahrhundert*. Heide: Westholsteinische Verlagsanstalt Boyens.

Griep, Wolfgang and Jäger, Hans-Wolf (eds) (1983) *Reise und soziale Realität am Ende des 18. Jahrhunderts*. Heidelberg: Winter.

Grivel, Charles (1994) 'Travel Writing'. In: *Materialities of Communication*, eds Hans Ulrich Gumbrecht and K. Ludwig Pfeiffer. Stanford, CA: Stanford University Press, pp. 242–57 ('Reise-Schreiben', 1988).

Hamalian, Leo (1981) *Ladies on the Loose: Women Travellers of the 18th and 19th Centuries*. New York: Dodd.

Harbsmeier, Michael (1982) 'Reisebeschreibungen als mentalitätsgeschichtliche Quellen: Überlegungen zu einer historisch-anthropologischen Untersuchung frühneuzeitlicher deutscher Reisebeschreibungen'. In: Mączak and Teuteburg (1982), pp. 1–31.

Heineman, Helen (1982) 'Anthony Trollope: The Compleat Traveller', *Ariel*, XIII, 1, 33–50.

Henderson, Heather (1991) 'The Travel Writer and the Text: "My giant goes with me wherever I go"', *New Orleans Review*, XVIII, 2, 30–40 (repr. in Kowalewski (1992), pp. 230–48).

Hentschel, Uwe (1992) 'Von der "ästhetischen Vollkommenheit wissenschaftlicher Werke": Theorie und Praxis der Reisebeschreibung bei Georg Forster'. *Zeitschrift für Germanistik*, II, 3, 569–85.

Hergenhan, Laurie and Petersson, Irmtraud (eds) (1994) *Changing Places: Australian Writers in Europe*. St Lucia, Queensland: University of Queensland Press.

Hibbert, Christopher (1987) *The Grand Tour*. London: Methuen.

Hindley, Geoffrey (1983) *Tourists, Travellers and Pilgrims*. London: Hutchinson.

Howard, Clare (1914) *English Travellers of the Renaissance*. London: John Lane/The Bodley Head.

Howard, Donald R. (1971) 'The World of Mandeville's Travels', *Yearbook of English Studies*, I, 1–17.

—— (1980) *Writers and Pilgrims: Medieval Pilgrimage Narratives and Their Posterity*. Berkeley: University of California Press.

Howell, James (1895) *Instructions for Forreine Travell*, ed. Edward Arber. Westminster: Constable (first published 1642).

Hudson-Ettle, Diana M. (1992) 'Approaching "Englishness": Jonathan Raban's *Coasting*', *Anglistik und Englischunterricht*, XLVI/XLVII, 305–18.

Hurd, Richard (1969) 'Dialogues VII and VIII on the Uses of Foreign Travel: Between Lord Shaftesbury and Mr. Locke'. In: *The Works*. Hildesheim: Olms, vol. 4, pp. 85–229 (first published 1763).

Jacobs, Michael (1995) *The Painted Voyage: Art, Travel and Exploration 1564–1875*. London: published for the Trustees of the British Museum by British Museum Press.

Jäger, Hans-Wolf (ed.) (1992) *Europäische Reisen im Zeitalter der Aufklärung*. Heidelberg: Winter.

Jarvis, Robin (1997) *Romantic Writing and Pedestrian Travel*. London: Macmillan.

Johnson, Samuel (1963) 'The Idler, Essay No. 97, 23 February 1760'. In: *The Idler and The Adventurer*, eds W.J. Bate et al. New Haven, CT and London: Yale University Press, pp. 298–300.

Kalb, Gertrud (1981) *Bildungsreise und literarischer Reisebericht: Studien zur englischen Reiseliteratur (1700–1850)*, Erlanger Beiträge zur Sprach- und Kunstwissenschaft, 67. Nuremburg: Hans Carl.

—— (1983) 'Travel Literature Reinterpreted: *Robinson Crusoe* und die religiöse Thematik der Reiseliteratur', *Anglia*, CI, 407–20.

Keay, Julia (1989) *With Passport and Parasol*. London: BBC.

Kirkpatrick, F. A. (1916) 'The Literature of Travel, 1700–1900'. In: *The Cambridge History of English Literature*. Cambridge: Cambridge University Press, vol. 14, pp. 240–56.

Koch, Dieter (1989) *Schönheit und Dekadenz: Die Italienerfahrung britischer Reisender im 19. Jahrhundert*, Grenzüberschreitungen, 1. Trier: Wissenschaftlicher Verlag Trier.

Kohl, Stephan (1985) 'Landschafts-Erfahrung: Von der sensiblen zur mechanischen Reise', *Anglistik und Englischunterricht*, XXVI, 87–105.

—— (1990) 'Travel Literature and the Art of Self-Invention'. In: *Anglistentag 1989: Proceedings*, ed. Rüdiger Ahrens. Tübingen: Niemeyer, pp. 174–83.

—— (1993) 'Reiseromane/Travelogues: Möglichkeiten einer "hybriden" Gattung'. In: *Radikalität und Mäßigung: Der englische Roman seit 1960*, eds Annegret Maack and Rüdiger Imhof. Darmstadt: Wissenschaftliche Buchgesellschaft, pp. 149–68.

Korshin, Paul J. (1990) '"Extensive View": Johnson and Boswell as Travelers and Observers'. In: McVeagh (1990), pp. 233–45.

Korte, Barbara (1994) 'Der Reisebericht aus anglistischer Sicht: Stand, Tendenzen und Desiderate seiner literaturwissenschaftlichen Erforschung'. *Zeitschrift für Anglistik und Amerikanistik*, XLII, 364–72.

—— (1996) '*Home and Away* – Perspektiven im anglokanadischen Reisebericht nach dem Zweiten Weltkrieg', *Zeitschrift für Kanada-Studien*, XXIX, 1, 16–35.

Kowalewski, Michael (ed.) (1992) *Temperamental Journeys: Essays on the Modern Literature of Travel*. Athens, GA and London: University of Georgia Press.

Krasnobaev, B.I., Robel, Gert and Zeman, Herbert (eds) (1980) *Reisen und Reisebeschreibungen im 18. und 19. Jahrhundert als Quellen der Kultur-beziehungsforschung*. Berlin: Ulrich Camen Verlag.

Krist, Gary (1993) 'Ironic Journeys: Travel Writing in the Age of Tourism', *Hudson Review*, XLV, 593–601.

Kröller, Eva-Marie (1987) *Canadian Travellers in Europe, 1851–1900*. Vancouver: University of British Columbia Press.

—— (1990) 'First Impressions: Rhetorical Strategies in Travel Writing by Victorian Women', *Ariel*, XXI, 4, 87–99.

Kuczynski, Ingrid (1992) 'Zum Aufkommen der individualisierten Wirklichkeitssicht in der englischen Reiseliteratur des 18. Jahrhunderts'. In: Jäger (1992), pp. 35–46.

—— (1993) 'Reisende viktorianische Frauen und der koloniale Diskurs', *Gulliver*, XXXIV, 2, 10–26.

Labarge, Margaret Wade (1982) *Medieval Travellers: The Rich and Restless*. London: Hamish Hamilton.

Lawrence, Karen R. (1994) *Penelope Voyages: Women and Travel in the British Literary Tradition*. Ithaca, NY and London: Cornell University Press.

Leed, Eric J. (1991) *The Mind of the Traveler: From Gilgamesh to Global Tourism*. New York: Basic Books.

Lévi-Strauss, Claude (1977) *Tristes Tropiques*, trans. John and Doreen Weightman. New York: Pocket Books (*Tristes Tropiques*, 1955).

Link, Manfred (1963) *Der Reisebericht als literarische Kunstform von Goethe bis Heine*. PhD thesis, University of Cologne.

Löschburg, Winfried (1977) *Von Reiselust und Reiseleid: Eine Kulturgeschichte*. Frankfurt am Main: Insel Verlag.

Lytton Sells, A. (1964) *The Paradise of Travellers: The Italian Influence on Englishmen in the Seventeenth Century*. London: Allen & Unwin.

MacCannell, Dean (1976) *The Tourist: A New Theory of the Leisure Class*. New York: Schocken Books.

MacLaren, I. S. (1990) 'Introduction', *Ariel*, XXI, 4 (thematic issue 'The Literature of Travel'), 5–7.

MacLulich, T. D. (1979) 'Canadian Exploration as Literature', *Canadian Literature*, LXXXI, 72–85.

McVeagh, John (ed.) (1990) *All Before Them: Attitudes to Abroad in English Literature 1660–1780*. London: Ashfield.

Mączak, Antoni and Teuteberg, Hans Jürgen (eds) (1982) *Reiseberichte als Quellen europäischer Kulturgeschichte: Aufgaben und Möglichkeiten der historischen Reiseforschung*. Wolfenbüttel: Herzog August Bibliothek.

Maquerlot, Jean-Pierre and Willems, Michèle (1996) *Travel and Drama in Shakespeare's Time*. Cambridge: Cambridge University Press.

Martels, Zweder von (ed.) (1994) *Travel Fact and Travel Fiction: Studies on Fiction, Literary Tradition, Scholarly Discovery and Observation in Travel Writing*. Leiden etc.: Brill.

Masello, Steven J. (1985) 'Thomas Hoby: A Protestant Traveler to Circe's Court', *Cahiers Elisabethains*, XXVII, 67–81.

Matos, Jacinta (1992) 'Old Journeys Revisited: Aspects of Postwar English Travel Writing'. In: Kowalewski (1992), pp. 215–29.

Mead, William Edward (1972) *The Grand Tour in the Eighteenth Century*. New York: Benjamin Blom (first published 1914).

Melchett, Sonia (1991) *Passionate Quests: Five Modern Women Travellers*. London: Heinemann.

Meyers, Jeffrey (1987) 'Lawrence and Travel Writers'. In: *The Legacy of D.H. Lawrence*, ed. Jeffrey Meyers. London and New York: St. Martin's Press, pp. 81–108.

Michelsen, Peter (1981) 'Die Reisen der Lady: Zu den türkischen Briefen der Lady Mary Wortley Montagu', *Arcadia*, XVI, 242–65.

Middleton, Dorothy (1965) *Victorian Lady Travellers*. New York: Dutton.

Miles, Peter (1982) 'A Semi-Mental Journey: Structure and Illusion in Smollett's *Travels*', *Prose Studies*, V, 1, 43–60.

Mills, Sara (1991) *Discourses of Difference: An Analysis of Women's Travel Writing and Colonialism*. London and New York: Routledge.

Moir, Esther (1964) *The Discovery of Britain: The English Tourists 1540 to 1840*. London: Routledge & Kegan Paul.

Müllenbrock, Heinz-Joachim (1982) 'Die politischen Implikationen der "Grand Tour": Aspekte eines spezifisch englischen Beitrags zur europäischen Reiseliteratur der Aufklärung', *Arcadia*, XVII, 113–25.

Mulvey, Christopher (1983) *Anglo-American Landscapes: A Study of Nineteenth-Century Anglo-American Travel Literature*. Cambridge: Cambridge University Press.

—— (1988) 'Anglo-American Fictions: National Characteristics in Nineteenth-Century Travel Literature'. In: *American Literary Landscapes: The Fiction and the Fact*, eds Ian F.A. Bell and D.K. Adams. London: Vision Press, pp. 61–77.

—— (1990) *Transatlantic Manners: Social Patterns in Nineteenth-Century Anglo-American Travel Literature*. Cambridge: Cambridge University Press.

Nichols, Ashton (1989) 'Silencing the Other: The Discourse of Domination in Nineteenth-Century Exploration Narratives', *Nineteenth-Century Studies*, III, 1–22.

Nixon, Rob (1992) *London Calling: V.S. Naipaul, Postcolonial Mandarin*. New York and Oxford: Oxford University Press.

Omasreiter, Ria (1982) *Travels Through the British Isles: Die Funktion des Reiseberichts im 18. Jahrhundert*. Heidelberg: Winter.

Ousby, Ian (1990) *The Englishman's England: Taste, Travel and the Rise of Tourism*. Cambridge: Cambridge University Press.

Parkes, Joan (1968) *Travel in England in the Seventeenth Century*. Oxford: Clarendon Press (first published 1925).

Parks, George Bruner (1954) *The English Traveler to Italy*. Rome: Edizioni di Storia e Letteratura.

—— (1961) *Richard Hakluyt and the English Voyages*. New York: Ungar (first published 1928).

—— (1974) 'Tudor Travel Literature: A Brief History'. In: *The Hakluyt Handbook*, ed. D.B. Quinn. London: The Hakluyt Society, vol. 1, pp. 97–132.

Pelz, Annegret (1988) '". . . von einer Fremde in die andre?" Reiseliteratur von Frauen'. In: *Deutsche Literatur von Frauen*, ed. Gisela Brinker-Gabler. Munich: Beck, vol. 2, pp. 143–53.

—— (1991) 'Ob und wie Frauenzimmer reisen sollen? Das "reisende Frauenzimmer" als eine Entdeckung des 18. Jahrhunderts'. In: Griep (1991), pp. 125–35.

—— (1993) *Reisen durch die eigene Fremde: Reiseliteratur von Frauen als autogeographische Schriften*. Cologne, Weimar and Vienna: Böhlau.

Penrose, Boies (1952) *Travel and Discovery in the Renaissance 1420–1620*. Cambridge, MA.: Harvard University Press.

Pesman, Ros (1996) *Duty Free: Australian Women Abroad*. Oxford: Oxford University Press.

Pfister, Manfred (1991) '"The Fatal Gift of Beauty": Das Italien britischer Reisender'. In: *Reisen in den Mittelmeerraum*, ed. Hermann H. Wetzel. Passau: Passavia Universitätsverlag, pp. 55–101.

—— (1993) 'Intertextuelles Reisen, oder: Der Reisebericht als Intertext'. In: *Tales and 'their telling difference': Zur Theorie und Geschichte der Narrativik*, eds Herbert Foltinek et al. Heidelberg: Winter, pp. 109–32.

—— (1996a) 'Introduction'. In: *The Fatal Gift of Beauty: The Italies of British Travellers: An Annotated Anthology*, ed. Manfred Pfister. Amsterdam and Atlanta, GA: Rodopi, pp. 1–21.

—— (1996b) 'Bruce Chatwin and the Postmodernization of the Travelogue', *Literature, Interpretation, Theory*, VII, 2–3, 57–90.

Philip, Jim (1993) 'Reading Travel Writing'. In: *Recasting the World: Writing after Colonialism*, ed. Jonathan White. Baltimore, MD and London: Johns Hopkins University Press, pp. 241–55.

Porter, Dennis (1991) *Haunted Journeys: Desire and Transgression In European Travel Writing*. Princeton, NJ: Princeton University Press.

Possin, Hans-Joachim (1972) *Reisen und Literatur: Das Thema des Reisens in der englischen Literatur des 18. Jahrhunderts*. Tübingen: Niemeyer.

—— (1985) 'Englische Reiseliteratur des 18. Jahrhunderts (Forschungsbericht)', *Anglia*, CIII, 96–108.

—— (1986) 'Begegnungen mit Deutschland 1928-1934: Deutschlandbilder in englischen Reiseberichten', *Anglistik und Englischunterricht*, XXIX/XXX, 85–112.

Pratt, Mary Louise (1982) 'Conventions of Representation: Where Discourse and Ideology Meet', *Georgetown University Round Table on Languages and Linguistics*. Washington, DC: Georgetown University Press, pp. 139–55.

—— (1985) 'Scratches on the Face of the Country; or, What Mr. Barrow Saw in the Land of the Bushmen', *Critical Inquiry*, XII, 119–43.

—— (1992) *Imperial Eyes: Travel Writing and Transculturation*. London and New York: Routledge.

Prose Studies (1982), V, 1: Special Issue on The Art of Travel: Essays on Travel Writing, ed. Philip Dodd.

Pudney, John (1953) *The Thomas Cook Story*. Stuttgart: Tauchnitz.

Rennie, Neil (1995) *Far-Fetched Facts: The Literature of Travel and the Idea of the South Seas*. Oxford: Clarendon Press.

Robinson, Jane (1990) *Wayward Women: A Guide to Women Travellers*. Oxford: Oxford University Press.

Rogers, Pat (1997) *The Text of Great Britain: Theme and Design in Defoe's Tour*. Newark, NJ: University of Delaware Press.

Rojek, Chris (1993) *Ways of Escape: Modern Transformations in Leisure and Travel*. London: Macmillan.

Russell, Mary (1986) *The Blessings of a Good Thick Skirt: Women Travellers and Their World*. London: Collins.

Schadendorf, Wulf (1961) *Zu Pferde, im Wagen, zu Fuß: Tausend Jahre Reisen*. Munich: Prestel Verlag.

Schiffer, Reinhold (1986) 'Flüchtige Bemerkungen eines Flüchtig-Reisenden. Oder: Was sagen die Titel englischer Orientreisen aus über typische Formen des Reiseberichts vornehmlich im 19. Jahrhundert?' In: *Gattungsprobleme in der anglo-amerikanischen Literatur*, ed. R. Borgmeier. Tübingen: Niemeyer, pp. 125–39.

Schivelbusch, Wolfgang (1986) *The Railroad Journey: The Industrialization of Time and Space in the 19th Century*. Leamington Spa/Hamburg/New York: Berg (*Geschichte der Eisenbahnreise: Zur Industrialisierung von Raum und Zeit im 19. Jahrhundert*, 1977).

Segeberg, Harro (1983) 'Die literarisierte Reise im späten 18. Jahrhundert: Ein Beitrag zur Gattungstypologie'. In: Griep and Jäger (1983), pp. 14–31.

Shattock, Joanne (1982) 'Travel Writing Victorian and Modern: A Review of Recent Research', *Prose Studies*, V, 1, 151–64.

Spurr, David (1993) *The Rhetoric of Empire: Colonial Discourse in Journalism, Travel Writing, and Imperial Administration*. Durham, NC and London: Duke University Press.

Stafford, Barbara Maria (1984) *Voyage into Substance: Art, Science, Nature, and the Illustrated Travel Account, 1760–1840*. Cambridge, MA.: MIT Press.

Stagl, Justin et al. (1983a) *Apodemiken: Eine räsonnierte Bibliographie der reisetheoretischen Literatur des 16., 17. und 18. Jahrhunderts*. Paderborn: Schöningh.

—— (1983b) 'Das Reisen als Kunst und als Wissenschaft (16.–18. Jahrhundert)', *Zeitschrift für Ethnologie*, CVIII, 2, 15–34.

—— (1989) 'Die Methodisierung des Reisens im 16. Jahrhundert'. In: Brenner (1989), pp. 140–77.

Stannard, Martin (1982) 'Debunking the Jungle: The Context of Evelyn Waugh's *Travel Books 1930–9*', *Prose Studies*, V, 1, 105–26.

Stevenson, Catherine Barnes (1982) *Victorian Women Travel Writers in Africa*. Boston: Twayne.

Stone, Ian R. (1987) '"The contents of the kettles": Charles Dickens, John Rae and Cannibalism on the 1845 Franklin Expedition', *The Dickensian*, LXXXIII, 1, 6–16.

Stoye, John Walter (1952) *English Travellers Abroad 1604–1667: Their Influence in English Society and Politics*. London: Cape.

—— (1982) 'Reisende Engländer im Europa des 17. Jahrhunderts und ihre Reisemotive', In: Mączak and Teuteburg (1982), pp. 131–52.

Strelka, Joseph (1985) 'Der literarische Reisebericht'. In: *Prosakunst ohne Erzählen: Die Gattung der nicht-fiktionalen Kunstprosa*, ed. Klaus Weissenberger. Tübingen: Niemeyer, pp. 69–184.

Stummer, Peter O. (1994) 'An-Other Travelogue: Ferdinand Dennis's Journey into Afro-Britain'. In: *Southern African Writing: Voyages and Explorations*, ed. Geoffrey Davies. Amsterdam and Atlanta, GA: Rodopi, pp. 191–8.

Swinglehurst, Edmund (1974) *The Romantic Journey: The Story of Thomas Cook and Victorian Travel*. New York: Harper & Row.

Tabachnick, Stephen E. (1987) 'Art and Science in *Travels in Arabia Deserta*'. In: *Explorations in Doughty's 'Arabia Deserta'*, ed. Stephen E. Tabachnick. Athens, GA and London: University of Georgia Press, pp. 1–39.

Tallmadge, John (1980) 'From Chronicle to Quest: The Shaping of Darwin's *Voyage of the Beagle*', *Victorian Studies*, XXIII, 325–45.

Thieme, John (1982) 'Authorial Voice in V. S. Naipaul's *The Middle Passage*'. *Prose Studies*, V, 139–50.

Thubron, Colin (1986) 'Travel Writing Today: Its Rise and Its Dilemma'. In: *Essays by Divers Hands*, The Transactions of the Royal Society of Literature, NS, vol. 54. London: Boydell, pp. 167–81.

Tinling, Marion (1989) *Woman into the Unknown: A Sourcebook on Women Explorers and Travelers*. New York: Greenwood Press.

Trench, Richard (1990) *Travellers in Britain: Three Centuries of Discovery*. London: Aurum Press.

Vaughan, John Edmund (1974) *The English Guide Book c. 1780–1870: An Illustrated History*. Newton Abbott and London: David & Charles.

Whitlock, Gillian (1993) '"A Most Improper Desire": Mary Gaunt's Journey to Jamaica', *Kunapipi*, XV, 3, 86–95.

Wooden, Warren W. (1983) 'The Peculiar Peregrinations of John Taylor the Water Poet: A Study in Seventeenth-Century British Travel Literature', *Prose Studies*, VI, 1, 3–20.

Wuthenow, Ralph-Rainer (1980) *Die erfahrene Welt: Europäische Reiseliteratur im Zeitalter der Aufklärung*. Frankfurt am Main: Insel Verlag.

Youngs, Tim (1994) *Travellers in Africa: British Travelogues, 1850–1900*. Manchester and New York: Manchester University Press.

Zacher, Christian K. (1976) *Curiosity and Pilgrimage: The Literature of Discovery in Fourteenth-Century England*. Baltimore, MD and London: Johns Hopkins University Press.

—— (1986) 'Travel and Geographical Writings'. In: *A Manual of the Writings in Middle English, 1050–1500*, ed. Albert E. Hartung. New Haven: Connecticut Academy of Arts and Sciences, vol. 7, pp. 2235–54 and 2449–66.

Other sources

Addison, Joseph (1949) 'The Pleasures of the Imagination (Nos. 411–421)'. In: *The Spectator*, Everyman's Library. London: Dent and New York: Dutton, vol. 3 (first published 1712).

Appiah, Kwame Anthony (1991) 'Is the Post- in Postmodernism the Post- in Postcolonial?', *Critical Inquiry*, XVII, 336–57.

Bacon, Francis (1974) *The Advancement of Learning* and *New Atlantis*. Oxford: Clarendon Press.

Bagwell, Philip S. (1974) *The Transport Revolution from 1770*. London: Batsford.

Bitterli, Urs (1989) *Cultures in Conflict: Encounters between European and Non-European Cultures, 1492–1800*, trans. Ritchie Robertson. London: Polity Press (*Alte Welt, neue Welt: Formen des europäisch-überseeischen Kulturkontakts vom 15. bis zum 18. Jahrhundert*, 1986).

—— (1991) *Die 'Wilden' und die 'Zivilisierten': Grundzüge einer Geistes- und Kulturgeschichte der europäisch-überseeischen Begegnung*. Munich: Beck (first published 1976).

Bloch, Ernst (1986) *The Principle of Hope*. Oxford: Blackwell (*Das Prinzip Hoffnung*, 1954).

Boswell, James (1980) *Life of Johnson*. Oxford: Oxford University Press (World's Classics) (first published 1791).

Camden, William (1974) *Britannia*, trans. Richard Gough, reprint of the 1806 edition, 4 vols. Hildesheim: Olms (first published 1586).

Carter, Erica, Donald, James and Squires, Judith (eds) (1993) *Space and Place: Theories of Identity and Location*. London: Lawrence & Wishart.

Friedman, John Block (1981) *The Monstrous Races in Medieval Art and Thought*. Cambridge, MA and London: Harvard University Press.

Goethe, Johann Wolfgang von (1995) *Faust Parts I and II*, in a new version by Howard Brenton. London: Nick Hern Books.

Hartog, François (1988) *The Mirror of Herodotus: The Representation of the Other in the Writing of History*, trans. Janet Lloyd. Berkeley: University of California Press (*Le miroir d'Hérodote: Essai sur la représentation de l'autre*, 1980).

Herodotus (1922–4), with an English translation by A. D. Godley, 4 vols, Loeb Classical Library. London: Heinemann and New York: G. B. Putnam's.

Hyde, Ralph (1988) *Panoramania! The Art and Entertainment of the 'All-Embracing' View*. London: Trefoil Publications, in association with Barbican Art Gallery.

Hynes, Samuel (1976) *The Auden Generation: Literature and Politics in England in the 1930s*. London: Bodley Head.

Impey, Oliver and MacGregor, Arthur (eds) (1985) *The Origins of Museums: The Cabinet of Curiosities in Sixteenth-Century Europe*. Oxford: Clarendon Press.

Kaplan, Caren (1996) *Questions of Travel: Postmodern Discourses of Displacement*. Durham, NC and London: Duke University Press.

Kohl, Karl-Heinz (1986) *Entzauberter Blick: Das Bild vom Guten Wilden*. Frankfurt am Main: Suhrkamp (first published 1981).

Krishnaswamy, Revathi (1995) 'Mythologies of Migrancy: Postcolonialism, Postmodernism and the Politics of (Dis)location', *Ariel*, XXVI, 1, 125–46.

Kristeva, Julia (1991) *Strangers to Ourselves*. New York: Columbia University Press (*Etrangers à nous-mêmes*, 1988).

Loomis, Chauncey C. (1978) 'The Arctic Sublime'. In: *Nature and the Victorian Imagination*, eds U. C. Knoepflmacher and G. B. Tennyson. Berkeley: University of California Press, pp. 95–112.

Lowes, John Livingstone (1927) *The Road to Xanadu: A Study in the Ways of the Imagination*. London: Constable.

Manwaring, Elizabeth (1925) *Italian Landscape in Eighteenth Century England: A Study Chiefly of the Influence of Claude Lorrain and Salvator Rosa on English Taste 1700–1800*. London: Cass.

Merian, Maria Sibylla (1975) *Metamorphosis insectorum surinamensium*. Leipzig (first published 1705).

Noyes, Russell (1968) *Wordsworth and the Art of Landscape*. Bloomington and London: Indiana University Press.

Oettermann, Stephan (1980) *Das Panorama: Die Geschichte eines Massenmediums*. Frankfurt am Main: Syndikat.

Pliny (1938ff.) *Natural History*, with an English translation by H. Rackham et al., 10 vols. Loeb Classical Library. London: Heinemann and Cambridge, MA: Harvard University Press.

Richards, Thomas (1993) *The Imperial Archive: Knowledge and the Fantasy of Empire*. London and New York: Verso.

Rousseau, Jean-Jacques (1979) *Emile, or, On Education*, trans. Allan Bloom. New York: Basic Books (first published 1762).

Ruskin, William (1904) 'Of Modern Landscape'. In: *Modern Painters*. The Works of John Ruskin, eds E. T. Cook and Alexander Wedderburn. London: Allen, vol. 5, pp. 317–53 (the relevant part of *Modern Painters* first published 1856).

Said, Edward (1978) *Orientalism*. London: Routledge.

Sehsucht: Das Panorama als Massenunterhaltung des 19. Jahrhunderts (1993) Katalog zur Ausstellung der Kunst- und Ausstellungshalle der Bundesrepublik Deutschland. Frankfurt am Main and Basel: Stroemfeld/Roter Stern.

Shakespeare, William (1964) *The Tempest*, Arden Edition of the Works of William Shakespeare. London: Methuen (first performance 1610).

Shohat, Ella (1992) 'Notes on the "Post-Colonial"', *Social Text*, 31/32, 99–113.

Solinus, Gaius Julius (1958) *Collectanea rerum memorabilium*, ed. Theodor Mommsen. Berlin: Weidmann.

Sprat, Thomas (1959) *History of the Royal Society*, eds Jackson I. Cope and Harold Whitmore Jones. St Louis: Washington University Press and London: Routledge & Kegan Paul (first published 1667).

Sternberger, Dolf (1981) *Panorama oder Ansichten vom 19. Jahrhundert*. Frankfurt am Main: Insel Verlag (first published 1938).

Sterne, Laurence (n.y.) 'The Prodigal Son'. In: *The Works of Laurence Sterne*. London: Routledge, pp. 443–7.

Todorov, Tzvetan (1984) *The Conquest of America. The Question of the Other*. New York: Harper & Row (*La conquête de l'Amérique: La question de l'autre*, 1982).

Tuan, Yi-Fu (1979) *Landscapes of Fear*. New York: Pantheon.

Wallace, Anne D. (1993) *Walking, Literature, and English Culture: The Origins and Uses of Peripatetic in the Nineteenth Century*. Oxford: Clarendon Press.

Wittkower, Rudolf (1942) 'Marvels of the East: A Study in the History of Monsters', *Journal of the Warburg and Courtauld Institutes*, 5, 159–97.

Wolff, Janet (1993) 'On the Road Again: Metaphors of Travel in Cultural Criticism', *Cultural Studies*, VII, 2, 224–39.

Wollstonecraft, Mary (1929) *The Rights of Woman*, Everyman's Library. London: Dent and New York: Dutton (first published 1792).

Index

Abrahams, Peter, 158
Addison, Joseph, 5, 48–51, 62–3
African Association, 7, 87
Alexander romance, 28
apodemic writing, 8, 47, 49, 69
art of travel, 77–8
Auden, W. H., 139, 142

Bacon, Francis, 36, 45, 46–7
Baedeker, 8, 21, 85
Bainbridge, Beryl, 135
Beckford, William, 42, 58–61, 63, 99
Behn, Aphra, 8
Bell, Gertrude, 111
Belloc, Hilaire, 190
Bird, Isabella, 110, 115–18, 191
Birkett, Dea, 107, 108–9, 111
Blaise, Clark, 174
Bloch, Ernst, 179
Blunt, Anne, 110, 114, 121
Blunt, Wilfrid, 114
Boswell, James, 13, 42, 52–3, 55, 76, 187
Bougainville, Louis Antoine de, 37
Breytenbach, Breyten, 174, 195
Brydone, Patrick, 53
Burton, Richard Francis, 82, 86, 89, 90, 92, 103, 116, 153, 189
Butor, Michel, 146
Byron, Lord, George Gordon, 42
Byron, Robert, 129–30, 139, 141–2

cabinet of curiosities, 31, 184
Camden, William, 68
Cartwright, Justin, 195
Chatwin, Bruce, 2, 130, 142, 144–6, 155
Chaucer, Geoffrey, 14
Chaudhuri, Nirad, 150–1, 158, 160, 162, 195
classic traveller, 50
Claude glass, 78, 93
Cobbett, William, 74

Coleridge, Samuel Taylor, 113, 182
colonialism, see Empire, imperialism
Columbus, Christopher, 23, 184
Combe, William, 80
Conrad, Joseph, 103
Conrad, Peter, 172
continental travel, see Grand Tour
Cook, James, 37–8, 61, 87
Cook, Thomas, 85, 96
Coryat, Thomas, 40, 43–4, 46–8
critique of civilization, 18, 137, 138–44
Cunninghame Graham, Robert Bontine, 103–5, 137
curiositas, curiosity, 26, 28, 44, 68, 88

Dampier, William, 36–7
Darwin, Charles, 9, 15–16, 38, 61–2, 87, 90, 103, 146, 182
Davidson, Robyn, 195
Defoe, Daniel, 8, 72–4, 148, 182
Dennis, Ferdinand, 162, 170, 176–7
diary, 11–12, 46, 57, 113, 182
Dickens, Charles, 84, 93–5, 96–7
discovery, see exploration
displacement, 144, 152
Dobbs, Kildare, 171
domestic travel, see home tour
Doughty, Charles, 14–15
Douglas, Norman, 6
Drake, Francis, 30
Duff Gordon, Lucie, 110
Durrell, Lawrence, 142

East India Company, 30
Edgeworth, Maria, 84
educational travel, see Grand Tour
Edwards, Amelia, 96, 101, 106, 110, 191
Elizabeth I, 31
Empire, 18, 72, 88–93, 110, 177, see also imperialism

215

218 *Index*